Challenging China

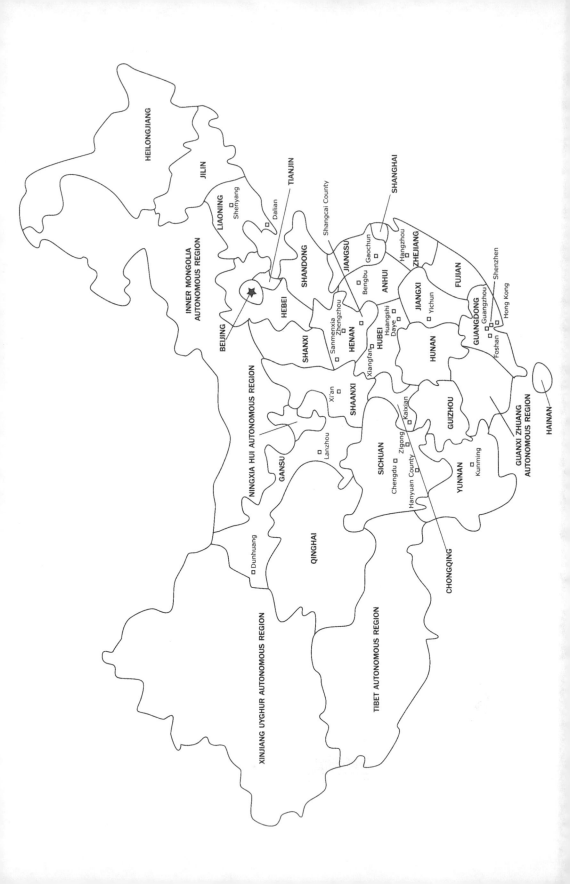

Challenging China

Struggle and Hope in an Era of Change

**EDITED BY SHARON HOM AND
STACY MOSHER**

Published in Conjunction with
Human Rights in China

THE NEW PRESS

NEW YORK
LONDON

NEW YORK
HONG KONG BRUSSELS

Requests for permission to reproduce selections from this book should be mailed to:
Permissions Department, The New Press, 38 Greene Street, New York, NY 10013.

Published in the United States by The New Press, New York, 2007
Distributed by W. W. Norton & Company, Inc., New York

LIBRARY OF CONGRESS CATALOGING-IN-PUBLICATION DATA

Challenging China : struggle and hope in an era of change /
edited by Sharon Hom and Stacy Mosher.
p. cm.
Includes bibliographical references and index.

ISBN 978-1-59558-132-7 (hc.)

1. China—Politics and government—2002–   2. China—Economic conditions—2000–
3. China—Social conditions—2000–
I. Hom, Sharon K.   II. Mosher, Stacy.
DS779.46.C4 2007
951.06-dc22
2006033822

The New Press was established in 1990 as a not-for-profit alternative to the large,
commercial publishing houses currently dominating the book publishing industry.
The New Press operates in the public interest rather than for private gain,
and is committed to publishing, in innovative ways, works of educational, cultural,
and community value that are often deemed insufficiently profitable.

www.thenewpress.com

Composition by dix!
This book was set in Bembo
Printed in the United States of America

2   4   6   8   10   9   7   5   3   1

This book is dedicated to the people inside China working and writing on issues crucial to China's future—and taking the considerable risks such work involves.

Contents

Acknowledgments

We would like to thank Andrew Hsiao and the other editors at The New Press for their enthusiasm for this project, and in particular for their encouragement, suggestions, and invaluable editorial guidance on this volume.

We would also like to thank our colleagues at Human Rights in China, especially Elisabeth Wickeri and Carol Wang, for their essential input and assistance, as well as various friends and colleagues who offered comments and suggestions.

Finally, we thank the writers who have generously shared their work with *China Rights Forum* over the years, the Chinese Web sites and magazines that publish them, and the translators who have helped us make these writings accessible to a non-Chinese audience.

INTRODUCTION

Sharon Hom

A dominant Western media image of China invokes the ultramodern skyline of Shanghai, or the capitalist bustle of Guangdong, the poster child of China as factory to the world. Through its expanding political, economic, trade, and military ties, China has become a major economic and political power. China's prominent international role is reflected in its hosting of the 2008 Olympics, membership in the World Trade Organization (WTO), and inclusion in the new forty-seven-member United Nations Human Rights Council. Demonstrating the Chinese leadership's sophistication and application of international norms and language, China has even issued white papers on human rights violations in the United States.

In this volume, Chinese commentators reflect on China's challenges to the world, and from its own people. As Liu Xiaobo observes, the Chinese leadership's clear policy decision to bifurcate economic and political reforms has hampered efforts to promote institutional change, greater democratization, or systemic protections for fundamental rights and freedoms. China's legal system is plagued by corruption, local protectionism, a low level of competence and professionalism, and the politicization of judicial processes through Party interference at all levels. As a powerful nondemocratic country lacking an independent rule of law, but offering the world's largest and most lucrative market, China poses difficult challenges for the international community.

At the same time, China is also being challenged by its own people, who are demanding greater accountability and an end to corruption, and who are rejecting the onerous human costs behind the "economic miracle" of China's rapid macro-economic growth and reforms initiated in the eighties. China's 700 million rural inhabitants, an estimated 140–200 million migrant workers, and more than one and a half million former employees of state-owned enterprises (SOEs) have been affected by the loss of jobs, homes, access to basic health care, and affordable education for their children. The UNDP's *China Human Development Report 2005* cites a survey of Chinese public opinion in which more than 80 percent of the respondents felt that China's current income distribution was either "not so equitable" or "very inequitable."[1]

Chinese leaders have been forced to recognize the threat to sustainability of economic growth and social stability posed by rising social unrest fueled by these growing inequalities and the collapse of social-safety networks. In July 2005, China announced its *Eleventh Five-Year Plan (2006–2010),* which shifts its economic emphasis from strengthening large cities to a plan for National Economic and Social Development aimed at agricultural areas.[2] Development rhetoric attributes social tensions to "economic struggles" among marginalized groups such as poor peasants and rural migrant workers, and advocates investment and preferential policies in agriculture to ease grievances among these groups. Recent official pronouncements call for a harmonious society that places the well-being of the people at the center and invokes democratic values and rule of law. However, maintaining social and political control remains the key policy imperative.

With almost 1.4 billion people, the challenges facing China's leaders are enormous and complex, and will require more than slogans and new rhetoric. Developing sustainable policies and solutions will require serious political will and resources, and must include the participation of all its citizens and civil society groups, including a vigorous and independent free press. However, instead of promoting free flow of information and debates, the Chinese government maintains a tight hold on information as a tool of political control, and invokes social stability as justification for repression and silencing of dissent and criticism.

Critical media reports on corruption in land appropriation and environmental damage were followed by intensified crackdowns on journalists throughout 2005 and the beginning of 2006, including several incidents of demotion or dismissal of chief editors, the closure of popular newspapers, and violent attacks on journalists attempting to cover sensitive stories. Government censorship and surveillance also increased in cyberspace in response to the Web's growing popularity and the rise of Internet activism in China. The government has invested heavily in network infrastructure that boosts filtering efficiency, and Web content is closely monitored. More than a dozen regulations relating to Internet governance are implemented by the Ministry of Public Security, the Ministry of Information Industry, the Ministry of Culture, and relevant departments of these ministries at various levels. The activities of U.S. and other foreign information-technology companies doing business in China have also contributed to official censorship and raise serious concerns about socially responsible corporate practices and policies.

Despite provisions in the Chinese Constitution protecting freedom of expression, freedom of the press, privacy of communication, and freedom of association, there is a clear gap between law and reality. Chinese journalists, lawyers, intellectuals, and activists who raise issues of official corruption, public health, and environmental crises, attempt to form an independent trade union, or engage in non-state-approved religious practices or groups, face persecution, prosecution, harassment and detention, or even torture and death. There is also an alarming trend of the use of Chinese mafia-like violence, with apparent complicity of local officials against activists or petitioners.

This volume brings together a range of voices and perspectives—including reporters, intellectuals, activists, former government officials, and poets. Organized thematically along five sections, these personal stories, memoirs, analyses, and reportage present a small window into the human struggles to speak out, to witness, to demand an accounting from those in power, and to critically interrogate the systemic causes enabling these abuses. Collectively, they offer insights into the China inhabited by the vast majority of China's people behind its gleaming urban facades.

Mineshaft: Like the survival—or not—of canaries in mines, China's most vulnerable groups also show warning signs threatening a sustainable and equitable future. Exposed to dangerous work conditions, challenging corruption, exercising their rights to air their grievances and petition the government, China's migrants, rural poor, and the victims of its legal system are digging themselves out of a great darkness. These voices of NGO activists, journalists, petitioners, and migrants are warning China's leaders that growing social unrest, corruption, and the poverty gap are ignored at risk of the survival of all of society. The message that what happens to the most vulnerable ultimately affects all of us echoes throughout the rest of the volume.

The Age of Mammoths: China is in the midst of a momentous transition. The system is changing in ways no one would have anticipated thirty years ago. In contemporary foreign media coverage, China is often portrayed as a dragon rising, awakening from centuries-long slumber. In popular Chinese songs, Chinese invoke a powerful self-image laced with Chinese nationalism and refer to themselves with pride as children of the dragon, the most noble and grand of all the animals of Chinese mythology. Yet, China is led by what is effectively still ironclad one-party rule, with a flawed justice system where torture and abuses are endemic, and little tolerance for criticism or calls for greater transparency and accountability. Will such rigidity and authoritarian impulse towards control end in a deadly prehistoric irrelevance? The contributors examine the urgent need for democratic reforms to ensure a peaceful China, and the abolishing of clan-based monopoly and Party power that has allowed massive corruption, pillaging of national resources, and tragic waste of human potential.

The Power of a Red Rose: In the summer of 2005, the Chinese leadership dispatched a research team to study the "color revolution" in Eastern Europe—more precisely, officials were concerned about how to avoid such a development in China. Yet, despite violent crackdowns and repression, just as in the Republic of Georgia, ordinary "acutely silent" Chinese people are gathering together and raising their own red roses. These individuals are intellectuals, students, and labor activists who spoke out in the democracy movement in 1989; they are the hundreds of thousands of petitioners raising complaints about the police, courts and prosecutors' offices, government corruption, and cases of injustice; they are the new social movements rising like a sea of red roses invoked by the poet Huang Xiang. Yet, these alone will not be enough to move China towards democracy. The international community has a role to play in generating pressure and attention, and supporting the expansion of a domestic space inside China for the blossoming of a civil society.

White Nights: Throughout China's history, mass social movements have resulted in long nights of mass suffering and social breakdown. The anti-rightist movement and the Cultural Revolution claimed millions of victims, invoking deadly designations such as "class enemies" to justify massive violations of human dignity and rights. The protests against corruption, calls for democratic reform, and efforts to organize independent trade unions in the spring of 1989 were designated antigovernment and counterrevolutionary and ruthlessly crushed in front of prime-time television cameras. In 2006, upon the fortieth anniversary of the beginning of the Cultural Revolution, the dangers and lessons of historical amnesia and the denial of public reexamination still persist in a culture of mistrust, fear, censorship, and self-censorship. The memoirs and interviews in this section offer reflections on the human losses—the suicides and deaths of loved ones, the loss of homeland—and examine how individuals carry these burdens of history.

The Shepherd's Song: Throughout China's modern social dislocations and upheavals, many Chinese persist in reclaiming their humanity and dignity through spirituality, literature, or art. As the stories in this volume powerfully testify, the human costs are enormous. Yet, everything has not been irretrievably lost. One contributor counters police oppression with forgiveness laced with a tinge of humor. Families struggle to hold onto their bonds. An artist against all odds, continues to create his paintings, while serving in labor camps. Writers explore the role of faith and the life of the spirit under severe religious repression. Gesturing towards the possibility of healing and spiritual reclaiming, this last section suggests the ways that individuals choose to heal themselves, their communities, the whole of the globe.

Notes

1. United Nations Development Programme and China Development Research Foundation, *China Human Development Report 2005* (Beijing: UNDP, 2005), http://www.undp .org.cn/modules.php?op=modload&name=News&file=article&topic=40&sid=228.
2. The plan was announced at the Fifth Plenary session of the 16th Central Committee of the Communist Party.

Challenging China

PART ONE

Mineshaft: Warnings from China's Most Vulnerable

We're all together in a long, long tunnel
Digging into an endless darkness.
From the time of our grandfathers' grandfathers,
It's hard to say how long we've been digging.
Slowly, we've dug our eyes black,
Dug our hair black,
Dug ourselves a black home.

from **Mineshaft, Our Black Home**
by Qiu Yueshou

On March 18, 2006, flooding at the Fanjiashan Coal Mine trapped and killed twenty-eight miners. Reports indicated that the mine, run by the government of Zhaoxian Township in China's northern Shanxi Province, was operating with an expired safety production license at the time of the disaster. Media coverage was brief—this was merely one of the catastrophic accidents that killed more than 6,000 miners in 2005. Although there have been some attempts to improve public access to information—for example, the number of deaths from industrial accidents was declassified as a "state secret" in 2002—many obstacles remain. Recent efforts by the Chinese government to tighten safety regulations and improve conditions in industrial workplaces do not address the impact of legal, social, and technological restrictions on access to and dissemination of information on key social issues such as corruption, or on attempts to address the dangerous working conditions faced by the millions who currently work in hazardous industries such as mining production.

The flawed implementation behind the rhetoric of smooth and cohesive plans for improvement in industrial safety is to a great extent echoed in the broader disjuncture between formal rights guarantees and actual practice. Just as central-government orders for the closure of unsafe mines are often thwarted by local officials in collusion with profit-hungry mine owners, so the Chinese Constitution's inclusion in 2005 of a clause guaranteeing protection of human rights is undermined by actual controls on free assembly and exchange of information. The obstacles preventing systemic improvements in human rights are multifaceted, but the government-instituted regime of information control is a crucial—and intended—barrier to the formation of a vibrant and independent civil society. Attacks on the independence of the press have ripple effects on society, and crackdowns on this sector discourage others, such as grassroots activists, petitioners, and dissatisfied workers, from voicing their concerns. The persistence of these diverse and critical voices against oppressive odds serves as a crucial reminder of the inadequacies of current CCP policies, and spotlights the concerns of vulnerable populations.

This section focuses on the intensification of crackdowns and the active responses of individuals, many of whom are armed with very limited tools with which to challenge the legal, social, and technological apparatuses controlling China's society. Hu Jia, a young activist who has been detained on multiple occasions, compares the government's treatment of the AIDS epidemic with its handling of the shorter and more internationally prominent SARS crisis, uncovering the lengths to which officials at all levels go to hide the human cost of AIDS. He Qinglian, a prominent Chinese scholar, describes the methods used to silence journalists. Zhang Youjie's piece addresses the flaws in China's legal processes by examining the stories of several young men who received disproportionately harsh sentences for petty crimes. Chen Guidi and Wu Chuntao's essay exposes the devastating effects of corruption at a village level. Yang Yinbo's description of a migrant family's daily existence reveals the insecurity that plagues this large and growing sector of the population. By addressing problems across the spectrum of Chinese society, these contributors illuminate the need for greater transparency and access to information, and greater government accountability for respecting and protecting human rights for all.

RULE BY TERROR

Chen Guidi and Wu Chuntao

This excerpt from the banned book Chinese Peasantry: A Survey *vividly describes corruption and violence in a small village in Anhui Province.*

It All Happened Within Five Minutes

With the current emphasis on commerce and materialism, most Chinese people like the number eight because of its pronunciation similar to the word meaning "prosper." For that reason, February 18, 1998, would have seemed an especially propitious date. But in fact, that day was to live on in infamy in the memories of the residents of Xiaozhang Zhuang in Tangnan Xiang, Guzhen County, Anhui Province.

Xiaozhang Zhuang was situated on a flood plane at the mouth of a river, and constant flooding in recent years had made the villagers' survival increasingly difficult. Exacerbating the villagers' misery was the egregious taxation imposed by local officials. But not all of the villagers of Xiaozhang Zhuang were willing to submit themselves to the officials' lawless bullying. Several stalwart men, Zhang Jiaquan, Zhang Jiabao, Zhang Hongchuan, and Zhang Guimao, submitted a request to the Tangnan Xiang Party Secretariat for the village accounts to be audited, and another villager, Zhang Jiachang, reported allegations of corruption to the Guzhen County Procuratorate.

This constant stream of petitions and reports was particularly infuriating to Zhang Guiquan, the "vice-head" of Xiaozhang Zhuang. Zhang Guiquan was a fearsome man considered capable of any evil deed, and although the main target of the complaints, he enjoyed enough support within the village that he could safely ignore his detractors.

One day he invited two members of the village's security squad to his home, then on some false pretext had someone tell Zhang Hongchuan, the instigator of the complaints against him, to come to his home with the accounts. Zhang Hongchuan, suspecting nothing, obligingly hurried over with the air of one who believes that virtue is rewarded. No sooner had he entered the door than Zhang Guiquan began hurling abuse at him, and ordered his two sons and the security officers to beat Zhang Hongchuan into a bloody pulp. If Zhang Hongchuan's nephew, Zhang Guiying, had not heard of the matter and rushed over to save him, who knows how things would have turned out?

Rather than discouraging the villagers from further action, Zhang Guiquan's violent threats drew the village's Party members, retired officials, and eighty-odd households into an unprecedented unity. They went twice to the Tangnan Xiang township government and five times to the home of the village Party secretary, forcefully demanding a full investigation against Zhang Guiquan and a thorough audit of the village's finances.

The villagers' repeated requests and appeals finally had an effect. The Guzhen County government was carrying out a thorough examination of the finances of all its subsidiary villages at the time, and the Tangnan Xiang Party secretary, Zuo Peiyu, told the petitioning villagers, "As it happens, our county has an audit drive in progress, and we've already done some research and decided that the secretary of the Tangnan Xiang disciplinary inspection committee, Wang Jiawen, will bring three accountants from his finance department to audit your village first."

The villagers of Xiaozhang Zhuang rejoiced at the news. On February 6, 1998, Wang Jiawen arrived in Xiaozhang Zhuang with three accountants and the township official responsible for Xiaozhang Zhuang, Xue Zhaocheng.

On February 9, under the direction of Wang Jiawen, the village's eighty-seven households conducted a lively and democratic discussion through which they selected a group of representatives to form an auditing committee. Those elected included Zhang Jiabao, Zhang Guiyu, Zhang Hongchuan, and Zhang Guimao.

As everyone was familiar with Zhang Guiquan's proclivities, they anticipated that the audit would not progress smoothly. Apart from laying down a strict system and discipline for the audit, the twelve committee members agreed that if Zhang Guiquan showed up at anyone's home to raise a fuss, all of the other committee members would immediately rush to the scene and prevent any mishap.

Right from the start, Zhang Guiquan did everything in his power to impede the audit. He started out by trying to divert attention with a false rumor that someone wanted to kill his sons. Then on several occasions during village meetings he declared, "Those twelve representatives want to tally my accounts and make trouble for me, but they won't find it so easy! They have no way to get rid of me, and if they can't get rid of me, I'll make their lives miserable—if I don't kill them, I'll grind them to pieces!" A couple of days later, Zhang Guiquan's daughter-in-law, Zhang Xiufang, spread the word that her father-in-law was planning to kill someone.

But the leaders and officials of Xiaozhang Zhuang and Tangnan Xiang didn't take Zhang Guiquan's threats seriously. The audit committee representatives likewise thought this was just Zhang Guiquan's attempts to intimidate them and paid no attention.

No one could have guessed that on the ninth day of the audit, early on the morning of February 18, Zhang Guiquan would actually wield his butcher's knife.

On that day, rain pelted the rooftops of Xiaozhang Zhuang in a steady, hypnotic patter. Although it was already daylight, most of the villagers remained snuggled in their homes. Fifty-eight-year-old Wei Surong was one of the few who rose from her bed as early as usual and bustled to the kitchen. She knew that her husband, Zhang Guiyu, like the other eleven village representatives, would have to go off to examine the village accounts, regardless of the weather. Rather than delay this momentous occasion, Wei Surong made sure that breakfast was prepared first thing in the morning.

Much to their surprise, just as Zhang Guiyu and his son, Zhang Xiaosong, had sat down at the table shortly after seven, Zhang Guiquan appeared at the door with two of his sons, Zhang Yuliang and Zhang Dongyi. They were joined soon afterward by the village accountant, Zhang Jiahui, and his son, Zhang Jie.

Zhang Jie, whose father, as the village accountant, was implicated in the investigation of the accounts, started out by imitating Zhang Guiyu sarcastically, asking, "How are the accounts? How about a share for me?"

Zhang Guiyu was a sensible person, and picking up on Zhang Jie's insinuation, he rose from the table and coolly replied, "The others told me to look at the accounts. How could I refuse?"

Zhang Guiquan immediately snapped back, "Let's not waste any more words," and then shouted to his two sons, "Beat him up!"

Zhang Dongyi snatched up a wooden pole resting next to the door of Zhang Guiyu's home, while Zhang Yuliang grabbed a sickle. Zhang Dongyi danced over to Zhang Guiyu, brandishing the pole, and the village accountant, Zhang Jiahui, grabbed Zhang Guiyu around the waist and held him tight. Zhang Guiyu managed through frantic exertion to free himself and picked up a brick from the floor. Wei Surong saw the village official's sons preparing to beat her husband to death, and quickly grabbed a vegetable knife from on top of the stove. The two sides eyed each other wildly, ready to leap at each other at a moment's notice.

The racket alerted neighbors on all sides. Afraid to attack in front of so many witnesses, Zhang Dongyi and Zhang Yuliang retreated to the backyard. Joining them, Zhang Guiquan, still not satisfied, shouted, "Xiao Qiao (Zhang Guiyu's nickname), you son of a bitch, if you have the guts, come out with me!"

Zhang Guiyu was an easygoing, honest man. When he saw the village official acting like a madman, he displayed no fear, but followed him behind the house and challenged him: "Tangnan Xiang officials want to audit your books, and the people here chose me as their representative. What have I done wrong? Zhang Guiquan, you should watch your language. Even if I want to audit your books, what can you do to me?"

During the argument, Zhang Guiquan had motioned for his son, Zhang Dongyi, to go home and fetch reinforcements. Soon two more of Zhang Guiquan's sons, Zhang Jiazhi and Zhang Chaowei, arrived at the scene with concealed weapons. Zhang Chaowei ran over and struck Zhang Guiyu, while Zhang Yuliang snatched the brick from Zhang Guiyu's hands. Zhang Guiyu continued to fight back empty-handed until Zhang Chaowei whipped knives out of his boot and waistband and began slashing savagely at Zhang Guiyu's head and chest. Caught off guard, Zhang Guiyu dropped without a sound.

Rushing to the scene, village representatives Zhang Hongchuan and Zhang Guimao found Zhang Guiyu lying prone in a pool of blood. Zhang Hongchuan angrily demanded of Zhang Guiquan, "How could you be so vicious? Why haven't you sent him to the hospital?"

By then, Zhang Guiquan had completely lost all rationality. With a demented grin, he said to Zhang Hongchuan and Zhang Guimao, "Damn, you came just in time! We've been waiting for you!" Then he charged at Zhang Guimao yelling, "I'll teach you for trying to get rid of me! I'll kill every one of the twelve who are auditing me!"

At the same time, Zhang Yuliang slashed savagely at Zhang

Hongchuan's chest, abdomen, and thigh, and Zhang Hongchuan fell lifeless to the ground.

Meanwhile, Zhang Guiquan had picked up an umbrella and grabbed Zhang Guimao from behind, yelling at him, "Here's what you get for your audit!"

Zhang Guimao, a tall, big man, defended himself vigorously. Finding himself at a disadvantage, Zhang Guiquan called out, "Dongyi, hurry, he's getting away!"

Zhang Dongyi danced over with a vegetable knife in his hand and managed to fell Zhang Guimao with blows to the head. Zhang Jiazhi finished the job by stabbing Zhang Guimao in the back three times with a butcher's knife. A subsequent coroner's report noted that Zhang Guimao suffered five wounds to his head, with some penetrating the skull bone, and that his left lung was punctured.

Meanwhile, Zhang Guiyu, lying on the ground near death, uttered a groan of pain, and the rage-maddened Zhang Jiazhi rushed over and stabbed him five more times in the chest.

In an instant, three village representatives had been felled behind Zhang Guiyu's house. Blood mixed with rain coated the earth, and the air was heavy with the stench of slaughter.

Zhang Guiyu's elder brother, Zhang Guiyue, heard of the attack on his brother, and filled with grief and outrage, he ran over with a small wooden feed pole. Hopelessly nearsighted, he was practically in front of Zhang Jiazhi before he saw his brother lying on the ground. "Is that Qiaozi?" he cried, but almost before he finished the sentence, Zhang Jiazhi had plunged his butcher's knife into Guiyue's chest.

Zhang Guiyu's sixteen-year-old son, Zhang Xiaosong, had managed in the confusion to reach his father's side in hopes of getting him to the hospital. Zhang Chaowei grabbed his bloodied knife and slashed at Xiaosong's head, but at an onlooker's cry of warning, Zhang Xiaosong turned just in time; Zhang Chaowei's knife struck him in the shoulder instead, and Xiaosong fled with his life.

In a matter of only five minutes, the blood of four dead and one wounded mingled with the wind and rain in Xiaozhang Zhuang.

As Zhang Guiquan's fourth son, Zhang Simao, took up a knife and arrived panting at the scene, the village loudspeaker sounded with the voice of village Party Secretary Zhang Dianfeng urging the village representatives to continue their audit. . . .

The Village Tyrant Phenomenon

According to modern economic theory, the power of a social organization is related less to its size than to its level of organization. Organizations connected with political authorities are that much stronger. China's peasants are numerous, but they are too widely dispersed, and they lack the organizational resources to withstand oppression. On the other hand, village officials arise from a highly cohesive organization, and enjoy the authority of the state. If even a small percentage of these representatives betray national interests and employ their organizational resources for personal gain, the results can be horrifying.

Even though Zhang Guiquan received no more than a primary school education, he was still able to attain a powerful official position as vice-chairman of the village council. Combined with the enormous power of his clan (including seven sons), Zhang Guiquan was able to assume complete control over Xiaozhang Zhuang and effectively become a "village tyrant."

He raised grain quotas and taxes and imposed family planning fines according to his own caprice and pocketed most of the proceeds himself, while cunningly evading his own obligations to the public coffers.

Zhang Guiquan also drew local wrath by abusing his position to appropriate land and fish ponds, public property, and funds. How could such a villain become so powerful? What were the committee chairman and the village chairman doing all this time? Were they sharing in his corruption or simply turning a blind eye? Our inquiries were never able to determine the truth of the matter.

Ultimately, Zhang Guiquan's history is bound to strike us city dwellers as inexplicable. But in fact, the ills that plagued Xiaozhang Zhuang were not limited to its chaotic financial management; even more shocking were flaws in its basic organizational structure. Back in 1992, Zhang Guiquan had been sentenced to a suspended prison term on charges of corruption and sexual assault. But, while serving his suspended sentence, he retained his then post as chairman of Xiaozhang Zhuang's village committee, while also being appointed vice-chairman of the village committee of neighboring Zhangqiao Village, against the will of village residents. This official endorsement hardly encouraged

Zhang Guiquan to reform his evil ways, but rather made him even more fearlessly rapacious.

The behavior exhibited by Zhang Guiquan, while typical of the local bully phenomenon that used to plague villages in feudal times, is also different in a number of fundamental ways. In the feudal period, the village bully was only able to lord it over a small turf, and he usually had very limited liquid assets at his disposal, not to mention not enjoying the legitimacy gained through the support of local public authorities. Zhang Guiquan enjoyed both power and legitimacy, making him a much greater threat to society than any feudal bully.

Although the murders committed by Zhang Guiquan and his sons might be called an "individual case," the "Zhang Guiquan phenomenon" is something that should make our hearts tremble. In the course of our inquiries, we discovered that the phenomenon of "rule by terror" in the villages has already reached shocking proportions. Zhang Guiquan is merely a living example of a particular product of modern China's grassroots village power structure.

It is all too easy to reach these conclusions and reflections after the fact. The quandary is how to prevent more such tragedies from occurring in the future.

Postscript: The authors go on to relate that Zhang Guiquan, Zhang Jiazhi, Zhang Chaowei, and Zhang Yuliang were arrested for the deaths of Zhang Guiyue, Zhang Hongchuan, and Zhang Guiyu (Zhang Dongyi, who had killed Zhang Guimao, escaped).

With Zhang Guiquan and his family in custody, the village audit proceeded apace, and many irregularities were found, implicating not only Zhang Guiquan, but also the village Party secretary, village council chairman and village accountant.

Zhang Guiquan and his sons eventually went to trial. Zhang Guiquan and Zhang Jiazhi were sentenced to death for killing Zhang Guiyue, and Zhang Chaowei and Zhang Yuliang were sentenced to life in prison for killing Zhang Hongchuan and Zhang Guiyu. The villagers felt the life sentences were too lenient, and were particularly incensed at implications in the court records that the killers had been acting in self defense. Family members of the victims applied for a review of sentence by a higher court. In the meantime, the magazine Democracy and Rule of Law *published an exposé that brought the events at*

Xiaozhang Zhuang to national attention. After the story broke, local officials made efforts to assist the victims' families. On September 8, 1998, the Anhui Supreme People's Provincial Court, in its review of the case, ruled that Zhang Guiquan and his sons had not been acting in self defense when they caused the deaths of their victims.

Translated by Stacy Mosher

This translation is based on the Chinese text of *Chinese Peasantry: A Survey* as posted on the Web site of Beijing University of Posts and Telecommunications: http://www.bupt.edu.cn/news/book/jsh/032/.

A TALE OF TWO CRISES: SARS VS. AIDS

Hu Jia

An AIDS activist provides a glimpse into the challenges of addressing China's AIDS tragedy, and of keeping the outside world informed of the true situation.

On May 15, 2003, the day of the International AIDS Candlelight Memorial, China's Vice Premier and Minister of Health, Wu Yi, met with World Health Organization Director-General Dr. Gro Harlem Brundtland in Geneva to outline the Chinese government's efforts in controlling the SARS epidemic. On that same day, a team of WHO experts observed SARS prevention measures in AIDS-stricken villages in Henan Province's Shangcai County. Tonight by the light of a candle, I record how local officials made every effort to ensure that the truth was concealed from visiting WHO experts.

The Preparations

Beginning on May 15, a number of residents of Shangcai County's AIDS-affected villages contacted me and reported unusual activities usually preceding the arrival of a VIP delegation. On May 16, news circulated from the local health department that a delegation from WHO and China's Ministry of Health would be visiting Shangcai County to observe what measures were being taken to prevent the spread of SARS.

Over the previous two months, Chinese officials had hindered WHO efforts by providing falsified information. Now, in order to prevent such deception, WHO officials had adopted the strategy of surprise inspections; they had obtained permission from the central government to visit Beijing, Shanghai, Guangdong, and other affected areas, providing no more than five minutes' notice at any location so that local officials would not be given the opportunity to cover up the actual circumstances. For this trip to Henan the central government had instructed local officials to provide the WHO team with unimpeded access to any areas they wished to examine. But what this order actually did was to give local officials implied permission and opportunity to prepare for the WHO team.

On May 17, portions of Shangcai County were placed under curfew while local officials had village doctors set up SARS inspection points at various traffic intersections to demonstrate the extensive efforts being made to prevent SARS from entering the area. All through the night of May 17, the Party secretary of Shangcai County personally accompanied local officials in delivering AIDS medications to affected households in Wenlou Village, the most significant measure taken on behalf of Wenlou residents to date. Regardless of whether the medication was appropriate for individual patients, it was duly distributed, with officials instructing the villagers to stay well away from the official delegation due to arrive the next day.

On the morning of May 18, more than 200 plainclothes law enforcement officers from neighboring localities surrounded Wenlou Village, and along with a posse of county and village officials, prevented any contact between villagers and the visiting WHO delegation. The "villagers" that the WHO team was allowed to see were in fact the very plainclothes police officers who were preventing actual villagers from speaking with them.

The Villagers

On that morning, when a few villagers went to the village clinic to pick up some medication, law enforcement officers required two AIDS-infected women to leave immediately under threat of arrest. Half an hour before the arrival of the WHO delegation, two more villagers came out to talk with the visitors (the villagers didn't know who was in the delegation, only that senior officials would be present), but county officials had them arrested immediately and taken to the police station, where they were detained from 10 A.M. until 4 P.M. Witnesses say these actions were carried out under the orders of County Secretary Yang Songquan, who threatened to fire any local official who failed to seal off the village.

Villagers who were denied access to the clinic spotted more than a dozen vehicles entering the village, but knew nothing more than that some senior officials had come to inspect SARS prevention measures. Local officials confined AIDS patients to their homes, and every street and lane was guarded. Some villagers were able to observe the proceedings from their homes, but only at a distance of at least one hundred yards, and public security officers closely monitored their every move. We were in telephone communication with some villagers at the time, but right up until the WHO inspection team left the village at 11:20, the villagers could say little but that the delegation included foreigners.

On June 26 we interviewed one of the people detained, a 40-year-old woman named Yang Nidan, to hear her version of events. Yang is already suffering from the symptoms of AIDS, and at the time of her arrest had just come back from an examination at the county hospital. With considerable emotion, she described how, on the morning of May 18, she had gone to the village clinic to obtain medication. The clinic was chronically short of medicine, and when Yang heard of the visiting VIP delegation, she decided to wait near the clinic to tell them of the situation. When low-level officials failed to deter her, the county Party secretary had police officers load her roughly into a police vehicle, after which she was detained at the police station until 4 P.M. Yang demanded the reason for her detention, but was told by a police officer, "You want to know what law you broke? I'll kick you to death and then you'll know!" Four police officers then loaded her back into the police vehicle and escorted her home.

We really would like to know what law this woman broke. According to article 37 of the PRC Constitution, "The freedom of person of citizens of the People's Republic of China is inviolable. No citizen may be arrested except with the approval or by decision of a people's procuratorate or by decision of a people's court, and arrests must be made by a public security organ. Unlawful deprivation or restriction of citizens' freedom of person by detention or other means is prohibited; and unlawful search of the person of citizens is prohibited." Article 38 states, "The personal dignity of citizens of the People's Republic of China is inviolable. Insult, libel, false charge or frame-up directed against citizens by any means is prohibited." And according to article 5, "No organization or individual may enjoy the privilege of being above the Constitution and the law."

At the time of the interview, Yang Nidan was still suffering from bruised elbows and an injured back. Yang is an average farmwife who does not stand out in any way among her neighbors in Wen-lou Village, and she is not an activist. Her father-in-law, now in his seventies, is an old Party member who participated in the revolution. The family is poor and their home run down, but they have never asked their government for anything, and the old man borrows money if necessary to pay his Party dues. When he learned of Yang Nidan's arrest, the old man, who seldom leaves his bed, made his way on crutches to the police station to reason with the police, but they would not let him in. The old man remarked bitterly, "The Party is no longer what it was."

Yang's husband has never mustered the courage to have an HIV test, but he is constantly ill with symptoms of AIDS. He said that if he could obtain legal aid he would sue the county Party secretary. The couple has two sons and a daughter, who, at fifteen years old, has already gone out to work. The Yang's situation is a very common one in Henan's AIDS villages, and Yang Nidan wishes no more than to voice the concerns of others like her. More recently Yang has tried to talk to county officials, but without success.

A few more examples show some of the special features of SARS prevention efforts in Shangcai and other AIDS-affected parts of Henan Province.

Fake Quarantines

During the weeks immediately following the outbreak of SARS in China's northeast, more than fifty workers left Shandong, Beijing, Guangdong, and other affected provinces to return to their homes in Shangcai County's Shilipu Village. None of them were put under any form of quarantine. As late as May 15, just before the WHO visit, workers were returning directly to their homes from SARS-infected Shanxi, and many circulated freely throughout the village, much to the horror of other villagers. Village officials in Shangcai County were all well aware of the serious SARS situation in Shanxi, Beijing, and other places, and knew that returnees should be quarantined for twelve days, but they were unwilling to strictly enforce these measures. The powerless villagers, especially those already weakened from the symptoms of AIDS, could only pass each day in fear of a local outbreak.

A quarantine tent on the road north of Shilipu Village was overseen by a village official from 8 A.M. until 6 P.M. This official also manned two examination stations north and south of the village, but no one picked up the work when he was off duty. At the end of April, a few returning villagers were obliged to stay in the quarantine tent for three to five days, but only during the day—at night they went home to sleep, hardly an effective quarantine. A few people were staying in the quarantine tent when provincial and city officials came to inspect it on May 16, but they all returned home that same afternoon.

When the big inspection team arrived, someone made a great show of sterilizing the roadside by spraying it with alcohol and then setting it ablaze. Once the inspection team left about half an hour later, the sterilization work ended. It appears that this was the only time any such activity was carried out. Some of the villagers at Shilipu remarked in disgust, "Those Communist Party officials aren't good for much, but at least they put on a good show." When I asked them if they thought similar performances were being carried out in other villages, the villagers replied, "All crows are black!" Indeed, it seems that similar activities were carried out in the neighboring Houyang and Wenlou villages. More than one hundred people returned to Houyang Village from SARS-infected areas, most of them construction workers in Shanxi.

Wenlou Village also had a steady stream of at least fifty returnees from Shanxi, Guangdong, and Beijing. Each returning villager had his or her temperature taken when entering the village, and then was allowed to return home without any quarantine or other follow-up precautions. In the opinion of many villagers, the examination stations were not so much for passing a health check as they were for passing an inspection by higher officials. Some HIV/AIDS patients observed that during the height of the SARS crisis many doctors and nurses at local hospitals were still not bothering to wear masks.

Experts on communicable diseases have noted that respiratory diseases such as SARS tend to die out naturally during the hot summer months. One of the great mercies in the SARS disaster was that there were no major outbreaks in China's villages. In Beijing, Guangdong, and Hong Kong, where medical services are at their best, the disease still hit medical workers hardest. With far inferior medical facilities and manpower, the hinterlands would have been devastated by a major outbreak. Shanxi, which has an equivalent economic standard to Henan's, was seriously affected by SARS. We can only thank the hard efforts of other provinces for the lack of an outbreak in Henan. Along with certain preventative measures taken locally, the other factor we must thank is dumb luck.

The Cover-up

Earlier in 2003, there was an inspection of Shangcai County by provincial and national health officials, for which local officials prepared by repairing every pothole in the local roadways, and by paying each AIDS patient 200 yuan in hush money. The incorporated village of Houyang comprises five natural villages and seventeen administrative villages with a total population of 3,864.

In the mid-1990s, more than 1,800 villagers took part in the government-sponsored blood-selling program. This was 95 percent of the village's most vigorous populace aged sixteen to fifty-five. Of these, 450 villagers tested positive for HIV at the Shangcai County Epidemic Prevention station. Taking into account results at other HIV testing centers in Wuhan, Zhengzhou, Beijing, and elsewhere, a total of 670 villagers were eventually found to be HIV positive. A good 65 percent of the villagers who sold blood were never tested for HIV because of financial or psychological pressures.

Quite a few people went for blood tests only after they developed symptoms of AIDS. Only in portions of Houyang is the number of HIV-positive test results reasonably close to the actual number of infected people. A total of 260 deaths in the village between 1998 and 2003 were officially attributed to AIDS, but this number does not include the deaths of people who, hoping to avoid discrimination against themselves and their families, never took blood tests or admitted having the disease.

At the time that news began spreading of Henan villagers contracting AIDS from selling blood, more than 1,400 of the 3,170 residents of Wenlou Village in Lugang Township had sold blood, and only 550 (around 40 percent) of them subsequently had their blood tested for HIV. More than 80 other localities in Shangcai County present similar statistics.

In fact, Wenlou Village was by no means the worst affected. A better example is Lugang Township's Chenglao Village. At the beginning of 2000, it was estimated that 188 of Chenglao's 308 villagers had sold blood in the mid-1990s. This figure included women who had come to or left the village through marriage. Only fourteen people who were tested were found to be free of HIV, and as many as 93 percent of those who participated in the blood-selling program later tested positive for HIV, not to mention children subsequently born with AIDS to infected mothers. Between 2000 and 2003, thirty villagers died from AIDS-related illness. Of these, five died in 2000, and sixteen in 2002, with the number of deaths expected to reach its peak in the next three years. Seven children below the age of eighteen and five children over eighteen have been deprived of both parents through AIDS-related deaths. Thirteen more children have lost their fathers to AIDS, and eleven their mothers. Given that at least one parent from every household in this village sold blood, and in most cases both parents have tested positive for HIV, the future number of AIDS orphans is hard to estimate.

Let's look at how the local government took care of these sick villagers. None of the taxes on the villagers were reduced, and if any family failed to pay the taxes in full, they lost the 100 yuan per month allowance paid to each infected person. Only when all the taxes are paid up is the AIDS allowance reinstated. The AIDS allowance is not provided in cash, but is only exchangeable for medication, and as it does not cover the full cost, AIDS patients are obliged to make up the difference with what little money they have. Children who have lost both parents to AIDS are allowed to attend school free of charge, but those who have lost only one parent to AIDS, or have two sick parents, must come up with all of the necessary fees for school and books.

Henan provincial and health officials were well aware that the visiting WHO team would be examining the province's handling of both AIDS and SARS. The Party secretary of Henan Province, Li Keqiang, is said to have at one point telephoned central authorities and asked them not to let the WHO experts visit Henan. But by then the Chinese government had already committed itself and could not withdraw its permission, so

Henan had no choice but to accept a joint inspection by the WHO and the Ministry of Health.

The tendency in Henan Province has been to provide inaccurate statistics on AIDS. Officials in charge of Shangcai County's epidemic control are not going to suggest there is no incidence of disease—otherwise they would have no work. But one official instructed health workers in Houyang to report only 450 cases rather than the actual 670. Likewise Wenlou Village was told to report 306 cases rather than the local estimates of more than 700. Adding in those who did not have their blood tested, the officially reported figures fall short by at least 1,000 cases. We already know that as early as April 20, the Ministry of Health announced in a press conference that the central government would not tolerate any further inaccuracies in figures relating to SARS, but similar strictures do not seem to have been applied to figures relating to AIDS.

On June 18, patients were rushed out of the clinic in Wenlou Village, leaving only a handful of carefully selected, docile individuals to be presented to the WHO delegation. In addition, all of the medical personnel had been trained to faithfully regurgitate facts, policies, and figures relating to AIDS and SARS. After the WHO inspection team left, several Wenlou villagers sought out the township leader, Yue Qiaohe, who had accompanied the inspection team. When the villagers commented on the overblown performance, Yue laughed bitterly and said, "You all know how it is. There's no way around it."

But even Yue felt the arrangements were unconvincingly contrived. She also worried about the consequences of a slip she herself had made by stating that there were more than 600 AIDS patients in Wenlou, when she had been instructed to say 300.

Given the emotional responses of many villagers, I decided to seek out a more objective observer, and found a longtime Party member, sixty years old and not infected with HIV/AIDS. Although he had no personal stake in the situation, this man still noticed some serious problems. "We had no idea who these people were," this man said. "All of Wenlou Village was put under curfew, with all of Shangcai County's law enforcement officers on hand to impose it. No patients or doctors were allowed to go to the clinic, and we were not allowed to speak. Jiang Zemin's Three Represents policy calls for officials to trust the masses and seek truth from facts. But now they still don't let the masses speak—if you try to say a word they beat you up."

I told the old Party member that the visiting delegation had included WHO experts, and asked if any of the villagers had seen their faces. The man replied, "No villagers came forward to speak. If anyone asked where all of the sick people were, I don't know how they answered. That WHO delegation came here to look around, but if not for AIDS, who would come to Wenlou Village? Henan's provincial Party secretary, Li Kejiang, has come here before, but one time he didn't even step out of his car, and another time he stopped for about five minutes and then left. He didn't spend any time with the villagers or listen to their views."

This Party member added, "Actually, I think the central government's policies are good, but anyone who tries to follow them honestly at the lower levels is persecuted. There is no way for officials in Beijing to know what the actual circumstances are down here, because local officials say that everything is fine. In 2002 they gave only fifty-eight yuan to each AIDS patient in Wenlou Village for the whole year. The government announced that it donated more than 5 million yuan to AIDS patients, and that schooling for children and medicines were all provided free of charge. That's complete rubbish."

It cannot be denied that Henan Province actually took unprecedented measures to prevent SARS, having been warned that if the disease spread to AIDS-affected villages, official heads would roll. Medical personnel who came across anyone with a fever or other symptoms of SARS immediately treated the case as a possible communicable disease.

But it is equally clear that in the eyes of many officials, especially in Shilipu Village and Wenlou Village, the main defenses needed to be erected against the people and the WHO inspection team rather than against SARS. If as much effort had been directed against the corona virus, villagers would have felt much less worried about the disease.

Discriminatory Treatment

At the end of April 2003, Shangcai County spent 500,000 yuan on respirators and other equipment for the treatment of SARS, even though it is uncertain that anyone knows how to operate the equipment. Given the long-term inadequacy of resources available to treat AIDS, such a large national subsidy for an impoverished county to deal with a single disease is unprecedented.

If not for the urgings of the central government, it would have been difficult for local governments to move so quickly in a concerted nationwide effort. Is there any hope of similar attention being devoted to AIDS?

A few weeks ago a worker infected with AIDS returned to his home village from Shanxi. When he was found to be feverish, local officials were alerted and immediately had the man picked up for a thorough physical examination. When it was found that he was suffering from AIDS rather than SARS, the man was immediately released without further treatment. Two more Houyang residents returned to the village with fevers, but were sent home once it was learned they were registered as HIV positive. On May 24, a 28-year-old worker with HIV collapsed upon his return from Shanxi. The man suffered from diarrhea and a high fever and had difficulty breathing. It is amazing that someone with those symptoms was not stopped at one of the examination stations somewhere along his journey home. This young man, the only son of his parents, died of AIDS complications the morning after his return. There have been more than a few cases in recent years in which AIDS sufferers have died in detention centers, in transit, or within a day of returning home.

There has never been a public health policy developed to provide impoverished AIDS patients with the kind of cost-free care given to SARS patients. AIDS patients in Henan's Sui County have gone two months without their monthly medical stipend, and the stock of medication in the local clinic has run out. The government's explanation is that resources had to be diverted to SARS, and Sui County AIDS patients have been left to battle the disease on their own. Two representatives of local AIDS patients went to the county seat to explain to officials the difficulties AIDS patients are experiencing, but they were barred from entering the county council building by more than ten security officers enforcing SARS prevention measures. All they could do was keep returning day after day in hopes of being granted an audience with an appropriate official.

Long-term Planning

Another issue that has arisen among Shangcai County's AIDS patients is whether the results of villagers' HIV blood tests have any legal effect. If there is a positive HIV reading from a blood test in Henan's Zhengzhou Disease Prevention Center, this is stated explicitly on the test results. But the blood test certificate from the Shangcai County Disease Prevention Center only instructs the patient to take adequate nutrition and rest, accompanied by the center's official seal. There is no explicit acknowledgement that the patient is HIV positive. Some AIDS patients suspect this is to limit legal liability in case they decide to sue the government blood-drive centers.

Many AIDS patients have already died, but the lack of information on their certificates makes it hard to have their deaths officially attributed to AIDS. Some villagers hope to go to Zhengzhou to have their blood tested, but lack financial resources for the trip. Others have likened their situation to that during the Nanking Massacre, and feel that it is important for them to have solid evidence so officials cannot evade responsibility.

Every major blood-testing drive in Shangcai County discovers another batch of HIV-positive villagers, causing a statistical headache for government officials. Recently some villagers who previously tested positive for HIV were told they were HIV negative. This has led some villagers to believe that test results are being falsified in order to reduce the number of officially recognized cases. That has made villagers feel it is even more important to have their blood tested in Zhengzhou before going for another test in Shangcai County, so there will be evidence of the Shangcai County government's attempts to evade responsibility.

Every year the Chinese government attacks the China sections of *Country Reports on Human Rights Practices,* published by the U.S. and other Western governments, and emphasizes that the most important human rights are survival and development. But in fact these two civil rights are routinely denied to impoverished villagers, who live and die without ever knowing that they could even hope for such rights.

Related Incidents

Let us continue by looking at some related incidents. In early March, the central government began considering the problem of AIDS orphans. The Beijing Aizhixing Institute submitted a report to the National People's Congress and the Chinese People's Political Consultative Conference, which caused considerable nervousness in the Henan provincial government. The Henan authorities sent the vice-director of the Henan Health Department's Epidemic Prevention Center, Wang Zhe, who had met us before, to meet me along with the new vice-director of the provincial Center for Disease Control. The Henan government was very worried that our work would harm the province's image. Their meaning was plain: they did not want us revealing the Henan provincial government's flaws, but wished for us to communicate with provincial health officials first and give them an opportunity to solve the problem. Because Wang Zhe has spent a lot of time in the field, and has always been relatively frank, I was inclined to accept their suggestion of going to them first and seeing if they could handle the problems locally.

On March 5, the National People's Congress began their meeting. We were expecting a petition signed by people with HIV/AIDS from Shangcai County's Shilipu Village calling for free schooling for their children. One of the villagers, after collecting the signatures, had taken the petition to the Shangcai County post office to send it by express mail to our office in Beijing. While at the post office, the villager ran into the head of Shangcai County's AIDS Prevention Office, Feng Shipeng. Feng asked the villager what he was doing, then warned him not to cause any trouble around the time of the meeting in Beijing or there would be serious consequences. The villager was speechless with anger. As it turned out, we never received the petition from the Shangcai post office.

On April 16, an elderly resident of Shangcai County's Shilipu Village brought his daughter, Chen Yue, and her four-year-old daughter to Beijing to petition the central authorities. The mother and daughter had both been infected with AIDS, and Chen Yue's husband had recently died of complications from AIDS. A Party official responsible for distributing the monthly stipend to villagers infected with HIV/AIDS had brutally beaten Chen Yue, who reported the assault to the Public Security Bureau. But the police were familiar with the Party official, and, in the end, Chen Yue received only 1,500 yuan in compensation, including the stipend money that was due her. Chen Yue suspected corruption and decided to petition Beijing.

The family came to our office along with a photographer who was recording their journey. But as a local civil society organization, we were unable to offer much substantive assistance. I decided to refer the case to Wang Zhe, and Wang was of the opinion that it could only be settled locally. He asked Aizhixing to provide the family with financial assistance to return home. At that time Beijing's municipal government was still covering up the extent of the SARS crisis, but because our group regularly deals with communicable diseases, we were by that time well aware of how serious the problem had become, and I was one of the few people already wearing a face mask. We were very worried that the family, already weakened by illness, age, and travel, might easily contract SARS while trying to deliver their petition.

Even worse, they might unknowingly contract the illness and carry it back to their home village, where SARS might have a devastating effect among those already suffering from AIDS. Some mainland doctors have noted that the rate of infection by SARS among people with AIDS is actually very low, but given that much remains unknown about both diseases, we worried that infection with SARS would ultimately speed the demise of people with AIDS.

For that reason, we agreed with Wang Zhe's advice to assist the family in returning to Shangcai County as soon as possible. But Chen Yue was unwilling to leave the Aizhixing office, even though it was already 8:30 P.M., and knelt pleading at my feet. The family had no confidence in local officials to solve their problem. My colleague and I tried to impress on the family the danger of SARS, but people who come from the hell of AIDS have already seen so much death and pain that they no longer regard death as a serious threat. Finally at 9 P.M., I led them out of our office to the garden of a nearby temple. Chen Yue continued to bow at my feet, in spite of my protests. Her elderly father sat under a tree, smoking and occasionally sighing and wiping away a tear. The small girl watched her mother's travails in silence. She was a sweet, bright-eyed child, and the whole time she never spoke a word.

I gave them all the money I had with me, except for three yuan that I needed to take the bus home. There was nothing else I could give them but my own face mask and my best wishes for their safe journey.

A few days later, I inquired about Chen Yue among other villagers of Shilipu. I learned that we had dashed all of her remaining hopes. I was very sorry, but there was nothing else we could have done. After repeated disappointments, in the end, there may be nothing left for them to seek but death.

On April 20, it happened that Wang Zhe was in Shangcai County, and I notified the villagers of Shilipu that they should approach him for assistance in solving the problem of school fees for AIDS families. Wang Zhe passed the matter on to Nie Yong, the county vice-chairman responsible for AIDS. Nie Yong told the villagers that the school-fee situation would take some time to resolve. Nie said, "When you sold blood back then, you were paid for it." A villager said, "If not for the urging of local officials, we wouldn't have sold our blood and contracted AIDS." Possibly Nie felt he had lost face in the presence of local reporters and health workers. Later he privately arranged for that villager to be arrested and taught a lesson, and terrified the villager and his family.

On May 16 at 10 A.M., the provincial government sent an advance SARS inspection team to Shilipu Village, and the Shangcai County leadership arranged for a welcoming party composed of the village party secretary, township head, and township party secretary. Each examination station and clinic put on its own show. Everything went smoothly.

On May 19, SARS was one of the leading topics at the fifty-sixth executive committee meeting of the WHO in Vienna. On May 20 the team of WHO experts held a press conference in Zhengzhou and proclaimed Henan's efforts against SARS effective. How much did the experts know about the even greater efforts that had gone on behind the scenes in connection with their visit?

Some Strange Opinions

Last Christmas, we brought some clothes donated by Beijing residents to help the AIDS orphans of Shangcai County pass the winter. During this time we experienced some ideological conflicts with local officials. We had heard several rather peculiar conclusions that had been drawn regarding AIDS. According to a county secretariat official responsible for national security, for example, AIDS patients were not people, but demons. One can only wonder how an official can serve the people effectively with such an attitude. But having seen the conditions that some AIDS patients live in, I had to concede that in fact they were effectively living in a different world from the rest of us. I said to that official, "If what you mean is that people infected with AIDS live in a hell on earth, then perhaps they are not far from demons."

Another interesting opinion was voiced by the head of Shangcai County's AIDS Prevention Office, Feng Shipeng: the situation of the AIDS epidemic is a state secret. Quite apart from the fact that the laws relating to communicable diseases make it very clear that AIDS is not a state secret, simply from the aspect of the people's right to know, this assertion can only make one's blood boil with anger.

The SARS epidemic started out as a secret kept by the Ministry of Health and the Beijing municipal government, with the result that Beijing soon became one of the places most seriously affected by SARS. On April 20, the Ministry of Health announced that the number of cases of SARS in Beijing had leapt from 37 to 339. People were horrified, and began stockpiling goods or fleeing the city in droves. The fact is that it was not the epidemic that caused social chaos, but rather the government itself, which had lost the people's trust because of its deception and which had failed to give people and medical facilities adequate opportunity to prepare a defense against the disease. This lost opportunity resulted in the greatest and most visible price Beijing has had to pay for an error in public health. But in fact, AIDS is yet another invisible killer, and serves as an even better example of the disastrous consequences of secrecy. With China facing the cost of AIDS ten or one hundred times greater than that of SARS, who will take the responsibility for this fatal error?

Another conclusion reached by Feng Shipeng was that news of the illness would cause anti-China sentiment and damage China's image abroad. It is true that the highly contagious nature of SARS led to calls overseas for a quarantine on China. But we need to recognize that because of the limitations placed on news issued by the national health system and the Guangdong provincial government, the international spread of SARS put unprecedented pressure on the public health facilities of the mainland, Hong Kong, and Taiwan, and added extra frost to an already chilly world economy. I cannot understand why China gives the world so many pretexts on political, human rights, environmental, religious, and now public health grounds, to corner and isolate it. As a Chinese citizen I feel that I and the entire country have lost face.

According to article 27 of the PRC Constitution, "All state organs and functionaries must rely on the support of the people, keep in close touch with them, heed their opinions and suggestions, accept their supervision and work hard to serve them." And article 41 states, "Citizens of the People's Republic of China have the right to criticize and make suggestions to any state organ or functionary."

Government officials, you must face the fact that your fiercest critics are your own citizens, who are most hurt by your actions. Because local media are too tightly controlled to provide all of the necessary information, the overseas media have been extremely helpful to us on many occasions. For example, Dr. Jiang Yanyong's interviews with CCTV and Phoenix Satellite Television exposing the extent of the SARS crisis were like dropping a stone into the sea. It was only after the April 8, 2003, issue of *Time* magazine alerted the whole world to the actual situation in Beijing that the government began mobilizing the public. Should this be considered anti–China? I believe the people who hurt China the most are those cruel local officials who treat the people like so much grass.

Numbers Games

Let's look again at some figures. In August 2002, the Henan Province Health Department passed a secret report to the provincial government. The report states that 23,100–33,500 people have become infected with AIDS in Henan Province as a result of blood sales. In August 2002, the Shangcai County government said that 48,000 people had sold blood in twenty-two villages, and estimated the number of infected persons at 14,000. And around the same time, the Henan provincial government reported through the China News Service that Henan Province discovered its first case of AIDS in 1995, with a total of 2,065 infected persons identified, 335 ill and 238 dead. It is very suspicious that there should be such a wide discrepancy in these figures, especially between external and internal sources.

Listening to the villagers leads me to wonder if there is any hope for Shangcai County. The impression this place gives to people with AIDS and to outside observers is of a hell on earth where snow falls in June. The Henan government asks why we always make trouble for officials. It is because the government has so horribly wronged the people of Henan. Only if we lose our conscience, or become deaf and blind, can we possibly consider leaving the Henan government in peace. We are supporting the villagers in their efforts to record the visit of the WHO delegation to Shangcai County, and we will continue by passing this record on to the WHO office in Beijing. We have also assisted some of the more daring villagers to install phone lines and go on the Internet, and we are helping with the education of AIDS orphans. We have provided cameras and computer equipment to the villagers so they can record the tragedy around them and become witnesses against officials who attempt to evade the truth.

In the short term, we call for the WHO team of experts to return to Shangcai County and other AIDS-affected areas of Henan Province and allow us to assist them to understand the true situation of AIDS and SARS. Or as an alternative, we could arrange for villagers from AIDS-affected villages to visit the WHO office in Beijing and testify regarding the local situation. In the meantime, the central government should remove from office all local officials who have been responsible for covering up the true situation of AIDS in Henan Province all these years.

In the long term, China's people, research institutions, domestic and overseas media, and the international community must increase their monitoring of the government to ensure the preservation of precautions enacted after the SARS scandal was revealed, and public-mobilization efforts deployed against SARS should be similarly applied to fighting AIDS. In addition, given the importance of civil participation in fighting AIDS and SARS, the central government should immediately relax the present conditions for registering nongovernment organizations (NGOs) and nonprofit organizations (NPOs). Finally, the government should disband the Central Propaganda Department and allow independent media reporting of social problems and the views of the people. This would help prevent future social, public health, and ecological crises.

Tip of the Iceberg

Once the SARS crisis has passed, we will visit Shangcai County again and directly ask the head of the AIDS Prevention Office, Feng Shipeng, if he dares to say again that AIDS is a national secret. I am willing to enter a public dialogue with the officials of Henan Province. If they can prove me wrong, no one will be happier than I. If any of my facts are wrong, I will accept full responsibility.

Is Shangcai County too small and unimportant, are its residents' voices too far away and too weak, to warrant disciplinary measures against any of its officials? The fact is that in Shangcai County alone, more people have died of AIDS than the total number who died of SARS worldwide. Many villages see several deaths from AIDS on any given day; a corpse is not even cold in one house before cries of mourning rise in the next lane.

At the end of 2002, we visited several AIDS-stricken villagers in Houyang Village, aged five to sixty years old. Within two months, all were dead. The five-year-old was a boy named Zhou Mao who had been battling the disease since birth. On February 15, 2003, his parents took him to watch the fireworks in a nearby town, and a few hours later he breathed his last. There is no way of knowing whether he suffered in death or if death released him from suffering.

Last summer the United Nations published a report called, "HIV/AIDS: China's Titanic Peril." We believe that SARS will come under control internationally by July and will quickly recede from memory. But AIDS will remain with us for the long term. SARS is a mere bee sting compared with the cobra bite of AIDS.

During the height of the SARS crisis, the news media reported thoroughly on SARS every day, and the Ministry of Health held a daily press conference at 4 P.M. to brief the media on the situation. We would like to see similar attention paid to AIDS. If there were some system in place to provide full and open information on AIDS, this would greatly improve the public's knowledge regarding the disease and help contain its spread.

I know that this report is likely to have little effect, but I hope that anyone who reads it will pass it along to others, and if possible that it might reach the hands of senior officials and the international community so they can understand what is going on at the local levels. In the past few days, I have been making an accurate record of all that the villagers tell me. They are so full of frustration that they cannot hold anything back. How can our people flourish under such officials? How will our country advance? These officials are like a cancer. They must be removed so our country will not collapse, but will be able to begin its recovery.

Postscript: Hu Jia has become an increasingly prominent human rights activist, and is regularly subjected to surveillance, house arrest, and detention. He was detained on February 16, 2006, and held for nearly six weeks in an undisclosed location after participating in a hunger strike to protest the abuse of rights activists and their lawyers.

Translated by Stacy Mosher

MEDIA CONTROL IN CHINA

He Qinglian

China's economic modernization has allowed the government to camouflage its pervasive control under the glossy facade of consumerism, with a shift from ham-fisted censorship to an elaborate architecture of Party supervision, amorphous legislation, stringent licensing mechanisms, handpicked personnel, and concentrated media ownership.

Who Owns China's Media?

In democratic countries, the news media industry has independent legal status. A media company's investors are its bosses; the market decides the life or death of a company, and a newspaper with no subscribers will fold. But this international principle does not apply to China. China's government agencies have designated the mass media as a special commercial activity, and no matter who its investors are, a news provider is a publicly owned resource. As a result, all news agencies have just one shareholder: the Chinese Communist government.

Before the opening up and reform of Chinese society, when all Chinese media were funded and controlled by the government, rights of ownership were quite straightforward: any private individual who wanted to start a newspaper was automatically branded a criminal. But China's market reforms have forced Chinese media providers to consider economics and income, and the bureaucratic nature of the Chinese media has thrown up obstacles on the road to marketization. In order to survive, government-sponsored media all over China have begun to think in terms of business strategies, opening a gap in the Chinese government's control of news media.

THE RISE OF POPULAR MEDIA AND THE FATE OF THE 2003 REFORMS

The Decline of Party-sponsored Newspapers

Before the reform period, the Chinese media had no relevance apart from propaganda. But under the reforms, market forces have brought about the rise of new media organs. These include evening and metropolitan papers that Hong Kong and Taiwan researchers refer to as "popular media," which began to enjoy ascendancy after 1992. These evening and metropolitan papers focus primarily on society, sports, and entertainment news, with content especially appealing to city dwellers. Even so, they have not been able to enjoy the same degree of openness as Western media because of the Central Propaganda Ministry's imposed rule of "Three Meetings, Three Nods of the Head" on any articles critical of any government or Party official. Under this rule, the reporter, the target of the criticism, and the target's superior all have to meet prior to publication, and the target and his superior both have to sign an authorization certifying that the article can be published.

However, fierce competition for readers has led industry players to engage in a new practice known as "blindsiding," which has made even the dry, monotonous, stifled Party-sponsored papers change the way they tell the news. The rise of the popular media also brought a decline in circulation for Party-sponsored publications. The circulation of *People's Daily* at one point fell to just a few hundred thousand copies, and almost all of its subscribers were public entities forced to maintain their subscriptions by government mandate.[1]

The drop in circulation for Party-sponsored papers can also be adduced from their share of advertising income. In 1978, China's mass media were reborn after the disruptions of the Cultural Revolution. The total income from ads jumped sharply from 73 million yuan in 1983 to almost 7.8 billion yuan by 1996, increasing at a rate of 39 percent per year. In terms of the share of ad income, Party-sponsored papers have clearly lost out to the popular papers. Before 1990, the top national paper, *People's Daily*, was the unquestioned winner in the contest to attract ads, but it lost advertising steadily as the 1990s progressed. By 1995, the paper was unable to maintain its ranking among the top ten, and in 1997 it dropped below the twentieth slot.[2]

Chinese news sources are fairly uniform, but the metro papers offer more attractive layout and photos as well as features on society and daily life. In the first half of the 1990s, the Chinese government still labeled the purely entertainment-focused tabloid *(bagua)* news as containing "unhealthy content," and occasionally imposed limits on the publication of stories relating to celebrity scandals and other popular tabloid topics such as get-rich-quick schemes, sex, and murders. By the end of the 1990s, however, the government's Propaganda Ministry came to the realization that in a society that could become politicized in the blink of an eye, tabloid news could effectively divert the attention of the public and induce them to fall in line. As a result, the bureaucracy has adopted a much more lenient attitude toward Hong Kong and Taiwan-style "scandal sheets," while reserving its strictest censorship and punishment for political offenses (with provincial governments following the example of the central leadership).

Media Reform and the Rules for Survival[3]
The burgeoning ranks of news providers has caused enormous headaches for official censors. A culling process was initiated among weak, low-quality papers through the 2003 reforms, which mandate criteria for the survival and extinction of newspapers and periodicals. The following types of publications must cease operations:

- Those with incorrect politics, or those that have broken the law within the past five years;
- Party bureau publications with similar content must merge, and those with paying private subscriptions making up less than 50 percent of total subscriptions must close down; and
- All newspapers and periodicals published by foundations, think tanks, and research institutions associated with administrative, public safety, financial, tax, commercial/industrial, life planning, traffic, public health, environmental, fire prevention, or any other bureaus at the provincial level or below.

Publications that do not belong to the Party system and are not being closed down are to be wholly absorbed into the Party-sponsored fold, or else merged with Party-sponsored papers at all levels.

It is not difficult to discern the true aims of this round of reforms. Cutting government bureau publications is a way of relieving financial burdens and concentrating the limited resource of publicly funded subscriptions on central Party publications, thereby restoring them to the pre-reform system of public subscription. But even more important is the drive to shut down papers with incorrect politics and with records of violating regulations. Based on my eight years of experience, the government has only political offenders in mind, and not financial offenders. Finally, the annexation of non-Party publications achieved by this executive order is nothing more than a reversion to total control by the Party.

WHO ACTUALLY OWNS THE POPULAR MEDIA?

It must first be noted that popular media production faces two limitations from the outset: 1) Official regulations clearly forbid private publications; every publication that applies for authorization must be run by the government or by government officials. This is set in stone. 2) Because of these restrictions, the funding of many publications must be concealed. For example, some publications don't receive direct government funding, but rather are offshoots of officially run publications (such as provincial papers) that have raised money through advertising and business sponsorships to launch papers more suited to the demands of the popular market.

Since China's media cannot be privately funded, all private investment in publications is illegal, and non-governmental money injected into a media company cannot be openly acknowledged. Investing under these conditions is extremely risky, as illustrated by the case of *Qingchun Shuiyue (Youth),* the monthly periodical of the Henan Communist Youth Group. The Youth Group was unable to maintain the periodical, so in November 2000, it signed a contract with a private businessman surnamed Xue, who agreed to provide backing of 300,000 yuan for each issue and to move the publication's offices to Shenzhen.

As the revamped magazine's articles managed to suit the tastes of the "new generation," Mr. Xue invested additional funds in sales promotion. After the second issue of 2001, with sales looking good, the staff of *Qingchun* demanded that their contracts be revised with increased pay and benefits. Mr. Xue felt that the publication was still in its formative stage—it had not yet begun to turn a profit—and asked staff to delay the discussion. When the two sides failed to reach an agreement, the magazine threatened breach of contract. The 800,000 yuan that Mr. Xue had already invested went up in smoke; he had no room for negotiation, since the whole transaction was illegal in the first place.

Actually, the thorny question of "ownership" was quietly settled by the Chinese government in 1999 by way of a "legal shortcut." On October 21, 1999, *Xinwen Chuban She (News Publishing)* reported a directive by the Public Affairs Bureau, the Ministry of Finance, and the News Publishing Bureau stating unequivocally that all of China's newspapers and periodicals are publicly owned assets. A publication's official sponsoring organization is the principal investor by law, and infusions of funding by individuals or groups must be treated as loans and debts.[4]

Chinese Journalists in Fetters

The relationship between the Chinese news media and the Chinese government is diametrically opposite that between the media and the government in democratic societies. In modern democracies, the media perform the function of a social watchdog. Government policy, the personal integrity of government officials, and foreign relations are all objects of critical debate by the media. In China, however, the government exercises tight control over public opinion, has designated many areas off-limits for public discussion, and has imposed penalties to restrict journalists' freedom of action.

Generally speaking, the central government controls the media by means of political power and a series of top-down coercive policies. Local governments, lacking the supreme power and authority of the central government, rely on a multiplicity of control methods: on their own local media they can exert direct political control. In respect of reporters outside their jurisdiction, they exert control either directly through violence or indirectly through what Chinese officialdom commonly refers to as "saying hello"—exerting pressure on officials from the reporters' place of origin to bring the offending organs into line.

Control is directed first of all at sources of information, a journalist's lifeblood. The essence of journalism is to collect information from all sources and then use a broad range of media, including newspapers, television, and radio, to disseminate news to the wider public. The government therefore controls news sources and restricts ordinary people from providing information to domestic and foreign media through various laws and regulations, as well as more arbitrary forms of control in accordance with the spirit of central government policy.

Long years of suppression have bred a habit of "self-discipline" in Chinese journalists, and most resign themselves to playing the role of "Party mouthpieces" or seek to exploit their social influence for personal gain. Journalists with a sense of social responsibility tend to adopt a sort of camouflage: they assume that the central government leadership is wise and that the Chinese socialist system is correct, and conclude that low-level corruption and its disastrous consequences can be attributed to the individual actions of a minority of officials. According to this line of thought, by revealing the facts, journalists can help the top leadership understand what is really going on so these problems can be dealt with effectively.

While these journalists believe their self-protective approach will guarantee their personal safety, events have proven that in reality the central and local governments are united in their views of how to deal with the news media. When journalists are framed and attacked by local officials, as happens all too often, and are courageously supported by other local media, the central government maintains a shameful silence that amounts to tacit consent to and encouragement of the local government's unscrupulous behavior.

CONTROL AT THE SOURCE

Since the 1990s, China has witnessed a period of widespread graft and corruption accompanied by shocking events such as mining disasters, mass poisonings, and labor uprisings, but these stories have very rarely been reported by the Chinese media. It is difficult for nonjournalists to appreciate the difficulties a journalist encounters, not only in getting to the bottom of a story, but in battling the various levels of the Chinese bureaucracy. When such reports finally see light of day and compel the Chinese government to declare that it will "resolve the problem," they bring no honor to the courageous journalists who fought for them, but more typically spell the end of the journalists' careers, or even land them in prison.

Generally speaking, the Chinese government employs the following methods to control the media:

Black Eyes and Blackouts
Since the 1990s, local leaders have demonstrated a growing tendency to instigate violent attacks against journalists in an effort to bring news-gathering activities under "unified control." While the people who carry out the actual obstruction of interviews and news-gathering activities are typically boozed-up layabouts, local bullies, and members of the criminal underworld, they inevitably have local authorities behind them. The central government's failure to speak out against violent interference with news reporting has only emboldened local governments in their abuses. Following a huge explosion at the Liupanshui coalmine in Guizhou Province, no less than the deputy provincial governor, Liu Changgui, ordered the arrest of journalists and the forcible exposure of their film. In notorious cases in Nandan, Guangxi Zhuang Autonomous Region, and in Yichun, Jiangxi Province, the people responsible for interfering with journalists' activities included local officials, public security officers, and public prosecutors.[5]

In the case of a massive explosion at a fireworks factory in Jiangxi, the cover-up by government officials was ultimately exposed by reports of the incident circulating in Internet chatrooms, and then-Premier Zhu Rongji was ultimately forced to make a public apology. Eighteen days later, at a news conference on production safety by the Chinese State Administration of Safety, some journalists raised the question of local government officials who had ordered journalists beaten for trying to inform the public. The agency's deputy director replied, "In principle, news reports should not make a big fuss about or exaggerate accidents affecting production safety. There must be unity for the sake of social stability." He added, "Unified news management ought to be observed with respect to reports from the scene of accidents, the number of casualties, and the handling of the situation."[6]

Gentle Persuasion
Violence is perpetrated against journalists all over China, but newspapers very rarely report such incidents. In one typical case, Zhao Jingchao and Lü Tingchuan, reporters for the *Jinan Shibao (Jinan Times)* and Yang Fucheng, a reporter for *Shandong Qingnian (Shandong Youth)* magazine, were detained by local officials on the afternoon of June 1, 2002, after following up on corruption complaints by villagers of Ximeng Village

in Ninyang County, Shandong Province. The reporters were forced to surrender all their film rolls, interview notes, and audiotapes, after which a dozen plainclothes policemen beat and kicked them, inflicting severe head injuries on Zhao Jingchao. It was only after midnight, when a group of journalists dispatched by the *Jinan Shibao* showed up, that the police released the journalists.[7]

The Blacklist

Some local officials attempt to legitimize their refusal to submit to public scrutiny by issuing their own regulations restricting media activities. For example, at the end of 2001, the Dunhuang City government in Gansu Province issued an "Opinion on strengthening the supervision of correspondents' offices in Dunhuang and journalists conducting interviews in Dunhuang." This "opinion" specifically stipulates: "Critical reports that involve the leadership of this municipality and cadres ranked assistant section chief and above must be submitted to the local propaganda department for approval, and must also be transmitted to the persons concerned and the relevant leaders."[8]

In August 2002, the Public Security Bureau of Lanzhou City, Gansu, sent a letter to all news media in Lanzhou naming sixteen journalists who had published "inaccurate" reports about law enforcement personnel breaking the law. These journalists, who were consequently banned from future interviews with public security officers, expressed shock and indignation over this blacklisting. Subsequent inquiries by journalists at another newspaper found that all of the original reports were accurate. This assignment of journalistic oversight to the Public Security Bureau (PSB) is probably unique to China.

Damage Control

On August 10, 2001, the weekend edition of *Gongren Ribao (Workers' Daily)* in Lushi County, Henan Province, published a long lead story exposing redundant and extravagant projects pursued by the county Party secretary. People in the hills and towns of the impoverished county rapidly spread the news and fell over each other in eagerness to buy copies of the paper. Within a few days, some 10,000 copies of *Gongren Ribao* had been sold or photocopied by local people.

But on August 15, the deputy head of the propaganda department of Sanmenxia City, Henan Province, made a long-distance phone call to the head of the Lushi County post office, instructing him to confiscate the weekend edition of *Gongren Ribao,* as well as the *Fazhi Wencuibao (Legal Miscellany)* newspaper and *Jinjian (Golden Sword)* magazine, which had reprinted the offending article, on the grounds that the reports had projected a "bad image" of the government and the Party.[9]

Declaring "State Secrets"

The international community first became aware of the spread of AIDS in China when it was revealed that Chinese peasants from Henan Province had become infected after selling their blood. Because this story was brought to light by Gao Lujie and other physicians of international renown, the Chinese government could only temporarily treat Gao as a "target of internal control." But AIDS had already spread beyond Henan Province, and journalists who reported on a serious outbreak in the Shangzhou district of Shaanxi Province were investigated and prosecuted.

In the spring of 2000, hundreds of residents of Shangzhou were found to be infected with AIDS, and spot tests indicated an infection rate of 4 percent, far exceeding that of some African countries. Alarmed by the seriousness of the situation, the Shaanxi provincial government issued orders that no further random checks be conducted on tens of thousands of potential victims.

Zhao Shilong, a journalist for *Yangcheng Wanbao (Yangcheng Evening News)* in Guangzhou, and several journalists for *Shanxi Ribao (Shaanxi Daily)* and *Sanqin Dushibao (Sanqin Daily),* decided to provide society with a true picture of the AIDS situation, and despite many obstacles managed to interview many AIDS patients. The results of their investigation were reported in the Guangzhou media in March 2001.

When Premier Zhu Rongji read these reports, he immediately wrote an official response, causing an earthquake in Shangluo government circles. By then, however, Zhu Rongji's influence was already on the wane, and his criticism had little effect on the Shaanxi government officials who had deceived their superiors and defrauded their subordinates. Instead, local officials diverted official wrath onto the journalists who had brought the administrative negligence to public knowledge.

Zhao Shilong, the *Yangcheng Wanbao* journalist in faraway Guangzhou, was beyond reach, but the local journalists and an editor were fired on accusations of "violating the State Secrets Law concerning unauthorized publication of information on serious epidemics." As an internal regulation of the CCP Ministry of Propaganda stipulates that such people may no longer work on the "cultural frontline," this put an end to the journalists' careers.[10]

Having carefully read the State Secrets Law (its full title is Law of the People's Republic of China on the Protection of State Secrets) upon which the local officials based the penalties they imposed, I have found that none of its seven articles stipulates AIDS as falling within the scope of a state secret. This makes clear that the Chinese government applies laws according to its own capricious whims.

The Iron Heel
Case 1: The death of Feng Zhaoxia
On January 15, 2002, Feng Zhaoxia, a 48-year-old editor and journalist for the Xi'an-based newspaper *Gejie Dabao (World Report),* died under mysterious circumstances after publishing a series of articles exposing corruption and organized crime in the region. The police concluded that Feng committed suicide, but his family and friends raised many questions and expressed suspicion that he had been murdered in retaliation by the mafia. The local public security bureau failed to pursue the matter, hastily ruling that it was a case of suicide that did not warrant further investigation.

Case 2: The jailing of Gao Qinrong
Gao Qinrong, 43, was a member of the Chinese Communist Party and a journalist for *Jizhe Guancha (The Journalist Observer),* a magazine published by the official Xinhua News Agency, when he exposed fraudulent waste of money and manpower in a major irrigation project in 1998. The article was published in the internal reference edition of the *People's Daily* on May 27, 1998, and Gao also reported the matter to the Central Commission for Discipline Inspection.

On the evening of December 4, 1998, Gao was detained while on his way to meet a friend, and on May 4, 1999, he was sentenced to twelve years in prison on fabricated charges of "taking bribes, procurement of prostitutes, and fraud." He is currently serving his sentence in Jinzhong Prison in Shanxi Province.

Case 3: Recall of a "reactionary book"

The heavy tax burden shouldered by China's farmers has strained relations between cadres and farmers to the point of physical confrontation in many localities. Gui Xiaoqi, deputy editor of *Nongcun Fazhan Luncong (Commentaries for Rural Development),* a magazine published by the Jiangxi Rural Areas Work Commission, decided to compile a manual consisting of all of the central government's statements and documents directing local governments to lighten the peasantry's burden. The idea was to familiarize farmers with their own rights and duties and ultimately reduce conflict between cadres and the people. The result was the *Jiangqing Nongmin Fudan Gongzuo Shouce (Work Manual on Reducing Farmers' Tax Burdens).*[11]

Even before the manual was available in bookstores, farmers rushed to the offices of *Nongcun Fazhan Luncong* to buy copies, with some 12,000 sold between July 29 and August 11, 2000. The farmers used this compilation of government documents as legal substantiation for their claims against subcounty cadres, and in determining which taxes and fees were legal and which were arbitrary.

On August 21, 2000, the book's editors received an order from higher authorities to stop selling the *Work Manual* and to confiscate copies that had already been sold. Within six months, 11,000 of the 12,000 sold copies were confiscated, and a schoolteacher who photocopied the manual and distributed it to farmers was arrested on charges of "distributing a reactionary book."

Gui Xiaoqi was suspended from his post and managed to flee the locality just before he was to be placed under arrest. Jiangxi officials ordered that if Gui returned to Jiangxi, he was to be thrown in jail, and as of May 2001, he was still a fugitive.[12]

Case 4: Jiang Weiping, jailed for subversion

From 1998 onward, Jiang Weiping, bureau chief of the Northeast China office of the Hong Kong newspaper *Wen Wei Po,* wrote a series of articles exposing the corruption of the top leadership in Liaoning Province. Because such news cannot be published in mainland China, Jiang Weiping published his articles in various Hong Kong–based political magazines, such as *Front-Line,* which are considered "anticommunist" by the CCP.

Although Jiang used a pseudonym, identifying him presented no difficulty for China's security services. In December 2000, he was secretly arrested by the Dalian City Public Security Bureau, and on January 25, 2002, he was tried and sentenced to eight years in prison on charges of "revealing state secrets to foreign nationals" and "incitement to subvert state power." A cause célèbre in the West, Jiang eventually had his sentence reduced, and was released early in January 2006.

Case 5: The arrest of Ma Hailin
It is common knowledge that children of senior cadres exploit their parents' influence in business deals for personal financial gain. However, Chinese media have avoided reporting on these shady dealings, since it would accomplish little apart from bringing endless grief to those involved in the exposé. It was therefore quite astonishing when *Zhengquan Shichang Zhoukan (Stock Market Weekly)* published an article by Ma Hailin entitled, "The Mysterious Huaneng Power International, Inc.," detailing how former Premier Li Peng's family had acquired its considerable wealth.[13]

Zhengquan Shichang Zhoukan was immediately censured by the Propaganda Department of the Communist Party Central Committee. All copies that had already been distributed were impounded, and the magazine's December 1, 2001, issue published a "correction" apologizing for Ma's article. Bizarrely, this new issue was also confiscated as part of the Party's efforts to obliterate every trace of the original article. The magazine's editor-in-chief, Wang Boming, son of CCP veteran Wang Bingnan, had to make several self-criticisms. Ma, who was also a cadre with the People's Armed Police, was put under house arrest by his unit, and the unit commander wrote a letter to Li Peng voicing unanimous accord with the Central Committee and claiming that Ma's wife had actually written the article.

The cases presented above amply illustrate that in recent years the Chinese government has failed to deal with the culpability of local officials, while busily jailing and censoring journalists and news media that have the courage to report the facts.

As everyone knows, the Chinese Communist Party has a long tradition of thought and speech control. Since the 1990s, the CCP has dealt with "crimes of conscience" involving questions of ideology and free speech according to a secret directive Jiang Zemin issued in Shanghai in

1994: "Handle political questions by non-political means." Whenever possible, criminal convictions that ruin the reputation of offenders are preferred (such as visiting prostitutes, fraud, graft and corruption). Failing that, it is preferable to charge the person with revealing state secrets, incitement to subvert state power, or endangering national security.

Unlike journalists in the West, whose most dangerous assignments are usually in war-torn countries, Chinese journalists encounter danger in their own country during peacetime. The people who harm Chinese journalists are none other than China's rulers, and guarding against this sort of danger can be even harder than dodging bullets. Journalists who sacrifice themselves to tell the truth don't even enjoy the consolation of social recognition, as the Chinese government deploys the full might of the state to smear their reputations. This is the inevitable fate of journalists in a country where human rights are ignored.

Translated by Paul Frank and Jonathan Kaufman

Notes

1. "Central papers do not compete with local papers," *China Economic Times,* December 24, 1998. This piece of information was provided by the National Statistics Bureau, the China Economic Prosperity Center, the New Generation Market Research Company, Ltd., and Britain's Market Research Bureau.

2. Chen Huailin and Guo Zhongshi, "Analysis of the Gap in Advertising Income Between Party-Sponsored Newspapers and Popular Newspapers," *Journalism Studies Research* (Taiwan) 57 (1999).

3. All information for this section is from "On Effecting the Adoption of the Provisions of the CCP Central Committee and the Ministry of State Central Committee's 'Notice on Enhancing the Management of Overabundance of Party Bureau Publications,' and 'Using Official Authority to Promote Distribution and Lighten the Burden of Grassroots and Agricultural Units,' " *China News Publishing,* July 31, 2003, carried in *Chuanmei Guancha* [*Media Observer*], August 2, 2003, http://www.chuanmei.net.

4. *News Publishing,* October 21, 1999, 1st ed.-

5. Guangzhou journalist Zhao Shilong, who has covered a number of significant national events, has written a vivid essay recounting his own experiences in a "high-risk profession." Zhao Shilong, "Shi shui zai zurao caifang?" ["Who is stopping journalists from conducting interviews?"], *Nanfeng Chuang* [*Southern Exposure*], February 2002.

6. Editor's note: On February 20, 2004, the Xinhua News Agency reported that Wan Ruizhong, a former county Party head in southwestern Guangxi, was executed after

being found guilty of taking 3.2 million yuan in bribes from the operators of the Lajiapo tin mine in return for concealing a fatal flooding of the mine, which killed at least eighty-one people in 2001. The Xinhua report said that armed thugs were hired to keep reporters away, as a result of which the incident was not reported until two weeks after it occurred. *Fazhi Ribao* [*Legal Daily*], January 17, 2001.

7. "Shandong jizhe fang tangwu'an zao jingcha duda" ["Shandong Journalists Savagely Beaten While Investigating a Case of Corruption"], *Pingguo Ribao* [*Apple Daily*], Hong Kong, January 8, 2002.

8. *Zhongguo Qingnianbao* [*China Youth Daily*], January 14, 2002.

9. "Pilu xianweishuji dagao xingxianggongcheng Gongren Ribao zai Henan Lushixian bei tongzhi shoujiao" ["Unsold editions of the *Gongren Ribao* [*Workers Daily*] in Lushi County, Henan Province, are reported to have been confiscated for running articles revealing that the county Party secretary was pursuing redundant and extravagant projects"], *Zhongxing Wang* [*China News Service*], August 24, 2001.

10. Guangzhou journalist Zhao Shilong, who has covered a number of significant national events, has written a vivid essay recounting his own experiences in a "high-risk profession." Zhao Shilong, "Shi shui zai zurao caifang?" ["Who is stopping journalists from conducting interviews?]," *Nanfeng Chuang* [*Southern Exposure*], February 2002.

11. "Yiben qishu de qiyu" ["The remarkable adventure of a remarkable book"], *Nanfang Zhoumo* [*Southern Weekend*], front page, October 12, 2000.

12. Personal interview between the author and Gui Xiaoqi in Shenzhen, Guandong Province, in May 2001.

13. See Zhongguo zhengquan shichang sheji yanjiu lianhe bangongshi, [Chinese Stock Market Research Center], *Zhengquan Shichang Zhoukan* [*Stock Market Weekly*], 93, November 24, 2001.

AN INSIDE VIEW

Zhang Youjie

A former government lawyer witnessed firsthand how a rigidly legalistic approach to crimes of youthful error or financial desperation too often results in injustices that condemn people to a life with no future.

On January 31, 1994, public security police secretly detained Yu Meisun, secretary to the vice-chairman of the State Council's Environmental Committee, on allegations that he showed State Council documents to a Shanghai journalist. On November 10, 1994, the Beijing Municipal Supreme People's Court rejected Yu's appeal and upheld the original judgment by Judge Zhang Cunying, in which Yu Meisun was sentenced to three years in prison for "revealing state secrets." One week later, Yu Meisun was imprisoned in Beijing's No. 2 Prison in the suburban district of Dougezhuang.

Over the next two years, Yu Meisun, who had been engaged in legal work and research for more than ten years, personally encountered many cases of wrongful imprisonments. He formed lasting friendships with people who had been heavily penalized for minor crimes, or without having committed any crime at all. The following article is drawn from Yu Meisun's recollections, and all of the names mentioned are those of real people.

Li Shusen and Kan Yongtian

Li Shusen, born in 1968, was of above-average height, with wavy hair, fair skin, and large eyes framed by thick eyebrows—a good-looking and straightforward young man. His parents were both officials at a state-owned enterprise, and as the youngest of several siblings, Li enjoyed a comfortable home life. At the end of the 1980s, Li Shusen graduated with a major in foreign languages from a tourism school in Beijing, and went to work for the Holiday Travel Company in the Lido Hotel.

He found that he was more interested in working in a different department of that company, and obtained permission for a transfer. But the American manager of his department saw that Li was very capable, and when he learned of Li's contacts with the other department, he was unwilling to release him.

In a fit of pique, Li Shusen late one night took the manager's briefcase and concealed it in a washroom downstairs. When the manager returned the next day and found his briefcase missing, he filed a report. Li Shusen had told a few colleagues about what he had done, and eventually the police got wind of the truth and cracked the case. They noted that the misappropriated items, including a camera, were valued at more than 10,000 yuan, and that the victim was a foreigner, and classified the case as a major theft. On that basis, twenty-year-old Li Shusen was sentenced to twelve years in prison.

The American manager tried to have the charges dropped, but the police vociferously maintained that the law was inflexible, that Li Shusen was over eighteen and capable of taking responsibility for his actions, and that by so much as moving the goods he was already guilty of theft. They said the sentence already reflected the fact that this was Li's first offense, and that he might be sentenced more harshly if he appealed.

At that time, it was not common for defendants to have legal representation, and Li did not appeal his conviction. His girlfriend, a pretty young woman who worked at a foreign enterprise, initially visited Li every month in prison and insisted that she would wait for him to be released. Li Shusen's behavior in prison was exemplary, and each year he was named a model prisoner, resulting in his sentence being reduced to ten years. But in the eighth year, Li's girlfriend finally reached the end of her patience and left him.

After Li was released from prison, the best he could do was go to work for his elder brother's company. He gained a reputation as a key employee and tireless worker. The days and nights followed each other in a similar fashion, and Li eventually found himself having reached the age of thirty-two, without a penny to his name and still single.

Li Shusen's youthful indiscretion had caused no real harm to anyone. It was a personal dispute that could have been resolved through criticism and education. But because of foreigner worship in the judicial system, a fine young man was obliged to sacrifice his youth. Yu Meisun puts it this way: "Li was imprisoned for ten years for his malicious game involving goods worth 10,000 yuan, suggesting that the life of a twenty-year-old youth is worth only 1,000 yuan per year. It is clear that a civilized people-centered approach is inconsistent with a judicial organ that is a tool of autocracy."

A case such as Li Shusen's was by no means unique in Beijing's No. 2 Prison. Kan Yongtian's case and sentence offer a similar example. When Kan Yongtian was seventeen years old, he was sentenced to twelve years in prison for a prankish theft. Kan should have been dealt with more leniently because of his age, but because he had turned eighteen by the time of his trial, he was sentenced as an adult.

After Yu Meisun was released from prison, he looked up Kan Yongtian's father and said, "I was with your son day and night, and he helped me a great deal. He seems to be the kind of good person who enjoys helping others." These words moved the seventy-year-old father so much that his whole body trembled.

Kan Yongtian's father had been wounded while fighting in the Korean War. He later worked as a bodyguard, and after he was demobilized, he worked for a while as a guard at the Ministry of Culture. Now retired, he had fallen into a deep depression since his son's imprisonment, and after Yu Meisun's visit, he telephoned Yu every year to wish him a Happy New Year. In the spring of 2001, the old man rushed over from the eastern suburbs to the West City, and gasping for breath, he told Yu Meisun, "My son had his sentenced reduced again for good behavior. He's already been in prison for nearly ten years, and it looks like he may be able to get out by the end of the year."

Yu Meisun says, "I came across many people in prison who were sentenced more harshly than their crime warranted. These two young scamps fortunately had family members who regularly made the long trip to the suburbs to visit them in prison. The support of a happy and loving family allowed them to return to a normal life once they left prison and returned home. There are many people in prison who come from broken homes, and when they leave prison they have no way to return to a normal life, and may not even have a home to go to. They can easily develop a rebellious attitude and decide to revenge themselves on society, with the kind of results that don't bear contemplating.

"Law arises from common sense and is also held together by common sense. When the police write up a case, they should carefully analyze the circumstances. Judicial organs must not only avenge evil, drive out villains, and protect the virtuous, but must also show a broader concern for human fate and show leniency toward those who commit a crime in a moment of foolishness. Giving such people a chance to redeem their lives can help resolve social contradictions."

The Effect of Harsh Sentences on Families

Kang Bao, an illiterate peasant from Wangzuo Village in Beijing's Fengtai District, is a tiny and unprepossessing man. In 1994 he broke into the finance office of a local work unit and stole a check. By the time he took the check to a nearby brickyard to buy bricks a few days later, the theft had been reported, and he was arrested and sentenced to thirteen years in prison. The fact of the matter was that he never bought anything with the check he stole, and according to law he should have received a lighter sentence for intent.

After Kang Bao was sent to prison, his illiterate wife found it hard to support herself and her two daughters, and the best she could do was remarry. Forty-year-old Kang Bao, who attended literacy classes under Yu Meisun's encouragement, no longer had anyone at home to write to, and became deeply despondent in prison. At the time that Yu Meisun was about to leave prison, Kang Bao still had ten years of his sentence left to serve. In his deep respect for Yu Meisun, Kang Bao begged repeatedly for Yu to adopt his elder daughter, Xiaowei, of whom he had been granted custody in his divorce. Yu Meisun declined this request at first, and wrote a letter explaining the situation to Xiaowei.

Unfortunately, his letter was intercepted by the prison guards, and Yu Meisun was brought in for a reprimand, during which he was told that ex-cons were all bad people, and that such an arrangement would harm Xiaowei. When Yu Meisun was discharged from prison, he was carefully searched to make sure he wasn't carrying the contact information of Kang Bao's family, but in fact he had memorized Xiaowei's address.

Out of respect for his friend's wishes, Yu Meisun made an effort to locate Kang Bao's ex-wife soon after he left prison. The woman earned only 300 yuan per month at her job, so she had rented out the three-room family home to boarders at 100 yuan per month, and moved with her two daughters to live with her new husband twenty miles away. Because of the family's straitened circumstances, the younger daughter was unable to continue her primary education, and went out every day to sell flowers in the street. The elder daughter, Xiaowei, felt that Yu Meisun was a bad person, and was unwilling to go with him. Yu Meisun felt there was nothing more he could do, so he gave 200 yuan to the family and left. Yu Meisun made a point of going back to the prison to report back to Kang Bao that all of his efforts had been in vain. Kang Bao's face, twisted with grief, remained etched in Yu Meisun's memory for a long time afterward.

Early on the morning of September 1, 2000, Yu Meisun was awakened from his sleep by a telephone call from Kang Bao's ex-wife. She said her new husband was unable to support her and her two daughters, and they had divorced. Xiaowei had enrolled in a professional computer course that began that day, but the family was unable to pay the 2,000 yuan tuition. Yu Meisun borrowed the necessary funds from his mother and sped off on his bicycle to deliver it. When they met, Kang Bao's ex-wife told Yu Meisun that in order to support the family and to meet Xiaowei's tuition costs, she was arranging to sell their house and expected to get 10,000 yuan for it. She promised to repay Yu Meisun's 2,000 yuan as soon as she received the money.

Yu Meisun urged her not to sell the house, because then Kang Bao would have no home to return to when he left prison. He assured her that she didn't need to repay him right away, and that he would continue to subsidize Xiaowei's school expenses. One month later, he received a letter from Xiaowei urgently requesting another 1,000 yuan for computer usage fees. Yu Meisun immediately sent her the money. By then he had started carrying out legal research for a research organization and was pulling in a small monthly income.

A month later, Yu Meisun received another phone call from Xiaowei's mother telling him that Xiaowei's school performance had put her among the top five students in her class, and she had been awarded a scholarship of 60 yuan. Xiaowei's mother no longer planned to sell their home, and would wait to remarry Kang Bao when he was released from prison. Yu Meisun was very gratified that his modest efforts had managed to rescue this troubled family.

Yang Jun Loses Everything

Yang Jun, a handsome young man who slept in the bunk bed above Yu Meisun's, was a frail bookworm. He persisted in his studies in prison, and had already passed the national exams for self-study in several subjects. In 1988, when he was only eighteen years old, Yang Jun and two friends were on a trip, and they ran out of money in Hangzhou. In the middle of the night, they broke into a shop and stole some money and goods, which started off a theft spree that continued as they traveled for another month or so. Finally they were caught in Tianjin and sent to the Public Security Bureau. Their series of thefts, involving goods with a total value of a bit more than 20,000 yuan, was designated as a roving crime ring operating under serious circumstances and involving a large sum of money, and after being sent back to Beijing, the young men received suspended death sentences. Realizing the deadly implications of their pranks sent Yang Jun into despair, and he attempted suicide several times.

Yang Jun took out his judgment, saved all these years, and showed it to Yu Meisun. When Yu Meisun examined it closely, he found that the death sentence had been imposed through a judgment that was overly simplistic in its review of the facts of the case. He also noted that the judge was Zhang Cunying, the same judge who had sentenced Yu Meisun himself. Yu Meisun eventually discovered that many people in the prison had been harshly sentenced by this same judge over the past ten years. Those who had been sentenced early on compared notes with more recent arrivals, and they consulted Yu Meisun on legal points.

Yu Meisun sympathized with them, but could only do his best to console and pacify them: "You have been punished more than you deserved under the law. But the best you can do now is to finish your sentences, and after you're released from prison, maybe you can find Judge Zhang and discuss the matter with her."

The prisoners, hungry for vengeance, said, "After ten or twenty years, this Judge Zhang may have already retired. If we all stand before her as a group, even without saying a word, we might well scare her to death!"

Yang Jun's father was originally the head of a state-owned factory, and his mother was a worker. His sister was married, and there was only a younger brother left at home. Yang's father, before his death, had entrusted the younger brother's future to Yang Jun even before he gradu-ated from high school. Once Yang Jun found himself on death row, his conscience was plagued by his inability to fulfill his father's death wish. By the time Yu Meisun left prison, Yang Jun had served eight years, and had heard nothing from home for two years. He obsessed over his belief that he had caused the ruin of his family, and pleaded with Yu Meisun to contact them.

After leaving prison, Yu Meisun went to the address he had memo-rized, No. 12, Lane 3, Taifeng Road, but he could not find Yang Jun's family. The local committee chairperson, Wang Shuying, told Yu Meisun, "Yang Jun's mother went mad and spends all day wandering the streets. She can't find her own way home and has to be helped by neigh-bors all the time. Whenever there's a major festival or a meeting of the National People's Congress or the Chinese People's Political Consulta-tive Conference, the local Public Security dispatch station detains her for the sake of maintaining security and order. Yang Jun's younger brother was caught stealing, and after being convicted, he was sent to the Chadian *laogai* (reform through labor) farm. His elder sister is a bit weak in the head and lost her job, and has to be supported by her worker husband. Their life is very hard. Yang Jun's girlfriend married someone else a long time ago."

Mrs. Wang added that Yang Jun had always been a good student, and she didn't understand what would lead him to commit such a serious crime. She hoped Yu Meisun could find some legal loophole that would allow Yang Jun to be released early and come home to take care of his mother, which would greatly reduce the burden on the local committee and PSB dispatch station.

Yu Meisun sighed, "With a suspended death sentence, Yang Jun will have to serve at least twenty-five years before he can be released, so it'll be another ten years before he can come home. According to clauses 81 and 82 of the Criminal Procedure Law, there are various circumstances under which someone can be released early, but all of these require money and *guangxi* (official relationships). From what I saw when I was in prison, each year cut from a sentence requires the payment of at least 10,000 yuan in bribes, so Yang Jun would need more than 100,000 yuan to get out—and even then the results aren't guaranteed. This process is out of the reach of the vast majority of ordinary people."

Before he left, Yu Meisun gave Mrs. Wang 100 yuan to pass along to

Yang Jun's sister so she could go visit Yang in prison. A year later, Yu Meisun visited Yang Jun's home again, and this time Mrs. Wang took him to see Yang's mother. He found an unkempt old woman, her clothes hanging in tatters on her bony frame, her eyes dull and clouded—a frightful apparition. She incoherently claimed that she had no son, that her son had died, and fearfully babbled on about how someone wanted to grab her and take her away. There was nothing in the kitchen but a bowl of cold rice, not even any seasoning or vegetables.

Water gushed from an open faucet. Yang's mother was not willing to turn off the faucet because she believed someone had poisoned the water. In order not to affect the water meters of the entire neighborhood, the local committee had connected the old woman's home to its own water source. Yu Meisun marveled at the waste and expense resulting from the endless water flow.

Seeing the condition of Yang's mother moved Yu Meisun to tears. As an experienced legal practitioner, he felt too ashamed for words. Surely this was not the desired result of China's penal and corrections system! This could not and should not be the spirit and purpose of the law. With the help of Mrs. Wang, Yu Meisun telephoned Yang Jun's brother-in-law, who said he had received the 100 yuan Yu Meisun left a year ago, but had not gone to visit Yang Jun. He demanded impatiently, "Why are you butting into other people's business? What's it to you?"

Yang Jun was eventually transferred to Xiangfan Prison in Hubei Province, and Yu Meisun continued to send him goods and funds. He never told Yang Jun about his visits to his family, and Yang Jun fortunately never asked, treating Yu Meisun as his only family.

Yu Meisun observed, "Prisoners love to sing 'The Sailor' by Zheng Zhihua:[1] 'What is the pain of wind or rain to us when we still have our dreams?' When Yang Jun leaves prison and finds out that his family is destroyed and his dreams are shattered, he's sure to go mad with despair. His leaving prison will do no good to himself, to others, or to society. I don't dare to think about or even hope that he will survive to leave prison. . . ."

On the Trail of a Hanging Judge

In November 1998, at the Annual National Symposium on Criminal Law Research, Yu Meisun heard one lawyer say that Zhang Cunying, the judge at Beijing's No. 2 Supreme People's Criminal Court, was preparing to become a lawyer. In 2002, Yu Meisun found Zhang Cunying, now in her 50s, listed on a Chinese lawyers' Web site as a lawyer working at a certain law office. When veteran lawyer Zhang Sizhi heard of this he was shocked, and immediately asked Yu Meisun to accompany him to meet this harsh judge turned so-called lawyer before whom he had presented so many unsuccessful cases.

In early 2004, Yu Meisun found out from a legal Web site that Zhang Cunying had moved to a different law office, and he took down her address and telephone number, but never made an appointment to see her. Yu Meisun worried that if he actually met Zhang Cunying, he would feel compelled to bring up her unlawful judgments, and would become so enraged that he might attack her and even kill her. In order to avoid such a disaster, and for the sake of long-term goals, he felt it was best to take a more low-key approach and endure his humiliation.

Although many of the people Yu Meisun met in prison have since been released, some victims of injustice, such as Kang Bao, remain incarcerated in the Beijing No. 2 Prison, and every year Yu Meisun goes to visit them.

Postscript: Since his release from prison, Yu Meisun has become a well-known rights advocate, providing legal advice especially to rural activists. He frequently writes articles for overseas Web sites and publications on human rights issues.

Translated by Stacy Mosher

The original Chinese article was posted on HRIC's *Ren Yu Renquan* Web site: http://big5.hrichina.org/subsite/big5/article .Adp?article_id=5937&subcategory_id=174.

Note

1. "The Sailor" *(Shuishou)* is a popular song by Taiwanese singer Zheng Zhihua, born in 1961, who has inspired many young people by gaining success in spite of being handicapped by polio at the age of two.

A MIGRANT FAMILY'S ACCOUNTS

Yang Yinbo

Migrant workers are an indispensable element in China's drive toward economic reform, yet enjoy few of development's long-term benefits. This article describes the vulnerability of a relatively well-off migrant family that faces destitution if circumstances of employment or health change even slightly.

Zheng Wanxian, Wu Wanqin, and Zheng Zhongjie make up a migrant worker family from a village near Zigong City, Sichuan Province. Over the years the family has endured all manner of hardships, supporting and depending on each other as they've moved from Zigong to Guiyang, then to Kunming, Nanning, Xiamen, Ningbo, and Beijing. Most recently they moved to Foshan, Guangdong Province, where they live in the suburban town of Nanhai.

Zheng Wanxian, born in 1953, is a construction worker with no fixed wages. During a busy season he may earn 30–35 yuan (approximately $4) per day. Wu Wanqin, his wife, born in 1958, was forced to give up working four years ago for health reasons. She now looks after the family's home and has no income. The couple's son, Zheng Zhongjie, born in 1980, graduated from a vocational school and began working at the age of 17. He learned to drive and now has quite a good job making deliveries for a peanut oil factory. Adding in bonuses and extra income, his monthly income can reach around 3,800 yuan ($475).

Zheng Wanxian's family enjoys a measure of prestige among the residents of Nanhai. Their standard of living is no worse than that of the average urban resident, and they make a point of helping out neighbors in difficulty. They are considered honest, amiable, and generous. Because they have made friends locally, they don't have to pay rent, an enviable situation. However, they actually face the possibility of financial ruin at any moment, as I learned through more detailed discussion with the family after having the good fortune to make their acquaintance at a meal. The main evidence of their impending peril is in the careful household accounts kept by Wu Wanqin.

Huge Expenses

In 2004, the family's expenses totaled 21,792.50 yuan ($2,724), including medical expenses of 4,590 yuan ($574) for Wu Wanqin. In the first half of 2005, the family recorded total expenses of 9,365.30 yuan ($1,170), including 2,009 yuan ($251) in medical expenses for Wu Wanqin.

These expenditures do not include the money the family donates to others in need. Zheng Wanxian's family readily extends a helping hand to those facing hardship, and routinely passes along numerous additional small sums of money that they don't bother to record. Their more substantial donations totaled 13,050 yuan ($1,631) between February 2004 and June 2005.

When all of these expenditures are tallied up, the Zheng family spent a total of 44,207.80 yuan ($5,526), averaging 2,555.30 yuan ($319) per month or 85.20 yuan ($11) per day, during the period of January 1, 2004 to June 9, 2005.

A HEAVY BURDEN
There are three problems that become apparent in examining the family's accounts:

1) Zheng Wanxian's family eats well. They have a balanced diet of vegetables, meat, fruit, nutritional supplements, snacks, and sometimes eggs, and their home is stocked with a 40-liter bottle of mineral water and several six-packs of beer. They enjoy entertaining guests, and it is not unusual for them to purchase 35 yuan to 75 yuan worth of meat for a meal, while a typical three-member household can enjoy a meal of meat, vegetables, and beer for about 10 yuan per day.
2) The Zheng family has very high medical expenses. From January 2004 to early June 2005, Wu Wanqin's medical expenses came to an average of 12.70 yuan per day. In June her medical expenses increased to an average of 19.40 yuan per day. Because of her frail condition, Wu opts for medical regimens that put additional pressure on Zheng Zhongjie's meager financial resources. And Zheng Wanxian

and Zheng Zhongjie have their own medical expenses. In 2004, Zheng Wanxian required medical treatment costing a total of 420.50 yuan ($53), while Zheng Zhongjie's medical expenses totaled 496 yuan ($62).

3) A large proportion of the Zheng family's expenditure is made up of their contributions to others. The following chart shows the percentage of total expenses devoted to each type of expense from January 2004 to early June 2005:

Type of expense	Percentage of total
Charitable contributions	29.52
Living expenses	28.93
Other	26.62
Medical	14.93

In fact, there is another expenditure not recorded in the family's accounts: financial support for Zheng Wanxian's parents (Wu Wanqin's parents have passed away), which includes basic living expenses as well as medical expenses. The family sent a total of 2,300 yuan ($288) to Zheng Wanxian's parents in 2004, an average of 132.90 yuan ($17) per month.

The Family's Background

This is a very strong family unit. Twenty-five-year-old Zheng Zhongjie is currently the family's main earner. In October 2002, Zheng Zhongjie, who was twenty-two at the time, resigned from his factory job and started from scratch in Foshan. He hands his entire paycheck over to Wu Wanqin to manage, and never carries more than 100 yuan.

Zheng Zhongjie observes, "Our family definitely operates on a collective system; father operates as a private enterprise, mother as a shareholder enterprise and aid organization."

As to why the family runs this way, Zheng says, "My parents are around fifty years old. From a personal standpoint, I'm repaying my obligations to them; from a family standpoint, this responsibility is growing heavier by the day, and I have to carry the bulk of it for now."

"How much?" I asked.

"At least 90 percent."

The family accounts bear this out. From October 2002 to June 2005, Zheng Zhongjie earned 116,000 yuan ($14,500), an average of 3,591.30 yuan ($450) per month or 119.7 yuan ($15) per day. But his father spends the money as soon as it comes in; Zheng Wanxian is a gambling addict and loves to socialize, and his income can hardly keep up with his spending. The piecework the elder Zheng picked up during an eight-month period should have brought a worker with his experience a net income of 10,000 yuan ($1,250), but he brought home only 3,430 yuan ($430), an average of 106.20 yuan ($13) per month or 3.50 yuan per day, about the price of a pack of cigarettes.

Zheng Wanxian is a rather unusual character in three respects: First, he has a particularly capable son; second, he has an unusually broad range of friends and acquaintances; third, he has the mindset and habits of China's traditional "knights errant" in his conception of fair play and shared interest. He involves himself in everything, and is able to rally support among workers from Guizhou, Sichuan, and Chongqing, allowing him to deal with matters in a way that few others can.

After experiencing much hardship in his life, Zheng has established many bonds of loyalty among his fellow workers, and operates largely on the basis that he should extend a helping hand to anyone in need, without any expectation of repayment, whether that person is a relative, fellow villager, or friend. Zheng Zhongjie has inherited this trait from his father; he operates more cautiously, more by the book and less by the rules of the road, and he thinks more than he acts, but when it comes to helping others, the father and son are of one mind in their willingness to do whatever is necessary.

Looming Perils

Assistance to Others

I would like to say first that I deeply admire the impressive support that Zheng Wanxian's family offers to those less fortunate. By devoting 29.52 percent of the family's expenditure to charitable causes without consideration of practical return puts this migrant worker family in a class of charity exceeding that of many philanthropists. But this only goes to show the dearth of resources offered to members of disadvantaged groups—migrant workers can only obtain help from each other.

The economic status of migrant workers really calls for a workable mechanism that they can embrace for regular assistance.

Ingrained Habits

It is with deep regret that I feel obliged to point out this problem, which helps to answer the question of why migrant workers find it so hard to integrate themselves into an urban environment. The migration of rural residents from the villages to the cities and suburbs is not only a shift of labor, but also of customs, practices, mentalities, and languages. The comparatively conservative village ways of life are imported wholesale to the margins of the urban system. The areas where migrants settle can be easily divided into two types: the first is an urban system, characterized by rules and procedures and a mainstream culture; the second is a rural system, characterized by provincialism and chaos and a marginalized, murky counterculture.

Zheng Wanxian's gambling and penchant for hospitality is a genuine calamity for his family. Zheng Zhongjie can deal with any kind of impediment except his father's intemperance, guilelessness, and extravagance. He has come to the deep conviction that migrants bring some of their ills upon themselves, and that there is a real need to gain a better understanding of this special disadvantaged class.

Future Risk

Zheng Zhongjie has already exhausted his best effort, and is unlikely to substantially increase his income in the short term, yet three major problems already loom before him: first, he has not yet married; second, he has no permanent home; third, his mother's illness is proving extremely difficult to cure. Zheng Zhongjie's savings currently total only 49,000 yuan. If any of the family's problems should become acute, Zheng will only be able to look on in horror.

Another factor is the complicated relationship between Zheng Wanxian and Wu Wanqin, whose marriage has encountered many a rocky road. As their son, Zheng Zhongjie plays a crucial role, not only as their financial bulwark, but also as his mother's protector and his father's communicator, as a decision-maker and as a sounding board for viewpoints, information, and feelings, and even as a teacher. If a major change takes place in Zheng Zhongjie's role, this family could very easily move toward collapse.

Every Family Has Its Inscrutable Side

My investigation into the Zheng family's situation eventually led the family to sit down behind closed doors and spend six hours discussing how they might reduce their expenditures.

I made the following suggestions: first, the family's financial resources are limited, so money should be spent efficiently and with as little waste as possible. Second, financial strength alone is not enough to guarantee the family's stability, just as economic prowess cannot guarantee a country's stability; even more important is an atmosphere of equality, unity, understanding, caring, acting according to one's capabilities, and exercising volition—in short, a free and democratic family system.

Third, one-way benefit is not the most desirable situation. The Zheng home is not a sanctuary or an aid station, but should establish itself as a place for developing mutual benefit and mutual aid. My meaning isn't that they should make money off of their fellow migrants, but rather that they should find a way by which they and other migrants could make money or otherwise benefit together. Otherwise, if someone loses his pants at gambling and comes to the Zhengs for a handout, they are not necessarily helping by giving him money.

I'm a charitable person myself, and others have often accused me of an unworldly and impractical outlook, so I can genuinely relate to the Zheng family. In solving our problems, we need to apply our brains as well as our hearts.

Translated by Stacy Mosher

This article was originally published in Chinese on the Web site of *China Monthly (Minzhu Zhongguo):* http://www.chinamz.org/ MZ_Magazine/142issue/142zx6.htm.

MINESHAFT, OUR BLACK HOME

(For the Victims of Mining Accidents)

Qiu Yueshou

You may be sitting in a cozy room
Surrounded by fresh flowers and fine wine,
Or squatting out in the open,
Buffeted by icy winds and rain;
You may be successful, settled and content,
Or a migrant with the police on your trail;
A Goldlion tie may sway on your neck,
Or a placard scrawled with your complaints;
We are still all coal miners;
The mineshaft is our common home.

We're all together in a long, long tunnel
Digging into an endless darkness.
From the time of our grandfathers' grandfathers,
It's hard to say how long we've been digging.
Slowly, we've dug our eyes black,
Dug our hair black,
Dug ourselves a black home.
In the boundless, limitless blackness
We have the choice of only one color,
And only one black song
That we've sung until we're hoarse.

Let others say what they will,
We won't believe we're stupid.
Let those above ground write their great literature;
Look—we're using blood and coal

To write a Chinese version of *The Red and the Black* that will shake
    the world.

We have a million ways to console ourselves
Braided into a silken cord twisting tipsily in the breeze;
Along the hempen rope of words our ancestors
    wove for us
We walk with light hearts toward the rosy sunset.
Slowly, we've learned to act deaf and mute.
Following the bandits' deceit-strewn path,
We cheerfully slide to our annihilation.
Gradually, we've learned artifice and cunning.

A thug's hand
Smears our faces black
While another hand—our own—
Blinds our eyes with a cinder.

In our effort to stand,
Our heads hit the ceiling
And our split crowns bloom with blood.
In our effort to survive,
Our hands become feet
And drag us along the ground.

In the human communities of this earth
Our distant cousins have long bathed in the light
    of freedom,
While spring rains have begun to shower the fields
Of our neighbors and near kinsmen.

Let us raise our heavy pickaxes
And smash through the thick wall of despair;
Open a great breach
And let in clear water
To cleanse our black home;
Break the thick partition

And let our heartfelt wails resound to heaven—
We want a new home.

December 4, 2004

Translated by Stacy Mosher

This poem was originally published in Chinese on the Web site
of New Century Net:http://www.ncn.org/asp/zwginfo/da-KAY
.asp?ID=61043%20&ad=12/5/2004.

PART TWO

The Age of Mammoths: Systemic Political Problems

On the great ocean
In our country, in our moment
We can all climb on deck;
This is the face of autumn—

This season more fiery than summer,
A face like glass.

The Age of Mammoths
by Yang Chunguang

Translated by Stacy Mosher

The original Chinese poem was posted on the Peacehall Web site:
http://www.boxun.com/hero/yangcg/7_1.shtml.

In the space of less than twenty years, China has transformed itself from a closed, Soviet-style planned economy into the world's fastest growing major economy. With reported GDP growth of 9.9 percent in 2005, China claims the second-largest economy in the world, recording a GDP of US$9.412 trillion in 2005. The gleaming skyscrapers of Shanghai and Beijing make it hard to believe that as recently as 1989, then-paramount leader Deng Xiaoping voiced worries about a "peaceful evolution" of socialist countries toward capitalism and "bourgeois liberalization."

Now Chinese leaders are pointing to China's "peaceful rise," powered by the very market-driven capitalism that resulted from Deng's economic reforms. China has become a world political and economic power through a transition so rapid and momentous that even the Chinese leadership seems to be struggling to keep up with it. Yet, where is this transition heading? Who are the winners and losers?

This transformation has brought material benefits, especially to the officially-connected and urban elite. At the same time, economic reform has left the vast majority of Chinese behind through unemployment, development disparity, and the collapse of social security safety nets, placing strains on a system that would be challenged even under the best circumstances, given China's immense size and population.

What remains unchanged is the Chinese Communist Party, which has retained its place in the center of power as the top seats of government have passed from aging Party veterans to what is referred to as the "fourth generation" of leadership under President Hu Jintao and Premier Wen Jiabao. Although democratic elections have been implemented at the local level, China remains a "people's democratic dictatorship" under which the formation of unauthorized political organizations or the voicing of dissenting views is subject to prosecution for subversion or other crimes considered a threat to state or public security.

Lacking a genuine voice in public policy, disadvantaged groups are increasingly resorting to public protest against the more oppressive aspects of China's economic and political development. Increasingly, the authorities are cracking down on these protests, instead of addressing the problems fueling them. In this section, writers highlight the systemic problems at the root of much of the unrest in China today: Liu Xiaobo describes a system in which the power elite converts public assets into private property; He Qinglian warns against the destabilizing effects of rampant pillaging of China's natural resources; Zeng Renquan portrays the tragedy of young girls fleeing rural poverty who become caught up in an underworld of prostitution and crime; and Leng Wanbao exposes flaws in the justice system that lead to the imprisonment or execution of innocent people.

In political terms, China is in an Ice Age, an "Age of Mammoths" in which radical environmental change threatens with extinction any of those—including the leadership—who fail to successfully address the challenges before them.

CHINA'S ROBBER BARONS

Liu Xiaobo

China's economic privatization has converted public resources into private wealth for an elite minority. Abolishing clan-based power monopolies is the only way to guarantee ordinary people a share in China's economic development.

The root of Chinese-style elite privatization, in which public assets are transferred into the hands of private individuals in the ruling elite, is not a capitalist market system centered on the protection of private property and free competition, but is the result of a dictatorial system that is itself a privatization of public political power.

Privatization of public power is not a special product of the reform era, but rather is characteristic of a political system that has allowed the Chinese Communist government to develop into the ultimate totalitarian regime. It could be said that clarifying the essence of the Chinese Communist Party's power is the key to understanding the current problem of property rights; but clarifying the essence of the Party's power is no easy matter since the Party has begun to accept market economy and private property rights.

The Privatization of Power

In my opinion, it is necessary to begin with the privatization of public power in explaining the essence of the Communist Party system and its crippled reforms. The distinctive feature of modern civilization, the concept that political power should be for the collective good *(tianxia wei gong)* and that property rights should be for private benefit *(tianxia wei si)*, is diametrically opposite to the situation in China, which is characterized by political power for private benefit and property rights for the collective good. Under the Chinese system public power has always been essentially privatized, with four distinctive features:

1) Public power is monopolized by special interest groups that will not share power with other groups, and will not allow the existence of any opposition party.
2) Dynastic succession and maintenance relies principally on violence, in effect private power relying on terror.
3) Any dynastic power transition takes place only within the privileged class; the other strata of society are not allowed to take part. In ancient society transfer of power was carried out within a dynastic clan; in modern society it is carried out within the Party.
4) All of society's resources, from individual people to property, are monopolized under the principle of "all for the collective."

The other essential qualities of China's political system, such as political conspiracy and ideological dishonesty, are mere by-products of the privatization of public power. Political conspiracy is the tool for distributing power within a despotic government. Ideological dishonesty serves as a despotic government's moral disguise. Whether we speak of the dynastic system of imperial times or the party system of modern times, whether it's the planned economy and collectives of the Mao Zedong era or the marketized power and elite privatization launched in the Deng Xiaoping era, the privatization of public power has not changed one iota—in all cases the nation's political power is transformed into the private tool of the elite class.

The Historical Basis of Clan Rule

In the imperial era, public power circulated within a clan *(jia tianxia),* and power was legitimized through violence. Whichever clan was victorious in battle took over the throne and retained power until a new clan wrested it away through violent means. Starting when the Qin Emperor united China through violence, China's 2,000 years of imperial history was a vicious cycle of clan rule, and the civil service exam system was nothing more than a means for the ruling clan to absorb serfs. Although backward ruling methods prevented clans from actually taking complete control of all property, and private ownership continued to exist among the people, the formal system of clan rule still only recognized ownership of property and individual persons by the ruling clan.

Although the revolution of 1911 overthrew dynastic rule and replaced it with a modern political party system, China's party system was little more than traditional clan rule in a different form. From the moment it entered China, the political party system operated along Leninist lines diametrically opposite to the Western concept of peaceful competition through votes, and depended on gaining and maintaining control through violence. Public power monopolized by a clan became monopoly by a party, and transition of power from one party to another was accomplished through violence just as it had been from one clan to another. Likewise, internal power shifts under party rule became an amalgam of clan and factional rule. In the eyes of a party chieftain, the most desirable transition of power was naturally within one's own family, from father to son. But lacking that opportunity, the next best thing was to ensure that power remained within the party and was not shared with any other party or political power.

The nationalist party system created in China under the leadership of Sun Yat-sen was developed further by Chiang Kai-shek into "one nation under one party under one leader" through the Kuomintang. Only the chaos of wartime prevented the Kuomintang from taking complete control. Although the Kuomintang authorities recognized private property rights, the privatization of public power resulted in a bureaucratic takeover of property, just another form of elite privatization.

After World War II, the Kuomintang authorities tried to implement a Western-style modern political party system, but the experiment failed due to lack of cooperation from the Soviet Union–supported Chinese Communist Party. After fleeing to Taiwan, Chiang Kai-shek passed on his dictatorial power to his son, Chiang Ching-kuo, and it was only in the 1980s that the Kuomintang authorities controlled by the Chiang family began to genuinely turn toward a modern multiparty system. In the year 2000, Taiwan for the first time implemented a transfer of power through competition between parties.

In mainland China, with the support of the Soviet Union, the Communist Party used a crippling civil war to replace the Kuomintang, but did not put an end to the one-party political dictatorship. Instead, the Communist Party creatively developed the nationalist party system by transforming the Kuomintang's one-party rule *(dang tianxia)*, composed of a mixture of bureaucratic resources and a party system, into a new one-party rule composed of a more peculiar mixture of property cooperatives and privatization of power. In addition, highly effective ruling methods resulting from the combination of a peaceful environment, a secretive organizational system, deceptive authoritarian ideologies, and technological advancement allowed the Communist Party's control to greatly exceed that of the Kuomintang era.

The spread of Party organizations and units to the grass roots allowed the Party's influence to permeate all of society, to the point that the entire country ultimately became the property of one person. Tens of millions of people became the experimental objects of Mao Zedong's personal ambition, and the Party devolved into little more than an organ for determining succession. In fact, Mao was by no means averse to family succession, as indicated by his strong support of Jiang Qing and Mao Yuanxin during his final years. If his son Mao Anying had not been killed in the Korean War, China would probably have had a family dynasty like North Korea's under Kim Il Sung.

After the death of the ultimate party boss, Mao Zedong, the Deng Xiaoping era came about through usurpation, with several oligarchs joining together to form a power balance within the Party and ruling out the possibility of clan succession. Succession determined by the Party bosses became the chief means of power transfer under Communist Party rule, and the periodic rejuvenation of the elite class was mainly carried out within the Party. But Party ownership of public power did not change at all; it simply shifted from individual totalitarianism to oligarchy, all the more easily becoming a private tool for the internal division of spoils among the privileged class.

Privatization of power and privatization of assets were mutually supportive, and ultimately resulted in a division of spoils among elite clans and individuals. The elite clans typically implement a division of labor—each clan has at least one senior official and one tycoon—that provides a systematic arrangement for the sharing of bribes and other plunder. As the veterans of the revolution have gradually died off, their descendants have assumed power through such internal distribution of spoils. The rise of the "princelings" is by no means an accidental product of China's current system, but rather is the natural result of Chinese Communist Party rule. During the Cultural Revolution, the children of top officials had already begun promoting the bloodline of "Heroic Elders Producing Virtuous Sons," nakedly presaging the ideology of elite privatization by a new generation of the Communist Party.

Now if an ordinary person aspires to a position in the Party hierarchy through which he can take for himself a share of the turf controlled by the elite, he must first turn himself into a "Slave of the Party." In addition, if an internal struggle or an anti-corruption campaign requires a sacrificial lamb, these "commoners" who have managed to ascend to elite status will be the first to be led to the altar, while the villains among the hereditary elite escape to continue satisfying their desires unimpeded.

The Invisible Power Structure

Shortly before his retirement as premier, Li Peng paid a high-profile tribute to his birth parents, apparently out of fear that upon leaving office he would become a target of revenge for his role in the June 4th bloodbath and for the participation of his family members in corruption scandals. Just over a year earlier, people defrauded in the Xinguoda Group case had raised the chant, "Return our money, Li Peng!" in demonstrations and petitions. By stressing his revolutionary credentials, Li Peng implied that anyone seeking revenge from him was a lowlife and a traitor to the revolution.

The case of Li Peng effectively proclaimed to society that elite privatization was not only a fact of life, but was also a traditional concept through which the new elite generation legitimizes the source of its power. In recent years economists have leveled subtle criticism at increasing clan control of China's private enterprises. But in fact the distinctively Chinese feature of clan control is not typified in the open clan control of private enterprises, but rather in the hidden clan influence at every level of the Chinese Communist Party's elite power structure.

Nowadays when people in China talk about power struggles within the leadership and the delineation of interest groups, one of the important factors is the clan. If it is said that political power struggles still involve the "Shanghai clique," the "Qinghua clique," the "Liusu clique" and the "princelings," then on the economic front elite interest groups are delineated by clans. In business, the elite's approach to apportioning state-owned assets and plundering society's wealth is largely clan-based; in politics, the elite's approach to apportioning power is even more clan-based. In each province, city, and county, ordinary people refer to the "XX clan" to denote the main group controlling the local level of elite power.

In recent years, under the "Three Represents" framework, the increasing clan domination of the Chinese Communist Party's elite interest groups has gradually led to a change from controlling state-owned enterprises to establishing private companies and thereby privatizing even more enormous amounts of state assets. A research report entitled "The Present Economic Situation of All Classes of Society"— produced jointly by the Central Research Office, State Council Research Office, and Chinese Academy of Social Sciences in 2003— revealed that China had 5 million people with assets of 10 million yuan or more, including 20,000 with assets of at least 100 million yuan. Among those with assets of at least 10 million yuan, the report's survey found that more than 90 percent were from the elite clans of the Chinese Communist Party. Only 5.5 percent were rich by virtue of being related to persons or operating businesses outside of China, and only 4.5 percent became rich from their own efforts. According to scholars who specialize in researching the highest levels of government, more than 200 "princelings" currently hold positions in the upper levels of the government.

The Economic Cost of Clan Rule

If we say that in regards to China's development the tendency toward clan control of private enterprises has done more good than harm, we still have to say that increasing clan control of the Chinese Communist Party's elite power cartels has done more harm than good. Objectively speaking, in terms of traditional inheritance practices as well as the current economic environment and marketization standards, clan control of private enterprises is only a natural result of tradition and popular preference, and is arguably especially beneficial in the early stages of marketization. Western commercial society similarly moved from family-controlled enterprises to more diversified shareholdings, and commercial regulations are an extension from blood-based relationships to contracts between strangers.

Under China's current system the prosperity of a private enterprise depends on developing relationships with those in power and buying influence, but private companies still require an enormous investment of private funds at the outset. Bribery is simply a means of defraying the "influence fees" and "system costs" that arise in the unlevel playing field of China's power-driven market. The perversity of the Chinese market is that its plentiful supply of cheap labor cannot compensate for the business costs exacted by officials. That is one of the main reasons that businesses routinely evade taxes. Foreign-invested companies compete with domestic private concerns, but both are equally dissatisfied with excessive administrative interference. Exorbitant trading costs run contrary to the market-economy principle of free and fair trade. Following China's accession to the WTO, one of the foci of economic reform has been to reduce excessive trading costs in accordance with the rules of a free market.

But the extortionate influence fees that so plague private enterprises are not something that the elite clans at any level of government are going to make any effort to address. That's because their privileged positions are the source of their fortune, what some refer to as making enormous profit from scanty capital. I say it is making huge profit from nothing at all, because the public power held by the elites actually belongs to society and should be used for the public welfare rather than as a tool for personal profit by officials and their families.

With the inability of the dictatorship to win the hearts of the people, the Chinese Communist elites are becoming increasingly shortsighted and sociopathic in their determination to grab as much benefit as they can before their privileged status disintegrates beneath their feet. This apocalyptic mentality, rooted in a paranoiac obsession with power and assets, has spread from the communist elites to the rest of the upper class, and has fueled opportunistic behavior such as extravagant lifestyles, emigration, and transfer of assets abroad.

The Moral Cost of Clan Rule

Even though opening and reform has gradually given ordinary members of society an opportunity to possess and distribute property, and has recognized the reality of privatization, the Communist Party still monopolizes the political resources of public power and has not allowed anyone else to share in them.

Their morally indefensible accumulation of personal wealth has led not only to the material impoverishment of the powerless masses and the moral impoverishment of the human conscience, but also to the utter bankruptcy of the greatest product of public welfare—social justice. Cronyism has become the general preoccupation of society as privatization of public power has made becoming an official a shortcut to securing personal benefit.

In recent years, one of the things the Chinese Communist Party points to with pride is the alacrity with which new university graduates are competing to join. But the reason for the students' interest is not unselfish idealism, but rather long-term personal aspiration. In China under the Communist Party, the best way to obtain personal advantage is through officialdom, which can only be achieved by joining the Party. Regardless of what one hopes to achieve in life, it is better to be a Party member than not. Even among students who "enthusiastically call for political progress," when the subject of Party membership arises, they abandon sloganeering and become extremely practical: China is run by the Party. If you want to accomplish anything in your profession, you definitely have to join the Party. That's the only way you'll have an opportunity to make money or achieve a position of influence. What's wrong with joining the Party, anyway? And what's wrong with becoming an official or getting rich? You can make a better living for yourself and your family, and contribute more to society than most other people.

Weary of paying the price for this extreme lack of public justice through crippled reform under elite privatization, the people have been spurred to civic consciousness; their power and dissatisfaction are increasing, and they are demanding their human rights. But as the system under privatized public power allows no legal organized means for the public to express its demands for rights, or any effective avenue for a direct response from within the system, movements must increasingly arise that will ultimately create a civil movement—or an alternative civil authority—outside of the system.

A political system monopolized by one party will never be able to satisfy these demands. But a common law system that could integrate and to a great extent accommodate the different interests and values of the bureaucracy and the people, if tolerant to criticism or opposition to the government, might be able to contain the conflict between different interests and values within a framework of legal competition. Such a system could also treat criticism and opposition toward the government as legal expression, and could ensure that the methods of competition and opposition remain peaceful. Otherwise, a one-party dictatorship will never be able to implement long-term social stability, and any other strategy will only be a temporary expedient. Once the opportunity for a thorough assessment of ill-gotten gains arises, there is a very real possibility of an economic cultural revolution in the order of the old land-reform movement.

In other words, if we don't change the system of privatization of public power that turns public assets into private property, any regime change under the existing system can only be accomplished under the chaos of violent revolution. And the price of violent revolution is high, and the results are uncertain—it could lead, not to the establishment of a modern political system, but to a reversion to dictatorship. This option will do more harm than good for all social classes.

Translated by Stacy Mosher

This article was first published in Chinese on HRIC's *Ren Yu Renquan* Web site (www.renyurenquan.org).

DRAINING THE POND TO CATCH THE FISH

He Qinglian

In October and early November 2004, tens of thousands of villagers from the Hanyuan Reservoir area in Sichuan Province staged a series of protests over their forced relocation to make way for the Pubugou Dam. In the course of the demonstrations, as many as 10,000 soldiers were reportedly deployed against the protesters. At one point the provincial Party secretary, Zhang Xuezhong, was surrounded and detained for several hours by protesters, and by the end of the clashes several villagers and two police officers had been reported killed, and scores injured. Although the Hanyuan uprising was one of the worst of China's recent mass protests, its root causes are in many ways emblematic of long-term systemic problems that will breed continued unrest in the future.

While the Hanyuan protest was staged to protect the livelihoods of 150,000 people, it was only one of a large number of similar popular protests that have recently been organized all over China in response to the Chinese government's plundering of the nation's natural resources, referred to as "draining the pond to catch the fish." Under China's new energy strategy, at least 50 million people will be forced to relocate in the foreseeable future.

Facing the twin crises of an energy crunch and riots at the bottom rung of society, the Chinese government is presented with a choice between developing energy resources to sustain economic development and protecting the basic livelihood of tens of millions of people. Put in plain language, it's a choice between sacrificing a minority's right to make a living in order to buy the Communist regime a few more years in power, or reducing the speed of economic development in order to cope with a variety of socioeconomic problems.

Many analysts attribute the Hanyuan riots to the fact that the compensation residents were offered was unreasonably scanty. But this explanation only scratches the surface. The deeper problem is that forced relocations destroy farmers' livelihood. Before they were relocated, these peasants had a few thousand *mu* of fertile land that enabled them to make a decent living. After they were relocated, they were given poor hillside land on which they could only plant corn and were unable to eke out an existence. Even if corrupt officials hadn't pocketed a penny of the so-called compensation, it was only a one-off payment, while each peasant family needs regular and uninterrupted income in order to support itself. The overall urban and rural unemployment rate in China now stands at approximately 30 percent. By ruthlessly driving the farmers of Hanyuan from their land, the government managed to increase the ranks of the jobless by more than 100,000.

The government fails to recognize the seriousness of this situation. Several months ago, a number of social scientists conducting an on-the-spot investigation warned that Hanyuan risked following the same disastrous path as the Manwan hydroelectric power station in Yunnan Province. They concluded that "a hydroelectric power engineering project designed to alleviate poverty and promote economic development has ended up impoverishing peasants who were previously relatively well-off." Why is it that while Hu Jintao chants lofty slogans about "governing for the people's benefit," the Chinese government repeatedly permits large-scale forcible relocations of ordinary citizens in a patent violation of their civil rights?

Sacrificing Individuals to the Interests of the State

Manwan and Hanyuan epitomize the destitution of peasants in the mad rush to build dams in western China. In the Yangtze and Yellow river areas of southwestern China, ten huge hydroelectric power stations are going to be built in the near future. Adding in the Ertan Hydroelectric Plant, which has already been built, these power plants will have a total installed capacity of five Three Gorges hydroelectric power stations. This hydroelectric boom is wreaking havoc on the natural environment and human society alike through a shortsighted policy that sacrifices the welfare of the general population to the interests of a small number of officials and power companies in the immediate term, and deprives future generations of their means of support in the long term.

According to incomplete World Bank statistics, over the past fifty years, major hydroelectric engineering projects in China have displaced 16 million people, at least 10 million of whom are now impoverished.

In 1956, when the Sanmenxi Reservoir on the Yellow River was under construction, the government forced 300,000 peasants to leave their home villages. In the twenty years that followed, the peasants staged organized attempts to return home under the leadership of four great leaders. Each time, the local government used armed force to expel them. The Chinese people have never been told the story, written in blood and tears, of these 300,000 peasants who took a stand for their rights.

During the reform period, the construction of hydroelectric power plants has been accompanied by widespread malpractice and corruption. Yunnan's Manwan hydroelectric power station, built in the 1980s, is one example of many. Before construction on the reservoir began, the provincial government did not bother to seek local residents' opinions. It simply assumed the right to sign an agreement with the hydroelectric power company and sacrifice fertile river land.

When construction on the Manwan Dam began in the mid-1980s, the local government's slogan was, "The Manwan power plant will bring prosperity to the common people," but the actual result was exactly the opposite. When the dam was completed, more than 10,000 people were forced to leave their homes and found themselves barely able to survive. Many men were forced to migrate in search of temporary jobs, and even more women and children had to pick through garbage in order to survive. According to one study, before the Manwan reservoir area was flooded, local residents enjoyed an average income 11.2 percent higher than the Yunnan provincial average. After the area was flooded, the average income of the dislocated population was less than half the provincial average. Before the area was flooded, residents paid 0.16 yuan per kilowatt-hour for their electricity. After the Manwan power plant went into operation, the dislocated population had to pay a staggering two yuan per kilowatt-hour.

An Unquenchable Thirst

Despite these problems, the Chinese government cannot stop building dams and hydroelectric power stations. On November 9, following the Hanyuan incident, the Minister of Water Resources, Wang Shucheng, declared in a speech to a group of scientists and engineers that in theory China has waterpower resources of 689 gigawatts, of which 395 gigawatts will be developed as installed capacity.[1] It is argued that China still needs to build many more dams in order to guarantee water supply to the cities, improve flood control, produce more hydroelectric power, and meet the country's huge energy needs.

This argument has alarmed the international community, where developed countries are currently pulling down their big dams in order to restore the environment. One international environmental organization after another has warned about the environmental disaster that will result from China's drive to build huge dams. The human cost may be even greater. According to UN data, China's current hydroelectric generating capacity of one hundred gigawatts has resulted in the forcible relocation and impoverishment of millions of people, suggesting that the construction of plants generating an additional 295 megawatts will force three times as many more people to leave their home villages, producing even more social unrest.

I have argued in numerous articles that before the 1990s, China relied mainly on its own natural resources for its economic development. But since then, economic growth has been accompanied by an ever-growing reliance on imported natural resources. Members of the Chinese government's brain trust know that there is a strategic window of opportunity of approximately six years during which natural-resource-based economic development can be maintained.

Since 2002, power shortages have been reported all over China. In many economically developed parts of the country, electricity is being rationed and factories are forced to follow a "three days on, four days off" production schedule. This energy crisis has spurred a search for alternative sources of energy. One of the goals of the Chinese government's new energy strategy is to achieve a structural diversification of energy sources during the first two decades of the twenty-first century. This will require vigorously developing hydroelectric and nuclear power as well as renewable sources of energy such as solar energy, bioenergy, and wind energy to reduce dependence on fossil fuels and achieve sustainable development.

With nuclear power posing serious challenges in terms of investment, technology, and the environment, the government plans to increase China's nuclear-energy generation capacity to forty gigawatts, or 4 percent of the country's total electric-power generation capacity, by 2020. Because the production of solar energy, bioenergy, and wind energy depends on favorable climatic and geographic conditions, these options will only be pursued on a prototype basis, leaving hydroelectric power as the principal source of alternative energy. At present, China's hydroelectric exploitation rate stands at only 15 percent, far below international standards, and even behind developing countries such as India, Brazil, and Vietnam. The development potential is huge.

Now that the construction of more hydroelectric dams and power plants has become state policy, all populations living in reservoir areas face forcible relocation. Appeals to public opinion have never stirred the government's conscience and sense of political responsibility. Even the Hutiao ("Tiger Leaping") Gorge on the Yangtze, a UNESCO World Natural Heritage Site, is slated to be flooded in the construction of another dam. With a drop of 3,000 meters, Hutiao Gorge is believed to be the world's deepest canyon. Its natural beauty and cultural significance make it one of China's most important tourist attractions. If even a natural treasure and World Natural Heritage Site such as Hutiao Gorge can be flooded, what hope is there for a humble place such as Hanyuan?

Plundered by a Privileged Elite

Economic development is the Chinese Communist dictatorship's last means of touting its legitimacy. For more than two decades, China has pursued an unenlightened path of rapid economic growth based on high energy consumption. To turn Shanghai, Beijing, Guangzhou, Shenzhen, and a few other cities into showcases of modernization, the government has sacrificed the countryside and countless middle-sized cities and towns. According to official statistics, in the mid-1990s environmental degradation cost China more than 8 percent of its GDP, which was exactly the nation's GDP growth rate at the time.

China is exhausting the world's limited natural resources, failing to address its mass unemployment, and wrecking the environment not only for future Chinese generations but also for its neighbors. Japan and South Korea have long suffered from Chinese sandstorms, Hong Kong's air is polluted by mainland industry, and the Mekong's downstream countries (Thailand, Laos, Cambodia, and Vietnam) complain that they are the victims of China's water resource problems.

It is fair to say that China is in a state of crisis, but the destruction of China's environment and the impoverishment of millions of Chinese people is largely ignored by the international business community. The popular uprisings that have become more and more frequent in recent years amply demonstrate that behind the flourishing coastal cities that showcase China's modernization there lies hidden another China, a China wrung dry and abandoned by privileged bigwigs who profit from the privatization of the economy: the real China in which most Chinese people struggle to make a living. The flames of protest are already rising from all directions. They may one day burn Chinese civilization to ashes.

Translated by Paul Frank

The original Chinese article was published in the December 2004 issue of Hong Kong's *Open Magazine (Kaifang)*.

Note

1. By way of comparison, a typical coal-fired power plant has a capacity of one gigawatt.

BROKEN FLOWERS

Zeng Renquan

With opportunities still limited in the countryside, many young girls find themselves caught up in the world of vice.

According to a report in *Chutian Metropolis Daily* on August 20, 2004, a sixteen-year-old girl nicknamed Lanlan was taken by the police to the Chongqing City emergency assistance station. She was covered in dirt from head to toe, her eyes full of panic and fear, and staff could tell in a glance that she was mentally unhinged.

Lanlan was from Xiangfangu City in Hubei Province. At the end of May 2004, she was tricked by a man known as "Bully Boy" into going to Chongqing, where she was forced into prostitution. She was reportedly discovered by police after she ran away. In the emergency assistance station, Lanlan kept scrawling drawings on the wall and babbling to herself until her mother arrived to take her home two days later. According to staff at the assistance station, in that month alone they had rescued six girls who had been similarly tricked; all six were under eighteen, and the youngest was only fourteen.

How many underage prostitutes are there in China today? Society at large has no means of estimating the number, and the government neither dares nor wishes to keep statistics, because there are too many troops in this army, the situation is too ugly, and too many reports would mean that those in power would lose face. Behind every underage prostitute there is a tragic story: when they were tricked into becoming prostitutes, police and local government officials managed to make matters even worse.

As it happened, while I was on the train home during the National Day holiday, the bunk above mine was occupied by a young man surnamed Li, about thirty years old. After his nap, Li climbed down for some food and drinks. He was very talkative, especially after knocking back a few. It turned out that Xiao Li worked in the "mistress" business;

he and his older sister had opened a restaurant at the corner of Tianmen and Yingcheng in Hubei. This so-called restaurant was merely a front for a brothel with three women, the oldest of whom was nineteen, and the others only fifteen and sixteen. Business was very, very good, and the three women couldn't keep up with demand, so Li was on his way to Sichuan to look for more. He had already established contacts, and a middleman had once again helped him find two fourteen- or fifteen-year-old girls. As we were talking, I began to develop a much better understanding of underage prostitution in China.

"Most of the young girls are from Sichuan, Hubei, and the remote mountain areas of Hunan. On the plains you won't find anyone. The flatland women are a bit smarter and more difficult to fool. The girls from deep in the mountains haven't seen much of the world, they're greener. They come from very poor homes, so they're easier to fool." Li talked exuberantly as he downed another glass. "We all have our ways, using a string of middlemen to make connections, and all the middlemen have their own methods. Some of them find a girl's father and swear that the girl is going to have a job with very good pay, and some parents think, if their daughters can earn some money and give the family some support, who can say no? Some women who have themselves worked as 'mistresses' go back to help recruit new girls; they're from the same village, and girls who've never been out of their own village before meet these women who have been around and have money for food and nice clothes—who can blame them for getting antsy? Working as a middleman is pretty good work; you can make as much as one or two thousand on one transaction."

"How old are the women you recruit?" I asked uneasily.

"The younger the better," Xiao Li said. "None of them will be older than eighteen—the older ones are tougher to manage. None of them have any education to speak of. The ones who've gone even as far as junior high are few and far between. Basically you're talking about girls who are fifteen or sixteen; the customers like them at that age," he said with a smutty leer.

My heart trembling, I asked, "But they're so young . . . are they really willing to do this kind of thing?"

"There's nothing else out there for them," he said. "First, we humor them a bit, buy them some pretty clothes, show them some porn movies, have some more experienced girls tell them about all the bene-

fits, and then it's usually fine. If this doesn't work, we slip a little something in their drink to knock them out. After the first time, the second
and third come pretty easy, and then you don't have to worry any more.
. . . But the fee for a 'first night' is pretty damn high—at least 1,800
yuan, with 200 or 300 going to the girl. The boss who put up the stake
naturally wants more money, but once that's over with it gets cheaper—
50 yuan per visit, with 20 for the boss and 30 for the girl."

"What kind of customer do you get down there?" I asked.

"Most of them are just passing through," he said with a laugh. "Truck
drivers, guys attending meetings, or officials out on business. Any restaurant with parking will have just about anyone, from petty officials to big
bosses. But senior officials won't come to a simple place like ours. Those
guys mostly go to four-star hotels for more high-class entertainment.
But a place like ours, once it gets started, draws a lot of word-of-mouth
business, and a lot of people will even take a detour to stop by because
of the great value. These guys are usually loaded in more ways than one,
if you know what I mean," he said with a laugh.

I had a hard time conjuring a smile, so instead I asked, "Doesn't the
PSB bother you guys?"

"We pay them off right away; otherwise, how are you going to open
a new place?" he said dismissively. "Haven't you noticed? Every national
highway, every provincial road is lined on both sides with restaurants,
and every doorway will have a couple of girls on display. They're all
'that kind of girl,' and they're all very young; otherwise, how are you
going to attract customers? After all, if these guys just want to eat,
they can do that anywhere. At the same time, every restaurant has the
protection of the local PSB. If you don't, how can you operate? Dealing with the PSB is a cinch. You treat them to a good meal, slip them a
red envelope, let them 'try out' your prettiest girls, and from then on
they'll give you a heads-up if there's a raid, and if you have problems
with a customer, you can give them a call and they'll stop by and set
things right."

I couldn't take it anymore and burst out, "Don't you know that what
you're doing is completely illegal? The women that you're setting up as
hookers, most of them are children!"

He just downed another gulp of booze and angrily replied, "Damn
it, these days it doesn't pay to be an official; agricultural taxes and fees are
down, village cadres would rather just confiscate the fields and farm

them themselves. There's nothing ordinary people can do about it, and if you don't stick your neck out you'll never survive."

Whether in big cities or small, in urban areas or in the countryside, massage parlors, karaoke bars, and hotels are everywhere. Look under the street lights, under the shining neon signs, and you'll see them: the fashionable young girls in heavy makeup with cigarettes between their fingers, hiking up their miniskirts to show off their legs, their lips warbling pop songs, their eyes measuring up the contents of a man's pockets. Their existence has become part of the scenic landscape of the city. Their customers are men with money who are successful in business and in politics; respectable, well-dressed men who under the shelter of nightfall answer their animal desires, with one hand gripping a wad of bills and the other arm curled around the waist of girls young enough to be their daughters. They don't care if the girl at their side is only fifteen or sixteen, if she has a sad past, if she was forced into her trade, and they care even less whether once their desires are satisfied, a broken child goes off to find a quiet place to weep.

According to sources within the PSB, nearly half of China's prostitutes are underage, and almost all of these children are forced into prostitution. Day after day, official newspapers and television proclaim that children are China's future, China's hope, but how many senior officials actually care about children? If local officials really cared about child development, would there be underage prostitutes like Lanlan tricked into work in China's cities and towns? If our officials actually paid attention to effective administration and really cracked down on this problem, would people like Xiao Li still have the space to run rampant as they do?

Translated by Tom Kellogg

"RESURRECTION" EXPOSES CONFESSION UNDER TORTURE

Leng Wanbao

In early 2005, several cases came to light of men imprisoned or executed for crimes they had never committed. The reports sparked public debate over capital punishment and systemic protection for the accused.

Recently the news media reported a shocking case of manufactured evidence exposed by the sudden "resurrection" of Zhang Zaiyu, a Hubei woman supposedly murdered by her husband, She Xianglin. Although She managed to escape a death sentence, he was sentenced to fifteen years in prison, where he remained until his wife's unexpected reappearance in early 2005.

This is by no means the only case of a man wrongfully convicted of killing his wife. In 1986, Li Huawei, a cement factory worker in Yingkou County, Liaoning Province, returned home and found his wife murdered. He immediately reported the matter to police, but was soon detained himself, and after three years in a detention center, he was convicted of murder and sentenced to death, suspended for two years, with permanent deprivation of political rights. He ended up spending fifteen years in prison.

In April 1998, Wang Xiaoxiang, a female police officer with the communications bureau of the Kunming Public Security Bureau (PSB), and Wang Junbo, the deputy director of Kunming's Lu'nan County PSB, were found shot to death in a car. Du Peiwu, Wang Xiaoxiang's husband and himself a police officer, was arrested on suspicion of murder. On February 5, 1999, the Kunming Intermediate People's Court found Du Peiwu guilty of murder and sentenced him to death. On appeal, the death sentence was suspended for two years, and Du Peiwu was sent to Yunnan Province No. 1 Prison.

In both cases the actual murderer was eventually apprehended and the truth came to light, but by then the innocent men had spent many years in prison. It is hard to know how many such wrongful convictions have occurred in China.

In all of these cases, the authorities manufactured their so-called evidence and then carefully embroidered it to develop the frame-up. Obtaining a confession by torture is one of the main methods used by police to make their case. Take, for example, how the investigations against these three men were carried out.

She Xianglin has described how he was tortured into a confession: "Take a look at this finger—one joint went missing in prison. Look at my toes—even now they still haven't straightened out. Look at my leg here, and here, these scars. Was there any way out for me? Once you're inside, you're lost. Think about it—they locked me up for ten days and nights and interrogated me around the clock, alternating beatings with haranguing. I wasn't allowed to sleep. Who could stand up to that? Finally, when I was dazed and confused, they thrust a pile of stuff in front of me and told me to sign it and stamp my fingerprint—you think you wouldn't have done it?"[1]

Li Huawei said, "The police said to me, 'There's blood on your collar, you're the murderer, admit it.' When I refused to confess, the police interrogated me under torture for three days and nights. . . . The lead investigator, surnamed Sun, said, 'This is what will happen: your father is a Party member, your mother's health is poor, your younger brother is preparing to marry. If you don't confess, they'll be rounded up, too, and it'll be even worse for you.' For days in a row they had me stand straight with my head against the wall while they took turns sleeping, drinking, eating, and torturing me. I couldn't bear the torture, the threats, the intimidation; especially when they detained my mom and brought her in—I couldn't take it any more. Sun told me to repeat everything he said, and he led me through a statement that would suit their needs."[2]

After Du Peiwu was detained, investigators Qin Bolian and Ning Xinghua interrogated him continuously without allowing him to sleep, and beat and kicked him or instructed other officers to do so. They hung him from the door by his handcuffed wrists, and repeatedly removed the stool from beneath his feet or yanked on a rope tied around his feet, so that his full body weight bore down on his cuffed wrists. When Du could no longer withhold his cries of pain, the officers tied a gag around his mouth, then made him kneel on the floor and struck him with electric batons until Du finally relented and admitted he was the murderer and identified the "crime scene."[3]

If even a police officer such as Du Peiwu could be subjected to such torment by his own brothers in the profession, the experiences of ordinary people can only be imagined with fear and trembling.

In the bleak history of China's political and legal system, these three innocent men can be considered "lucky," as the truth eventually came out. In She's case the dead woman was "resurrected," and in the others the actual killers were finally apprehended and brought to justice. But if the real killer or a "resurrected" victim is the only evidence that can vindicate the wrongfully accused, this burden of proof is horrific indeed. If the victim remains dead, and the real culprit is never apprehended, the authorities will continue to maintain they have an iron-clad case.

From these cases of wrongly accused men, it is easy to see that the authorities' handling of a case is dominated by initial suspicions and first impressions, and the Party's policy of heavier punishment for those who refuse to confess leads authorities to rely heavily on statements, while neglecting physical evidence that might vindicate the suspect.

For example, a year after She Xianglin's wife was supposedly killed, someone reported seeing the "victim" somewhere, but the authorities simply intimidated that witness and his family. Investigators, rewarded with promotions and salary increases for successful cases, are well motivated to burnish the image of official infallibility. Judicial officials are certainly aware that the use of confessions obtained under torture in processing cases is the rule rather than the exception in China. Courts are supposed to be the last bastion of justice, but because they are merely tools of the Party and the government, with political legal committees routinely serving as the real deciding force in a judgment, the courts regularly give the green light to abusive and unlawful actions by officials, aiding and abetting the authorities in their frame-ups of innocent people.

Since it is impossible to rely on present law enforcement bodies to eradicate the use of manufactured evidence and confessions obtained through torture, national legislative bodies need to establish new laws granting criminal suspects the right to remain silent, and the right to have a lawyer present during interrogation, and providing for audiovisual recordings of interrogations for presentation in court. These measures would help ensure that the personal and legal rights of criminal suspects are not infringed, and could provide evidence in support of the accused when coerced confessions are used. In addition, there should be more comprehensive stipulations against the use of unlawfully obtained evidence—not only should such evidence be banned from court, but the police officers responsible for obtaining it should be punished.

The central government should also better implement laws protecting the right of citizens and their families to appeal and petition. In the case of She Xianglin, when She's family attempted to appeal and petition on his behalf, officials refused to follow the appropriate legal processes, and even threw She's mother and elder brother into detention as a means of preserving their supposedly ironclad case. The government should not consider those who appeal and petition to be destabilizing factors in society, but rather as reflections of the true source of social instability: a political and legal system that frames innocent people, and officials that deprive them of their legal rights.

Of course, these suggestions are really just stopgap measures. What matters is whether the government leadership can set up an equitable system with genuine oversight. If not, any claims of protecting the rights of Chinese people are nothing more than empty words, and the authorities will continue to exist only as a bane rather than a defender of the lawful rights of Chinese citizens.

Translated by Stacy Mosher

The original Chinese version of this article was originally published on the Web sites of *Chinaeweekly:* http://www.chinae weekly.net/viewarticle_gb.aspx?vID=1201, and *Epoch Times:* ttp:// www.epochtimes.com.tw/bt/5/4/13/n887467.htm.

Notes

1. Quoted in Wang Xin, "She Xianglin an—yuan'an weihe bianchengle 'tie'an'?," published on the Web site of *People's Daily:* http://www.people.com.cn/GB/news/ 25064/3300177.html.

2. See "Jingshi yuan'an," published on the Web site of *Legal Daily (Fazhi Rebao):* http://www.legaldaily.com.cn/gb/content/2000-12/22/content_10791.htm.

3. An account of this case, published in *China Youth Daily* on August 21, 2000, is accessible on the Web site of *Epoch Times:* http://www.epochtimes.com/gb/1/7/20/n111283.htm.

ROTTEN ROPE

Yan Li

It has come loose!
Do you believe it?
History that has come loose from a piece of rotten rope
Will be clasped forever in a museum's arms
It has become loose
Those knots like fists are coming undone
A bundle of excavated death comes loose
From that rope that has no backbone
That strength that ancestors tied up in it is coming loose
According to the science of genetics
That strength
Has already come down to our hands
These hands
Even now are digging out words that ancestors forgot to tell us
But these words
Have come loose from that rotten rope
These words
Can't be tied up into sentences again
These words aren't fitting into prose that says what we mean
And that means
That we in the 20th century are victims of a great big trick
Oh man!
That rotten piece of rope is really rotten!

Translated by Denis Mair

PART THREE

The Power of a Red Rose: Protesters

Why is there dictatorship in this world? Because you consent to it
   and become its accomplice.
Why is there totalitarianism in this world? Because you recognize
   it and become its co-conspirator . . .
A red rose is a Liu Di, a Du Daobin,
A Huang Qi, an An Jun, a Yang Zili, a Tao Haidong, a Li Dawei,
   a Zhao Changqing,
An Ouyang Yi, a Yan Jun, a Luo Yongzhong, a Zheng Enchong,
   a He Depu,
A Ren Bumei, a Yu Jie, a Liao Yiwu, a Yu Shicun, a Wang Yi,
   a Fan Baihua,
A Donghai Yixiao, a Yang Chunguang, a Liu Xiaobo, a Mo
   Lihua!
One red rose is hundreds and thousands of red roses; it is millions
   of acutely silent Chinese people!

from **The Power Of A Red Rose**
By Huang Xiang

On January 19, 2006, China's Ministry of Public Security announced that it had recorded 87,000 cases of "disturbances of public order" in 2005, up 6.6 percent over the previous year. The upsurge in such incidents was first publicly acknowledged in July 2005, when Public Security Minister Zhou Yongkang revealed that the number of "mass incidents" in 2004 had risen by 30 percent from 2003 to 74,000, with a total of 3.8 million people taking part. The minister's use of the term "mass incidents" included any riots, demonstrations, and protests that involved more than 100 people.

A quick glance at worldwide headlines on China reveals a multiplicity of forces pressing for change in the economic, social, and political sectors as China's people become increasingly aware of their rights and of the fact that the vast majority are increasingly excluded from the benefits of development and denied access to housing, jobs, and health care. Incidents of unrest raise a spectrum of issues, with farmers and workers, AIDS and human rights activists, journalists and cyber-dissidents employing a variety of methods to challenge the regime. Some attempt to follow established paths of challenging social injustice through the Chinese tradition of petitioning the central government. Others turn to public demonstrations, both peaceful and violent, to make their voices heard. Still others form groups focused on environmental, religious, health, or other social issues.

How one group chooses to express itself creates ripple effects in society that then affect how the government deals with other groups and individuals. The Chinese authorities previously reacted to uprisings with harsh suppression across the board, but the failure of such measures to stem protests, and indications that they actually inflame public discontent, have led the authorities to respond more recently with a greater range of approaches. This section presents the experiences and struggles of individuals engaged in various forms of protest and activism.

Individuals, whether they work alone or as part of an organization, face harassment, surveillance, house arrest, arbitrary detention, and eviction if their action falls outside of the government's boundaries of acceptability, and the most serious offenders are arrested and imprisoned. Wang Juntao reflects on his experience in China's closed society, while exploring the PRC's strategy on the international stage and the role of human rights organizations. Liu Xiaobo's piece *provides a snapshot of China as social movements gain momentum despite Beijing's repressive regime. Yang Hongfeng interviews Zhang Xianling, the mother of a slain student, who continues the struggle for a truthful accounting of the June 4th crackdown through her participation in the Tiananmen Mothers group. Yi Ban describes the situation of petitioners who spend their nights in a makeshift camp beneath an overpass while in Beijing petitioning the central government. Lastly, Zhang Lin examines the situation in Bengbu, a city facing pressing issues such as unemployment, workers' rights, and discrimination against migrants. These authors survey the varying ways in which individuals are pushing for social justice with every protest, every open letter, and every new independent organization.*

By making examples of certain individuals and constructing numerous hurdles in the way of organizing, the PRC government is undermining the creation of an open and independent civil space necessary to address China's complex problems. Yet, rising awareness of the power of collective efforts is also fueling the growth of that civil society.

JUNE 4TH AND HUMAN RIGHTS IN CHINA

Wang Juntao

Through historical analysis and his own prison experiences, one of the "black hands" of the 1989 Democracy Movement explores tactics and mechanisms that might improve China's human rights situation.

Historical Background

The Tiananmen massacre of June 4, 1989, galvanized the cause of human rights in China, and marked a turning point during which the dissident movement and the Chinese people completely severed their emotional and intellectual ties with the Communist regime. Although China's economic achievements allowed it to reclaim much of its support domestically and abroad, by the mid-1990s, people dissatisfied with the communists made human rights part of the guiding principle that repudiated the ideology and theory of communist rule.

Human rights had reentered the mainstream of Chinese political thought during the late 1980s as China's social sciences and the humanities absorbed Western ideas, and theoreticians began to debate and disseminate the basic ideas of humanitarianism and individualism. Today's Chinese scholars are still debating whether traditional Chinese political thought includes the concept of human rights. Since the May 4th movement of 1919, enlightened intellectuals have argued that the inhumane elements of Confucian thought must be responsible for China's backwardness, while Neo-Confucians strive for a new interpretation of Confucianism and its significance for human rights.

China's affirmation of fundamental human rights concepts set forth in the Universal Declaration of Human Rights in 1948 was the result of nearly a century of creative reinterpretation of traditional Chinese thought and integration with modern political ideas. Even the Chinese Communist Party adopted the political line of Western human rights advocates to gain domestic and international support during its fierce struggle to overthrow the Nationalist government.

In spite of this harmonization of modern human rights concepts with China's political thought in the 1940s, fundamental human rights values were almost totally repudiated in the suppression of dissent under post-1949 Communist rule. The Anti-Rightist Campaign of 1957 and the various political campaigns that followed it completely eliminated all independent political, economic, social, cultural, and intellectual forces. During the Cultural Revolution, the very terms "liberal democracy" and "human rights" became synonymous with criminal conduct, and those who advocated these principles saw their families broken up or destroyed.

All this political upheaval utterly destroyed Chinese people's faith in the communist revolution. Mao Zedong's death in 1976 triggered a dramatic transformation in Chinese politics in which purged CCP veterans, led by Deng Xiaoping, began reassessing the Maoist revolution and making amends for its consequences. Although persecution continued against activists, intellectuals, and reformers, it enjoyed no support among ordinary people, and was hotly debated even among those in power. Legislation and the administration of justice served to constrain and standardize the instruments of dictatorship.

All the same, the concept of human rights was not widely accepted in the China of the 1980s, and during various campaigns against the "spiritual pollution" of Western ideas and capitalist liberalization, even the mention of humanitarianism and human rights was to be avoided. Political persecution did not stop, and judicial brutality became more and more severe. The dissident movement focused mainly on theory and reform of the political system, in part because the most influential elements in the dissident movement were people whose Communist Party background left them leery of the feasibility of human rights demands, but also because Chinese society as a whole had yet to accept the principle of individualism.

International norms adopted as part of international exchanges helped Chinese professionals learn more about human rights. As a result, human rights became a key rallying point domestically and abroad in the resistance to the political oppression that followed June 4th. My personal experience is a case in point.

A Personal Journey

I was born into China's top military academy. From childhood, I received a standard education in communist ideology. But as I was confronted with social realities, I discovered a huge gap between the poverty of the people and the ideological promises made to me, and I began to have my doubts about communist rule. In 1976, when Mao launched the last political movement of his life against reform-minded cohorts, I was one of a million citizens who took to the streets of Beijing in what is now referred to as the April 15th movement. For this I was imprisoned at the age of 17. When Mao died I was released from prison, and resolved to devote my life to working for the democratization of China. During the Democracy Wall period, I founded *Beijing Zhi Chun (Beijing Spring)* together with some people I had befriended during the Tiananmen Incident of April 5, 1976.

Later I tried to establish Peking University as a center of the democracy movement, organizing elections there in 1980. In the late 1980s, Chen Ziming and I and some other friends tried to establish an independent nongovernmental research and cultural enterprise trust. With the support of numerous individuals and organizations, in 1989 I founded the Capital Patriotic All-Sector Joint Liaison Group for Protection of the Constitution, which promoted comprehensive reform to break the political deadlock at the time. In 1991, after sixteen months in detention, I was sentenced to thirteen years' imprisonment with four years' subsequent deprivation of political rights.

Following my arrest in October 1989, I was kept in solitary confinement and could not engage in any activities other than trying to protect my own rights and interests. Since promoting democratization was impossible in prison, I resolved to press for the application of international norms in Chinese prisons and to establish minimum standards of treatment for political prisoners.

Hunger strikes were my most effective method of struggle, although fraught with danger and by no means assured of success. From the day of my arrest in August 1991 to my release in April 1994, I went on hunger strike on twenty-one occasions. My third and longest hunger strike lasted fifty-eight days, during which I was force-fed twice a day to keep me alive. A friend who visited me told me that my case had become an international cause célèbre, and thanks to my family's efforts to bring attention to my case and to pressure from the international community, I achieved my aim every time I went on hunger strike.

Experience taught me several things:

- *The need for determination and willpower.* You have to show courage and determination when you ask your family to tell the outside world what you are going through in prison. When the crunch comes, you must neither yield nor compromise. When I was force-fed while on hunger strike, I would often sing old frontier songs as loudly as I could to express my determination.
- *The need for a strong legal standpoint.* Every time I took a stand against my jailers, I stated clearly when and how my rights had been violated, citing chapter and verse of the relevant laws, and wrote legal briefs outlining the details of my case. This was the only way to get any support from a prosecutorial and judicial system that was established largely to give the international community the impression that China enjoys humanitarianism and international sophistication.
- When engaging in a form of resistance as drastic as a hunger strike, you can succeed in having your demands met as long as they are not too vague and uncompromising.
- *Take a softly-softly approach.* Show good intentions and state your demands orally at first, then in writing only if they are not met. Increase your demands little by little to give everyone involved time to solve the problem.
- *The importance of timing.* The Chinese government has its own work schedule, and the treatment of political prisoners only enters the leaders' field of vision at certain time periods when the issue can become a public relations disaster. State visits to China by foreign leaders often provoke heated debate about relations with China in their home countries. High-level talks between Chinese and foreign leaders often provided good opportunities to achieve progress and improve prison conditions.
- *The need for friends within the system.* The Cultural Revolution eliminated popular support for political persecution, making it easier to secure help from friends within the regime. The first time I tried to take a stand in prison, a *(Legal Daily) Fazhi Ribao* journalist, high-level officials from the Ministry of Justice, and the personal secretary of an influential politburo member, Qiao Shi's, all looked into my case. This

had a very positive effect, including improvements in my medical treatment.

- *The need for sympathy and support* from prison guards, doctors, and prison authorities. No matter how legally strong your case may be, the testimony of people directly in charge is critical in the review of an individual case. When I fought for my rights, I always cited the relevant laws and legal provisions, and left ample time to ensure that those acting on my behalf would be able to report my complaint in a comprehensive way in order to prevent their superiors from shifting responsibility onto them and forcing them to fabricate false evidence.

On one occasion, when the Public Security Bureau arrested a relative of mine, Yao Shuhai, the director of education at Yanqing Prison, gave truthful and factual evidence in several court hearings, despite the fact that a leading official from the Reform Through Labor Bureau (RTLB) had threatened him and colluded with others to give false evidence. Thanks to this testimony, my relative was released and the RTLB official was dismissed from his post. My medical condition was top secret, but doctors or high-level prison officials always told me my real situation, and senior staff in the prison hospital refused to sign diagnoses stating that I was in good health, as demanded by the RTLB. Whenever I went on hunger strike, a guard would take the risk of informing my family and friends about my condition, thereby alerting the international community.

On April 23, 1994, I was finally released from prison and sent into exile in the United States. When Chinese government officials took me to Beijing Airport and handed me over to an American embassy official outside of a United Airlines airplane, I realized that I, my family, and the people who had stood by me in my struggle had won. We had succeeded in making the international community protect political prisoners in China. This reality was hard to grasp for someone like myself who had been brought up under Maoism.

Meeting the New Challenges

Although human rights became a rallying cry of the Chinese democracy movement after 1989, and the Chinese government has accepted the concept of human rights in theory and in legislation, we cannot say that much genuine progress has been made in this area. Recent developments give particular cause for concern.

The cause of human rights in China is part of a larger international human rights movement driven by globalization and fueled by international pressure and friction. The way the government dealt with the aftermath of Tiananmen was far less brutal than had been the case in previous political crackdowns, mainly because of international and particularly American pressure. The policy of reform and opening up to the world had been underway for ten years, and suddenly cutting off contact with the world would have plunged China into an economic crisis. The regime could not have maintained such a policy, and when Chinese dissidents recognized this fact they adjusted their strategy. Whereas they had previously sought to mobilize China's elite and ordinary citizens by focusing on longstanding problems in Chinese politics, they now turned to the issue of human rights to win support from the international community and to get it to exert pressure on the Chinese government.

The basic process for the advancement of human rights is this: Chinese dissidents challenge those in power; the power holders respond by stepping up control and repression; Western human rights organizations, media, and NGOs respond with indignation and put pressure on their own governments; Western governments begin to exert pressure on the Chinese government in bilateral relations and international forums; the Chinese government responds to this pressure and makes some human rights improvements. In the final analysis, the catalyst for the advancement of human rights in China is international rather than domestic pressure, as I found in my own case.

Why and in what ways does the Chinese government respond to Western pressure by improving the human rights situation in China? One explanation often offered outside China is that China's rulers have a sense of shame, and that they improve human rights in order to avoid international condemnation. An explanation more in line with East Asian culture is that the Chinese government wants to save face. The trouble with this explanation is that it assumes that the Chinese government identifies with the human rights standards established by the West. The fact is that the Chinese government does not identify one bit with the theory of human rights, and therefore feels no shame or culpability.

On the contrary, it takes special pride in its resistance to Western pressure on this front.

When Chinese leaders do respond to Western pressure, they do so based on their own interests and assessment of the situation. The first thing we have to understand is their perception.

In the 1990s the Chinese government was undergoing transformation. On the one hand, its leaders realized that the communist ideology and system were things of the past, and that they needed new ideas and principles to build a new system; on the other hand, they remained constrained by old political interests and patterns of thinking that caused them to reject potentially destabilizing ideas and systems, particularly the democratization process expected by the West. China's rulers knew that since the Tiananmen crackdown had cost them all legitimacy in the eyes of the Chinese people, their political survival depended on maintaining economic development, which relied on Western technology, investment, and markets. In addition, although brutal repression saved them in the short term from being overthrown by their indignant populace, they knew that they had to take measures to reduce popular hostility.

It was in consideration of their own interests that the Chinese rulers shifted from their unyielding attitude during the Tiananmen crackdown to an attempt to accommodate Western demands for an improvement in human rights in China. But the Chinese government's response was subject to three restraints: First, there remained within the CCP some very stubborn conservatives who for ideological or nationalistic reasons opposed compromise with the West. Second, the concept of face prevented Chinese leaders from following the Western model too closely, and obliged them to shore up China's prestige and authority. Third, they could not allow concessions to threaten their own rule by giving the opposition movement more room to maneuver. For these reasons, China's rulers designed their post–June 4th foreign policy to maintain and renew cooperation with the West while preventing the development of the democracy movement in China.

A closer examination of China's ruling elite reveals that some leaders are more supportive than others of a positive response to human rights diplomacy from the West. Many were influenced by the CCP's professed aim in the 1930s and 1940s to build China on a foundation of freedom and democracy, and their experiences during the Cultural

Revolution had made them even more aware of the importance of human rights. These veteran Party members did not support political persecution, but advocated leniency, human rights, and political reform.

These complex mechanisms within the Party prompted the leadership to respond to Western demands for human rights progress with a new gambit designed to ensure the stability of their hold on power while relieving Western and domestic pressure to maintain economic growth. They improved the conditions of prominent political prisoners and even released some, engaged in human rights negotiations, enacted a window dressing of Western-style legislation, and allowed limited monitoring of human rights by the West by entering into diplomatic negotiations, and signing international treaties.

It should be noted, however, that the background and mechanisms of this interaction are currently changing in ways that seem detrimental to human rights progress in China. First of all, even as China was formalizing these relations, it limited their political impact to a particular sphere. Second, the release of prominent political prisoners is an increasingly isolated and ritualized phenomenon aimed at currying favor or reducing pressure from the West while having no constructive effect in China.

Third, the PRC links economic and security interests, provoking divisions between and within governments. International lobby groups representing Western business and professional interests also lobby their governments to pursue a more "balanced" China policy that furthers their interests and plays down human rights diplomacy. Fourth, the PRC adopts international human rights concepts and norms in a way that brings some aspects into contradiction with others, thereby provoking debate among human rights advocates. Lastly, the CCP's success at turning the issue of human rights into a seesaw-like international relations game has brought improvements in China's human rights situation to a standstill.

Political factors contribute to a weakening momentum in the international human rights game, while giving the Chinese authorities more latitude in playing it. First of all, mainstream Chinese public opinion is focusing less on human rights. After their initial indignation at the June 4th massacre, people have gradually lost interest in the issue. Young people who have grown up under deceitful government propaganda don't even know what really happened. Nationalism has also made many young people and members of the elite hostile toward Western human rights diplomacy. The rapid development Deng Xiaoping called for during his southern tour in 1992, although characterized by corruption, has provided the economic and intellectual elites with tangible benefits that have prompted them to forge an alliance with the political elite to maintain political stability.

Second, an increasing neo-conservatism among China's elites raises concerns that rapid Westernizing reform will result in collapse, and the belief that a great country such as China ought to follow its own development model without imitating the West.

Third, the opposition or dissident movement in mainland China is becoming increasingly divided. Some groups and individuals refuse to compromise with the regime and appeal to the West to exert pressure on the Chinese government. Their challenges to the regime provoke persecution, which prompts the West to exert pressure on the Chinese government to make policy and systemic changes. But consumerism and nationalism are causing this type of dissent to become an oasis of conscience as it is increasingly marginalized among the common people. This marginalization breeds ambivalence among erstwhile Western supporters, who increasingly have their own reasons to improve relations with China.

Already in the 1980s, some dissidents and professional elites of a traditional caste had begun to distance themselves from the opposition movement that was openly turning to the outside world, and cautiously began to develop new political and legal mechanisms to mobilize support within China (including among the leadership), and to promote China's reform by means of their professional activities. These divisions have weakened the capabilities of China's democracy movement. If people operating within the system and the forces of opposition are to come together in a united cause, a change must occur in PRC politics. Enlisting locally rooted political support and winning greater operating room within China may require eschewing sensitive and confrontational issues for those that appeal to the conscience and self-interest of the general Chinese populace.

Conclusions

Although mainland Chinese dissidents have become virtual professionals and specialists at challenging the regime, they have also become marginalized and enfeebled in the Chinese political context at the same
time that debates in Western societies about the benefits and value of a
China policy have diluted pressure from the Western media and human
rights organizations.

With Western governments increasingly promoting their own national and political interests through the international relations game
with China, human rights organizations are just about the only impetus
left for genuine human rights progress in China.

In the 1990s, human rights groups successfully exerted pressure on
Western governments to demand an end to the persecution of dissidents in China as a key element of foreign policy, and in recent years
they have sparked renewed debate on human rights issues. But preventing a regression in China's human rights situation under the current political realities will require more than stepping up international pressure
on the Chinese government. A substantial improvement in the human
rights situation is only possible if there is real pressure and action for it
within mainstream Chinese public opinion. Therefore, international
human rights organizations must consider how to promote human
rights mechanisms within China to create a domestic impetus for
human rights progress that will facilitate the efforts of the international
community.

In fact, changes that have taken place in China since the late 1990s
have in many respects created favorable conditions for the advancement
of human rights through support within the regime, greater debate en-
gendered by globalization and international human rights agreements,
the popular unrest caused by corruption and abuse of power, and the inclusion of human rights in research by Chinese academics and policy
analysts developing government policies to address these systemic cata-
lysts of unrest. Ultimately, there is the hope that human rights organizations that plan their strategies carefully will be able to enter and operate
legally in China.

Translated by Paul Frank

THE RISE OF CIVIL SOCIETY IN CHINA

Liu Xiaobo

Social movements are flourishing in China to fill the moral vacuum left by officialdom, but may not provide an adequate vent for public frustrations if political suppression and economic disparity continue unchecked.

The Fall of Official Influence and the Rise of Populism

Although the bloodshed of June 4, 1989, is long past, the incident has left an enduring legacy of public consciousness and a disillusionment with Communist Party values in the hearts of the people—including most officials.

While the Communist Party continues to monopolize public power and media, and to maintain its dictatorial position and political stability through suppression and ideological inculcation, the authorities have suffered a severe loss of prestige and credibility and can no longer hope for complete control of civil society in the long term. The top-down official policy of reform and openness is actually the result of pressure from the people below, and once the people become aware of their power, they will become harder and more costly to control.

In the reform era, as personal interest has become the greatest source of motivation for the masses, the concepts of "public" and "national" have surrendered much of their status to the concepts of "popular" and "personal." Public justice and morality have deteriorated as the bureaucracy has shifted its emphasis from moral obligation to personal advantage. The trend in recent years of graduates rushing to join the Party for reasons of personal advantage has accelerated a slide into systemic corruption and abuse of power. Official policies facilitating personal advantage have helped the Communist Party co-opt the social elite, but have simultaneously led to a siphoning off of public resources and increasing dissatisfaction among the lower classes, both of which have contributed to a decline in effective Party rule.

This debasement of official values has also resulted in a loss of respect for authority among members of the public, as reflected in the increasing popularity of political jokes with sexual connotations. Popular satire is now applied to every department and all levels of government. Official efforts to instill patriotism after June 4th have brought about increased nationalism among China's citizens, but only insofar as national interests coincide with personal interests.

The debased status of the public sector has been accompanied by a rise in prestige for people or organizations with populist tendencies. For example, international media and private news sources are treated with much greater regard and credibility than official media. Although the Chinese Communist regime does not allow private media sources, private capital and people from outside the system have become heavily involved in the broadcasting industry, even under the banner of the state-run media. Even the state-run media have begun to give their news coverage a popular slant; if this results in censure, they fall into line only as long as it takes for the storm to blow over. In particular, Guangdong's top three newspapers, *Southern Weekend, 21st Century Economics Journal,* and *21st Century Universal Journal,* and the bimonthly *Southern Exposure,* along with publications from other cities and provinces such as *Economic Observer* and *China Youth Journal,* all are diligently developing their popular appeal. The trends in reader subscriptions show clearly the people's appreciation for popular media and their loathing for Party mouthpieces. Even a senior Party official, Li Changchun, was reported during his stint as Guangdong's Party Secretary to have said, "Apart from *Southern Weekend,* I only read Hong Kong newspapers."

Another example of popular values overriding official values is the emergence of "people's champions." Such individuals began appearing as early as the 1970s and 1980s with the "May 4th heroes," "Democracy Wall heroes" such as Wei Jingsheng and Xu Wenli, and "intellectual heroes" such as Fang Lizhi, Liu Binyan, and Wang Ruowang. June 4th produced its own round of heroes, such as Wang Weilin, who stepped in front of a tank, Professor Ding Zilin in her fight for human rights, Wang Dan among the student leaders, and "black hands" such as Wang Juntao and Chen Ziming. Former top officials such as Zhao Ziyang and Bao Tong became important moral beacons after being expelled from official favor, and old Party members such as Li Shenzhi, Li Rui, Hu Jiwei, and Xu Liangying have become increasingly important and daring spokespersons for the interests of ordinary people.

Although these populist heroes are not recognized in the official values system, the values they represent have been greeted with solidarity and sympathy by many within China and by the international mainstream. While unable to spread their messages through the state-controlled media, such dissidents have attracted much attention outside of China, and through the growing popularity of the Internet they are becoming more widely known to their countrymen.

The Struggle for Rights and Values

Official policies aimed at diluting the influence of the 1989 Democracy Movement have contributed to a reformist retreat, but the silent majority continues to nurture values and notions quite different from the official mainstream. Unless the regime can reclaim its moral authority through a transformation consistent with the preferences of the masses, its downfall is inevitable. Russian scholars' analysis of the crumbling of the Soviet Union provides just such an example. They find that American pressure from the outside was of less importance than the corruption and decay of morale that destabilized the Soviet empire from within.

Because the masses lack any legal outlet to express their reasonable demands regarding rights and corruption, and receive no direct response from the authorities, they have increasingly resorted to demonstrations and protests. This has given rise to a new breed of dissidents and "people's champions" bearing the labels of "peasants' heroes," "leaders of industry," "anti-corruption heroes," and "martyrs of faith." They are not a product of political opposition movements, but rather of the people's struggle to protect their own rights, and as such they have deep grassroots support. Although the Party's censorship and repression have contained the influence of such heroes within limited geographical areas and populations, they have become important arbiters of morality and legitimacy. As the personal-rights movement gains momentum, ultimately the scattered popular forces will coalesce into independent organizations, and local heroes will unite to face down the morally bankrupt agents of tyranny.

Some "people's champions," in particular commentators in the economic field, have been given more credit among overseas scholars than their actual benefit to the people justifies. A few, however, have moved beyond theory to become the conscience of their profession. For example, Wu Jinglian, a member of an official think tank, has gained the reputation of a "people's champion" because of his concern for the rights of ordinary investors in the stock market. Others such as Zhou Qiren of Peking University have gained popular plaudits for rejecting the numbers game and expressing deep concern over the rights of peasants and systemic flaws. There is also Liu Junning, who was expelled from an official sociological institute because of his strong advocacy of constitutional democracy; Qin Hui, who was subjected to heavy criticism at Tsinghua University because of his outstanding comments on social justice; and Li Changping, who lost his official position in Hubei Province as a result of his advocacy on behalf of peasants.

In the legal community, lawyers such as Zhang Sizhi and Mo Shaoping have been honored as "champions of Chinese law" for their willingness to take on the defense of controversial political dissidents, including myself. They have been placed under surveillance, arrested, reprimanded, and otherwise harassed for their trouble. Chongqing lawyer Zhou Litai built a practice in Shenzhen specializing in legal services for workers, handling 1,019 cases of ordinary people suing officials and more than 600 workers' compensation suits. As a reward for the efforts of this "workers' lawyer" on behalf of the disadvantaged, his Shenzhen office was shut down by Shenzhen's Longgang District Court.

In discussing the rise of populism, it is impossible to ignore the recent trend of privatization of public power and public property, which has exacerbated the shift in public sentiment from public welfare to personal advantage. Unlike privatization among the general populace, which involves profiting from one's own efforts, China's privatization of public power and resources is a form of immoral and unjust profit and gain based on elite monopolies rather than fair and free competition. As a result, it inspires feelings among the disadvantaged not only of unfairness, but also of bitterness, and ultimately gives rise not only to corruption, but also to revenge.

The social divisions between the advantaged and disadvantaged in China in terms of power, opportunity, income, social security, access to resources, and modern standards of living are now so great that it is almost a matter of "winner takes all." In the years since June 4th, the perceived dichotomy of "morality residing in the civil sector and power lying with the bureaucracy" has become so widely accepted that the authorities have been forced to take corrective measures such as the "Three Represents" policy. Ultimately, however, maintaining social stability depends on brutality, lies, and bribery, with no pretense of morality. The by-product of a thoroughly discredited system and bureaucracy is a society dominated by artifice in every sphere.

The Development of Nongovernmental Organizations

The social stratification resulting from redistribution of wealth, and the proliferation of value systems stemming from the new ideological openness and its transformations, have become the major forces driving the diversification of society in terms of interests, lifestyles, and values. Serious conflict between a diversifying social structure and the homogenizing tendencies of a rigid governmental system is becoming unavoidable at the same time that increasing popular discontent, coupled with a lack of officially sanctioned outlets, is giving rise to civil movements outside of this system.

The Communist Party's persecution of political dissidents has led to political protest movements; its long-term blindness to the swelling ranks of the impoverished and disadvantaged has created industrial workers' and peasants' movements; its tolerance and even protection of official corruption has led to the anti-corruption movement; its suppression of systems of belief has generated religious movements; its refusal to grant freedom of assembly has fostered the emergence of secret nongovernmental organizations that operate outside of the system. Unable to satisfy popular calls for social justice or incorporate dissenting voices, this regime will one day find itself facing the complete loss of its systemic authority and the utter failure of its repressive power. That will be the moment when civil society, long excluded and suppressed by the regime, will burst forth.

The development of unauthorized civil organizations in spite of tight control and strict suppression by the Party is striking evidence of the gradual maturation of Chinese society. As long as the present system remains incapable of answering the people's demand for justice and providing expression of their legitimate needs, illicit social movements and civil organizations will continue to expand inexorably, flexibly, and in secret. The main types include the following:

RELIGIOUS AND QUASI-RELIGIOUS ORGANIZATIONS

Qigong associations and religious house-churches are the two types of social organizations that grew the fastest in the 1990s. The former rely largely on the resources of homegrown religious and quasi-religious organizations, while the latter draw resources from the West. Although Falun Gong, Zhong Gong, and underground Christian churches (both Protestant and Catholic) all come under varying degrees of pressure from the government, religious faith cannot be destroyed by strong-arm repression—as the saying goes, "Three soldiers can seize a general, but an entire army cannot overthrow a human will." Since the June 4th incident, as official ideological propaganda has totally lost its seductive power and the creation of independent organizations has been blocked by the government, homegrown religious organizations have triumphed over official repression, and their adherents now number in the tens of millions.

In terms of numbers, resiliency, and diversity of government-defying methods, Falun Gong practitioners provide an admirable model of non-violent resistance. Catholic and Protestant house-churches are spread throughout the cities and the countryside; official estimates number their membership at 30 million, but the true numbers far exceed government statistics. The main reason for underground churches is that the Communist Party has rejected modern civilization's separation of church and state, and forces churches to accept administration and clergy appointed by the regime. Under these circumstances, many Chinese Christians (particularly Catholics, who rely on the authority of the Vatican) turn to illicit, unofficial house churches to maintain the purity and integrity of their faith.

While the regime employs its authoritarian power to destroy churches and imprison parishioners, it has no way to prevent large numbers of people from assembling and praying every week, no way to make Protestants accept the God presented to them in the official "Three-Self" Protestant church, and no way to induce Catholics to abandon the Vatican's authority.

The development of China's underground religions alerts us to the fact that China's restriction of freedom of religion is contrary to the people's desire to have control over their own souls. It demonstrates a popular recognition of the fact that if people do not take the initiative to fight for their legally guaranteed freedoms of speech, assembly, and belief, but instead passively sink into the embrace of material satisfaction, they will have no escape from a life of terror and will never achieve the richness of an active spiritual life.

A discussion of religion in China has to include the Communist regime's relationship with Tibetan Buddhism and Islam in Xinjiang. It is interesting to note that on one hand, the Communist Party recognizes the legitimacy of all branches of Tibetan Buddhism, but on the other hand, it does not recognize the legitimacy of Tibetan Buddhism's highest spiritual leader, the Dalai Lama. This confusion arises from long-standing cross-cultural conflicts, and makes the relationship between Tibetan Buddhism and the Chinese Communist Party different from that between the Party and other religious organizations.

ENVIRONMENTAL PROTECTION AND AIDS ORGANIZATIONS

Since the spread of AIDS and the destruction of the environment are globally recognized problems, organizations dealing with these issues in China have attained a certain amount of influence. The environmental group Friends of Nature is recognized both at home and abroad; it often undertakes projects that involve international cooperation and receives donations from foreign sources. The group's founders, including Wang Lixiong and Liang Xiaoyan, often travel to remote villages and border areas to promote environmental awareness among schoolchildren in an effort to spread their message to the farthest regions of China. Dr. Gao Huijie and the civic organization known as the Aizhi Action Project have not only carried out much practical HIV prevention work, they also revealed to the world the AIDS-tainted blood-selling disaster in Henan Province, along with the subsequent cover-up by the local government. This accomplishment was a major factor in spurring China to develop its HIV–prevention program. The Chinese government no longer muffles its serious AIDS problem under a veil of silence, but talks openly about the ever-worsening HIV situation and seeks international help in dealing with it. However, the regime's chief motivation is merely to obtain more international aid.

It should be mentioned that none of China's legally authorized civic organizations are what would be internationally recognized as non-governmental organizations (NGOs). All are covertly manipulated by the Communist Party, and their very existence depends on the Party's estimation of how much of a threat they pose to its power. Superficially, the chartering and administration of these groups falls to the Civil Administration Bureau, but their survival actually lies in the hands of the Public Security Bureau, which immediately bans or obstructs any organization regarded as a threat.

For example, in 2003 the Public Security Bureau warned Friends of Nature to expel the dissident Wang Lixiong. The leader of Friends of Nature, Liang Congjie, immediately obeyed, first urging Wang Lixiong to withdraw willingly, and then expelling him when he refused. Wang Lixiong was a founder of the group and a member of its executive committee, and had made important contributions to its development, influence, and operations. Even so, his expulsion followed no formal administrative procedure or any democratic process through the executive committee, but was carried out under the direction of the Party. Such authorized civil organizations operate much like the eight showcase democratic parties; they are completely under the thumb of the Communist Party, and their internal affairs are controlled just like those of the Party through the completely unsystematic and disorderly rule of a few individuals.

Over the past few years, opportunism has become the Communist Party's guiding political philosophy. The Party has learned to become more flexible under international pressure; particularly when dealing with organizations that have a certain amount of international renown, its official policies adjust according to the perceived benefit. The transformation of the Aizhi Action Project from tragedy to success story in just a few short months illustrates this point. When the regime felt that the blood-selling scandal would damage the Party's image, officials banned the organization and jailed its leader, Wan Yanhai.

This occurred just as the World AIDS Conference was getting underway, and the Communist Party's barbaric behavior met with a major international backlash. Apart from the beating China's international reputation took, there was a real possibility that the United States would withdraw $10 million that it had pledged in support of China's AIDS prevention efforts. The regime reevaluated its actions, and with the dual aim of recovering the respect of the global community and the threatened aid funds, it released Wan Yanhai. The government also granted the Aizhi Action Project official status as the Beijing Aizhixing Institute and allowed Wan Yanhai to leave and return to China at will, facilitating the organization's solicitation of foreign donations. At the same time, the Beijing Aizhixing Institute lost its populist identity and became an officially controlled ornament of state authority. If the group once again transgresses state-imposed limits, it will almost certainly once again face official sanctions and repression.

INDEPENDENT AND OFFICIAL TRADE ASSOCIATIONS AND CULTURAL INSTITUTES

These civil organizations bring together a large number of intellectual leaders; some institutes are completely self-sufficient and have been able to reform themselves as civic associations. The most successful example is undoubtedly the Unirule Institute of Economics (*Tianze Suo*, www.unirule.org.cn) run by the economist Mao Yushi, which sponsors biweekly lectures where intellectuals can engage in free scholarly exchange and debate.[1] There are also groups such as the Beijing Dajun Economic Observation and Research Center (*Beijing Dajun Jingji Guancha Yanjiu Zhongxin*, www.dajun.com.cn), which often holds public events. In addition, in 2003, Liu Junning and other intellectuals founded an independent academic think tank called the Cathay Institute for Public Affairs (*Jiu Ding Gonggong Shiwu Yanjiu Suo*, www.jiud ing.org).

There are also some famous independent bookstores, such as All Saints Book Garden in Beijing and Sisyphus in Zezhou, that have been instrumental in promoting freedom of thought. All Saints often invites popular academics to give lectures, poetry readings, and even small-scale art exhibitions on hot topics such as societal transformation, disadvantaged groups, economic stratification, political reform, and cultural constructs. On May 19, 2002, this bookstore hosted a meeting where American legal scholar Ronald Dworkin debated with Beijing academics and intellectuals, a most rewarding experience for the entire Chinese intellectual establishment.

THE INTERNET

In the past few years, Chinese civil organizations have become increasingly aware of the usefulness of Web sites for consolidating information and human resources. The site set up by Liu Junning, Wang Yi, and Chen Yongmiao called "Pros and Cons of Constitutional Government," for example, aims to prove a public forum for popular topics, bring independent intellectuals together, and promote democratic constitutional reforms.[2]

INDEPENDENT AND SECRET WORKERS' AND PEASANTS' ORGANIZATIONS

Large numbers of workers facing unemployment and severe deprivations have begun to demand more independence and power for labor unions; peasants, too, have begun to call for independent agricultural unions. Although the Communist Party strictly suppresses independent labor and agricultural organizations and uses official unions to impose top-down control, it has been unable to dam the rising tide of self-organized unions. A spate of localized demonstrations and protests is providing the impetus and foundation for union organization, while regional protest movements are already taking on the aspect of fledgling unions, and have bred a new generation of labor leaders such as Yao Fuxin of the Liaoyang workers' movement, now in prison.

In the countryside, the government's heavy-handed methods of dealing with peasants and its inability to satisfy their demands for justice have led peasants to rely on their own strength and ingenuity to endure the unendurable. Under these conditions, "peasant heroes" have emerged under whose leadership protest movements are developing in strength and number.

In Renshou County of Sichuan Province, Zhang De'an led a coalition of peasants defying a corrupt faction in the county government that had set excessively high production quotas. Their cohesiveness, bravery, and hard and protracted effort enabled them to overturn the production quotas, and their workload dropped to the lowest level in the past ten years. The peasants' awakening to their own rights indicates progress beyond the old feudal mentality—instead of waiting passively for munificence from above, they take the initiative to fight for what is their due.

INDEPENDENT POLITICAL AND HUMAN RIGHTS ORGANIZATIONS

The most sensitive type of civil society group, these have come under the harshest repression, yet have produced impressive results. The Tiananmen Mothers, led by Ding Zilin, is an outstanding example of the people's power in urging the Communist Party to redress its wrong-doings and pursuing accountability and justice. Ding's association, formed by the parents, spouses, and children of those killed or injured at Tiananmen Square in June 1989, has sought international and domestic donations for the survivors, and under tremendously difficult and personally hazardous conditions, has collected evidence of the fates of the June 4th martyrs, and calls for justice and the rectification of the historical record. Even more astonishing, these people who suffered the most grievously as a result of the June 4th massacre conduct their resilient struggle under the motto of "Brotherhood, Forgiveness, Kindness, and Reason."

In 1998, the creation of the China Democracy Party was announced. Although the Communist Party immediately arrested key members of the organization and sent the rest into hiding or exile abroad, a small number continue the party's work in secret and regularly issue statements, giving the organization an enduring symbolic significance. The New Youth Study Group, founded by a small group of youths with humanitarian interests, was likewise designated an illegal organization; Yang Zili and three other members are currently in prison.

The Government's Stake in Freedom of Association

As explained above, there are no Chinese NGOs in the internationally accepted sense, and truly independent, self-governing organizations are not allowed to operate legally in China today. Most groups, whether they are legal and under government control or suppressed and illegal, lack the organizational ability to take advantage of their collective strength and remain in a scattered, embryonic state. With no safety valve for society's discontent and no official framework to accommodate a political opposition or allow the people any power to manage them-

selves, the masses and the bureaucracy have become increasingly polar-
ized. There is no way to build a common foundation of values shared by
both sides, or to create a new order in which public and private sectors
compete with and tolerate each other as equals.

In a system lacking legal, independent organizations to protect the
people, and in which opportunities exist only for those at the top, the
common ethical expectations for people, organizations, and governments to interact on a peaceful basis have been replaced by unrestrained,
extralegal, and amoral practices. Put another way, today's social order is
based solely on the employment of naked violence to protect the elite,
and it could be uprooted at any time by the long-buried resentments
and desires of the repressed.

The common trend was for these groups to move from the country
to the city, from the border regions to the central regions. Small and
scattered groups in villages and towns allied to form unions encompass-
ing entire townships, cities, or even counties, and the protest movements
became highly organized, showing considerable staying power. The
large-scale protests in the Daqing oil fields and Liaoyang in 2002 are
good examples of these trends. An even better example is that of the
Falun Gong, which has managed to launch a highly organized national
and international protest movement.

These examples show that China's independent protest movements
cannot revolve around the will of a few core members. Rather, China's
populist organizations can succeed only if they aim to channel the political power of the masses into a new, nonviolent societal order by providing the common man with a bit of flexible political space. The
crimes and excesses of the elite, coupled with the continual suffering of
the people over many years, have instilled in the people an eagerness to
participate in the political process that has already reached a point sufficient to transform society. The more tyrannical the suppression, the
more desperate the people's desire for empowerment, and the more
worrisome the potential for violence. The state of affairs in China today
is such that, even if we were to ignore the economic stratification and
the abuse of disadvantaged groups, and look only at the June 4th Massacre and the repression of the Falun Gong, the demands for justice
inspired by these travesties have been enough to trigger political mobi-
lizations on a national level.

The economic reforms launched in 1992 have allowed China's urban dwellers to suddenly enjoy a level of material prosperity most people never dared to imagine before. They have the modern amenities of a developed nation and even share in the postmodern age of globalization brought by the Internet and computers. Their material enjoyments far exceed—perhaps too far—those of the much more numerous people living in border areas and other poverty-stricken regions. Vacation homes, private automobiles, leisure time, and foreign vacations not only soothe the spiritual wounds inflicted during Tiananmen, but provide distraction from the human rights tragedies that occur around them daily and mask the primitive, cruel realities that still exist in China.

In the long run, the extreme disparity in wealth and resources already evident in China can only worsen with time. Even if a regime sympathetic to the common man comes to power, the competition for resources in a nation with a population as large as China's will remain fiercer than in other countries, with the majority of the populace continuing to yearn in vain for the benefits of modern life. Jiang Zemin's assertion that in twenty years every resident of China will be living above the subsistence level was nothing but a tyrant's glib, empty promise to temporarily distract the masses from the crises of the present and the hopelessness of the future. The truth is that China is trapped in a vicious circle, and there is no evidence of official commitment to developing a more benevolent system.

In this situation, it is incumbent on the Chinese Communist regime to initiate political reform. Rather than trying to maintain a system of rigid official controls that has already sprung innumerable leaks, the government should amend the "Societies Law" to provide legal guidance and leadership for civic organizations and ease its self-imposed burden of managing every aspect of society. This acknowledgment of the people's right to autonomy in their everyday lives would allow the effective tapping of human resources and channel the latent creative energies of the masses into a positive force for a stable society. With the government giving official backing to the independent development of civil society, a new order could eventually emerge in which people would have the power to conduct themselves, defend themselves, and coordinate their ideas and energies—in short, a free and benign society in which the government does not interfere in all aspects of daily life.

Translated by Jonathan Kaufman and Stacy Mosher

This translation is an edited version of an article that originally appeared in Chinese on the Web site of *China Monthly:* (http:// www.chinamz.org/115issue/115gfdl1.html).

Notes

1. Mao Yushi's Unirule Institute has since been closed down, apparently because of the controversial nature of its discussions and positions, and the organization's Web site has not been updated since late 2005. See interview with Mao Yushi in Li Weiping, [There will certainly be change within ten years] *"Shi nian zhi nei be you da bian,"* Open Magazine (Hong Kong), February 2006.

2. Since Liu Xiaobo wrote this article in early 2003, many more discussion forums and resource Web sites have been established in China, but are subject to periodic shutdowns depending on the political climate.

A TIANANMEN MOTHER VOWS
TO FIGHT ON

Yang Hongfeng

Epoch Times *reporter Yang Hongfeng interviewed Zhang Xianling by telephone on April 3, 2004, shortly after Zhang and two other Tiananmen Mothers, Ding Zilin and Huang Jinping, were released from several days' detention by Chinese authorities. April 3 was also the birthday of Zhang's son, Wang Nan, who died in Beijing on June 4, 1989.*

Yang Hongfeng *(ET)*: We're extremely happy that you finally returned. But in fact this should never have happened. Did the authorities arrest you through the appropriate legal procedures?

Zhang Xianling *(ZX)*: Yes, they followed proper legal procedures. That is, they produced a valid warrant, initially a summons and then a detention notice.

ET: What reason was given?

ZX: They stated that I was suspected of breaking such-and-such an article of the criminal law. I can't remember all the details, but the summons stated that I was a suspect in a crime, and that it was according to article 50 of the Criminal Procedure Law. The second one, the detention notice, stated the arrest was in accordance with article 61 of the Criminal Procedure Law, but didn't refer to me as a criminal suspect.[1]

ET: They said you received a package.

ZX: That's right.

ET: Did you ask someone to send it to you, or did someone just send it to you?

ZX: You could say that I was aware of this matter in advance. I knew in advance that someone wanted to send me some T-shirts, and I agreed—if I hadn't agreed, they wouldn't have known my address—and after I told them my address they sent the package to me. I felt it was only some T-shirts, just souvenirs, and I thought that if customs didn't agree to the T-shirts being sent, they would just confiscate them. But my thinking was too naïve, I see that now.

I feel this law is rather vague, because it doesn't provide any specifics about exactly how the law has been broken. One is Customs Law, I think. In relation to the Customs Law, they said what was sent were T-shirts, but what was written on the customs form was scarves, so there was a discrepancy in the documentation and that involved Customs Law. But I didn't fill out the customs declaration, so this shouldn't have been blamed on me!

Another accused me of "inciting subversion of state power," and I think this is wrong. We received a few T-shirts—in what way does that "endanger state security"? It simply doesn't make sense. So I believe this legal interpretation is quite vague.

I feel the Chinese government was not very sensible in doing this, because I think this kind of matter should be settled. If you see some problem with our T-shirts, you can confiscate them and then come over and talk to us about it. My husband recently had heart surgery and immediately experienced heart trouble and had to go to the hospital. If you had any sense of humanity, you shouldn't arrest us in this way, don't you think? A few mothers like us, even if we received not fifty T-shirts but as many as 500 T-shirts, could we overthrow the government? Could we endanger state security? It's impossible!

ET: When they released you, what explanation did they give?

ZX: They didn't really give any explanation, and I don't think they had one. They gave me the impression that originally they could have applied to put me under surveillance, but having taken into consideration my explaining the situation clearly, and that it tallied with their version, they would restore my liberty. Putting it simply, they had their reason for arrest and their reason for release. This is what is known as, "The charges have a basis, but evidence is lacking." I think if you've spent any time in China you're familiar with this phrase.

ET: Does that mean you've experienced this kind of harassment in the past?

ZX: I can't say it's been often. This is the first time I've been detained. Before, it was more like, if I went somewhere, they would follow me, or if I went to make offerings at the grave they would tell me not to do it, but if I insisted they'd allow it; and sometimes there would be a surveillance vehicle, that sort of thing. But this was the first time for this kind of situation. It's at least the second time for Ding Zilin! She was previously detained for forty-five days.

ET: Today is Wang Nan's birthday. What do you have planned?

ZX: It's our custom every year on this day to go to the Wan'an Public Cemetery, which is where Wang Nan's ashes are kept. Today was the same as always, we went this morning and made offerings and placed some fresh flowers. After we came back my mood was not very cheerful; this is inevitable, whenever we come to this time my emotions are very unstable. Because I can still see the day he was born as if it were happening before my eyes, and so when I think of it I find it very hard to take. At the same time I remind myself that I'm not the only person to meet with this tragedy; there are so many other mothers, fathers, wives, husbands, in different times and places who, even with the passage of time, still feel this pain.

Ai, what can I say, every time I think of it I feel very sad; I'll just tell you briefly about it. He was nineteen years old, a student at Yuetan Middle School. When the student movement first started he really didn't understand much about what was going on. But he rode his bicycle to school every day, and he would be on the road for more than half an hour, and as he rode he would encounter some university students, and he naturally talked with them about what was happening at Tiananmen Square, and eventually he became involved.

Later I heard from others that he went there every day at lunchtime and took pictures. He loved photography. That's why on that evening, June 3, he took his camera, and wearing khaki fatigues and a helmet that someone had left at our house, he rode his bicycle to Tiananmen. I've thought about what route he must have taken after he left; it should have been the route from the back entrance of Beihai, from Beichang Street, and then southward toward Nanchang Street, because he died at the entrance to Nanchang Street, and if he had come from Tiananmen he definitely wouldn't have been able to reach that point.

Before he left he had telephoned a fellow student and said he was going to record the true events for history, and at 10:30 P.M. he asked me whether I thought there would be gunfire. I said, "I don't think so." I said, "Even at the time of the Gang of Four they didn't open fire, why should they do it now?" But I said, "Don't go out, it's dangerous out there." He said, "Don't worry, I won't go out."

I never guessed he would actually go out, taking his camera and wearing a helmet and riding his bicycle toward the north end of Nanchang Street.

Later I found some eyewitnesses who told me that when the martial-law troops opened fire, he ran out to take a photo and was struck by a bullet. After he fell people in the crowd wanted to carry him away for treatment, but the martial-law troops wouldn't allow it; they said he was a hooligan, and whoever tried to help him would be shot, so the people had no choice, they could only back away. Just then an ambulance came from the north end of Nanchang Street on its way to Chang'an Street to save people, but it wasn't allowed through.

The doctors in the ambulance got out and tried to reason with the martial-law troops, saying, "We're doctors, we have to go to save the injured," but the martial-law troops said they were not allowed to go to Chang'an Street. Ambulances came twice, but their negotiations failed, and they had to go back from the north end of Nanchang Street, and for that reason the injured people on Nanchang Street could not receive treatment.

Eventually some medical students managed to carry my son behind the martial-law troops to a place where they could bandage his wound. They felt his breast, which was still warm, and they saw his old student ID from when he was at Huayuan Village Middle School, which said he was seventeen years old although he was actually nineteen. The medical students saw he was still very young, and they hoped they could save him, but the martial-law troops wouldn't allow them to take him away for treatment. They said, "If you want to help him, you'll have to do it here," so of course they couldn't save him.

Eventually around 3 A.M., after he had passed away, the medical students said, "He's dead, we're not taking him away for treatment, but to let his family come and identify the body." But the martial-law troops said they couldn't take him away. So all they could do was stay there with him until sunrise, around 6 A.M., and then the martial-law troops forced them to leave, and they had to just leave him there. Apart from Wang Nan there were also two other corpses, and the medical students had to leave them there, those three corpses.

One of the students telephoned the school, and that's how our family eventually received news of Wang Nan's death. In fact, by the time I found his body it was already more than ten days later, on the 14th. They contacted us to come and identify the body at the Huguosi Hospital for Chinese Medicine. The hospital told us that his body had been found buried outside the No. 28 Middle School next to Tiananmen Square, and that his had been one of three bodies found in that pit. Because he was wearing fatigues, they initially believed he was one of the martial-law troops, so they took him to the hospital. I think the others were probably cremated, because there was no identification on them and no one knew who they were. Eventually, after Wang Nan was brought to that hospital, they carried out inquiries and learned that he was not a serving soldier, and they notified the school, and then the school notified us.

Eventually someone gave me a photograph of him after he'd been dug up, and that was unspeakable; after I saw that photo the first time I couldn't sleep for more than a week. Such a good boy—whatever you might do, why did you have to kill him? Having wounded him, why not let him be treated, and after he died, why not let him be taken away, but instead just bury him, and in a common grave?

Among us petitioners there are thirteen people who up to now have still not found the dead bodies of their family members, and it's possible that the bodies were buried nearby and then cremated.

Even when two military forces fight each other, they won't prevent treatment of the wounded or the arrival of ambulances—that's basic human decency, isn't it? Someone has died, and you still don't let him be carried to the hospital, but just bury him.

I used to get very upset when I talked about these things; I've really wept my eyes dry. When I found my son's body, there was a bandage around his head, so I could see someone had tried to save him. As for his student ID from Huayuan Village Middle School, a teacher from the school told me the school had received a telephone call from someone notifying them that a student named Wang Nan, with the student ID number so-and-so, had been wounded at such a time, and had died at such a time.

Eventually I looked for that person and found him, and he came to our home and gave us the student ID card and the bicycle key Xiao Nan had been carrying, along with some other things. He also told me the details of what had happened, and that's how I know that the martial-law troops wouldn't let my son be treated and wouldn't let his body be taken away. The way things are in China now, I don't dare to reveal those people's names for fear of bringing harm on them. But I believe some day they will come forward and bear witness.

There was a period of time when I nearly went mad, but eventually I realized that I couldn't go mad and I couldn't weep myself blind, I needed to gain a clear understanding of what had happened. And later I found eyewitnesses, and found the doctor who had tried to save my son, and found the traces of his burial. During that time I came to know Ding Zilin, and we began devoting our energies to finding the people who had died.

ET: I'm sure I speak for our readers overseas when I say our greatest hope is that such a thing will never happen again.

ZX: Yes, my feeling now is that such a thing is unlikely to happen. But if the matter is never made clear, and if there is never a proper legal resolution, it will be hard to guarantee that it will never happen again.

ET: During the UN Human Rights Commission session, right after the Chinese government issued its white paper on human rights, it turned around and detained the three of you . . .

ZX: It's very stupid, I have to say. Someone said something to me that I think is true, which is that the Chinese leaders may have been blinded by certain well-known people acting in their own interests. I have to say,

I don't know, I'm just an ordinary mother, and it's only because I lost my son that I've stood up to fight for justice on behalf of my son, and it really opened my eyes. I don't know why they would want to arrest me, it seems a very simple and routine matter to me.

In fact, we've expressed our views repeatedly in hopes of gradually solving the problem. We're not advocating any kind of violence or social instability; Ding Zilin and I and the other Tiananmen Mothers have all along conducted our group activities in a lawful, open, and independent manner. We want to solve the problem, not make a big show or raise a fuss—this has been our principle all along.

ET: When you and Ding Zilin contact other family members, listening to their stories must be quite distressing.

ZX: That's for sure. Every time we listen to someone it's very upsetting. At the same time I experience an intuitive reaction, which is that when I find other people in a situation similar to mine, I also feel their pain. I read something somewhere that said sharing the pain of others is a way of reducing one's own pain. When I've sought people out I've found that I still felt pain, but it's not the same as before. I feel there are many people who share my unhappy fate. So I should work even harder to find others, and I should work hard to get to know these people.

Before it was as if you couldn't say anything, because if you did it was possible that others would discriminate against you, but now it's much better. When I first found them, some people wept bitterly and said, "All the mental anguish I've been suppressing all these years, now I can talk over with you!" We had a common language. There was an old granny of around eighty-five who was originally feeling extremely repressed, extremely anguished, cursing her fate and wondering why it was so bad, but after I found her she said, "It's not that my fate is bad, there's just too much wrong that is done." Since then we've been in touch regularly, and she was the original inspiration for the Tiananmen Mothers.

ET: Do the Tiananmen Mothers intend to continue their work seeking out family members?

ZX: Of course, we'll definitely continue. After we were detained this time, while I was in the detention center I really felt a lot of anxiety, because my husband's health was not good, and his spirits were low, and it caused me a huge amount of worry. I was also extremely worried about the other Tiananmen Mothers. I didn't know how upset they might be over Ding Zilin, Huang Jinping, and myself all being arrested at once. But after I got out and learned what was going on, I was extremely happy to learn that we Tiananmen Mothers could not be struck down. Detaining us for six days, six months, even six years, would not keep the movement from continuing.

ET: What do you think an ordinary, powerless Chinese can do to help you Mothers?

ZX: I believe ordinary Chinese are already helping us. Some people provide us with information; they know someone died in a particular place or was injured in a particular place, and they tell us, and we go and find out the full details from them.

Our goal is to verify what happened, because there are always rumors. My mother always says, "By the time news has been passed a third time, an immortal becomes a yellow dog." You say a certain person was killed, but is that actually true? And if so, was it the martial-law troops who killed him? And did he die on June 4th? Was he an ordinary citizen or a hooligan? We have to verify what happened, and we hope ordinary people will be willing to help us.

Another thing people do is donate money. There are some families who may not be starving to death, but who are still experiencing great hardship. There's a woman in a village near Beijing whose husband was killed, and raising two children on her own is extremely difficult—they really just have four walls around them and nothing more. When Ding Zilin went to see this woman the first time, she wept to see someone living under such hardship.

ET: How can people get in touch with you or donate money?

ZX: They can get in touch with Ding Zilin, and a lot of people in China know my telephone number. But I don't want to make our contact information known for overseas telephone calls.

ET: What can Chinese overseas do?

ZX: We hope you'll be concerned about us and support us, that will be very good.

ET: On behalf of our readers, I express deep gratitude to you for accepting this interview under your current circumstances.

Translated by Stacy Mosher

The original Chinese article was posted on the *Epoch Times* Web site: http://www.dajiyuan.com/gb/4/4/5/n501038.htm.

Note

1. Article 50 of China's Criminal Procedure Law outlines the different forms of detention available to police. Article 61 authorizes the police to first detain a person who is a prime suspect or who is apprehended in the process of or immediately after committing a crime under specific circumstances.

THE VIEW BENEATH THE BRIDGE

Yi Ban

In late 2003, more than 200 people took shelter from the cold beneath the overpass of Beijing's Second Ring Road, having come from all over China to seek justice through petitions to the central authorities.

An Early Morning in December Beneath a Beijing Overpass

"Wake up, time to go to work!" A woman, Liu Hua, crawls from a plank bed, shouting to her sleeping neighbor, a woman from Shaoguan, Guangdong Province. Today marks the winter solstice, and at a little after seven o'clock dawn has not yet broken in Beijing. As on other days, it is the roar of cars over her head that alerts Liu Hua to the start of a new day.

Regardless of whether she or the other woman wakes up first, their first remark is always, "Time to go to work." In fact, they have no place to "go to work"; rather, it is the person they will seek out today who is now preparing to go to work. As for the women, they have to prepare their belongings for their day's travels.

Soon afterward, a man beside the woman from Shaoguan crawls from the bed. He is also from Shaoguan, a former schoolteacher. Every night he squeezes in among the others and warms himself in their quilts. On Liu Hua's other side is her husband, a village head. Relying on his hardy physique, he allows the woman from Shaoguan his share of the quilt as he curls next to his wife night after night.

Gradually the entire area under the intersection comes alive. Li Dashu from Anhui Province, Xiao Qi from Hubei, Meng Yanjun from Hebei—one by one, each sits up on the plank bed. "Shit, it's freezing," Sichuan native Wang Erwa cannot help cursing as she opens her eyes. A blast of cold wind follows her words into the space under the overpass, and those who have left their beds shiver in spite of themselves. The last to awaken is an elderly woman, ninety-two years old. Supported by her grandson, she has managed to survive another long winter night.

Finally, all 200-odd people have roused themselves, and the air beneath the overpass fills with odors from the plank beds, people's bodies, and unwashed clothes, inducing coughs of protest from some of the elders. The five-year-old son of Zhang from Shandong is crying near the exit. "He wants to see his mother—his mother is dead," Zhang says angrily. "His mother was killed, and we haven't corrected the injustice yet."

Zhang says that three years ago, while he was working in a city far from home, village cadres came to his house and demanded money. His wife had none to give them, and was dragged away by the cadres. When Zhang learned of the matter and returned home, all he found was his wife's cold body. The child continues to weep, and Zhang falls silent. Rearranging a bag full of his belongings beneath his pillow, he says he and his son may never see justice in their lifetime.

Someone lights a stove, a discard from someone else's home recovered from a ditch. In this space beneath the intersection, three to five people usually share a stove, and at the moment several dozen stoves are lit, filling the space with black smoke and obliterating the first rays of sunlight. On these stoves they produce their breakfast.

Rush Hour Beneath The Overpass

The morning of December 22, 2003, marks the first day of winter. The central weather report forecasts the warmest first day of winter in Beijing for the past few years, but for the 200-odd people who have gathered from more than twenty provinces, cities, and districts here beneath the Majia Bao East Road overpass, the cold from the concrete beneath their feet chills them to the bone.

To the north of the overpass is the two-tiered Second Ring Road, which has eight lanes in each direction. Next to the Ring is a moat that has guarded the imperial city of Beijing for hundreds of years. Despite the relatively warm winter, the water in the moat has frozen almost solid enough to bear a person's weight.

Second Ring Road is one of the most important thoroughfares in Beijing, carrying more than a million cars to every district in the city. Regardless of whether people are going to the office from home, or from the office to bars or hotels, from South City to Tiananmen Square or from North City to the Temple of Heaven, they must pass along Second Ring Road.

At the same time, this is only one of many intersections within the 1,000-plus square kilometers of urban Beijing, and few people stop their cars to observe what's going on beneath. No one notices that human lives—cooking, eating, drinking, and living—are carried on beneath the overpass. As for me, one evening when I was hurrying from my office to dinner with friends at Feng Tai, I was caught in a traffic jam on the overpass; it was then that I noticed a sign stating "Refuge of the Wronged" and saw traces of smoke. A few days later I made a special trip there, and while walking through the area from west to east, I came upon this scene.

The space is about one hundred meters long and ten meters wide. People have erected simple wooden dividers, and within each division are piled worn quilts, clothes, and housewares. Inside some cubicles I saw people earnestly writing. "They're composing petitions," I was told.

Others were curled up in tatty quilts. "They're waiting here for a ruling." I heard dialects from all over China. Although the faces were of all different shapes and colors, they turned the same dull, blank expression to the interloper.

"We call this space our Bridge Home," said the woman from Shaoguan.

North of the overpass, within two kilometers of Second Ring Road, stands the National People's Congress. A cheap ride further north on the No. 20 bus will take you directly to the Ministry of Public Security. To the west is the Beijing South Train Station, where the cheapest trains arrive from all over China. A five-minute walk along a little street called Happiness Road to the west of Beijing South Train Station brings you to the National Supreme Court's Letters and Petitions office. Five minutes from Second Ring Road is the Petitioners Financial Assistance Office, and within fifteen minutes you can reach the Petitioners Reception Office of the National Procuratorate. Twenty minutes brings you to the reception office of the National Bureau of Letters and Petitions.

The location of the Bridge Home at the nexus of so many government departments has made it the most desirable refuge for people who frequently "go to work" at these departments, especially in subzero winter temperatures.

Seeking Security Beneath the Bridge

"When I first began staying here, there were only about ten people under the overpass," says Liu Hua, now one of the veterans of the group. On August 27, 2003, forty-year-old Liu Hua left her child and her home in the town of Hongling Bao, Shenyang Prefecture, Sujia Village, and came to Beijing to file a petition for her husband. "When I first arrived, the weather was warm, and I hadn't brought a change of clothes."

Liu Hua says that on her way to the National Supreme Court's Letters and Petitions office, she noticed people living under the overpass, and after talking with them she learned that they were petitioners like herself. That night, Liu Hua became a resident of the Bridge Home. Since Liu Hua had no quilt, she collected a big pile of black plastic sheets. "They're passable if you line them," she says casually.

After a couple of days, Liu Hua became acquainted with the woman from Shaoguan, as well as the eighteen-year-old Hebei youth, Meng Yanjun, and she curled up with them at night. On September 9, Liu Hua brought some documents to the Ministry of Public Security, where she was intercepted by eight officials from her home village. "They said they would get back to me with a settlement," and on the basis of that promise she accompanied them back to Shenyang that evening.

"I waited at home for three days, but no one came to deal with the problem, so I came back to Beijing again on the 12th." Liu Hua says that this time she brought a quilt with her, since the people she'd stayed with before had lost theirs. She shared her quilt with the woman from Shaoguan and the former schoolteacher for a little more than a month until October 21, when the woman from Shaoguan was taken away by Public Security officers from Guangdong who had been summoned by the National Bureau of Letters and Petitions. On November 10, the woman from Shaoguan returned to Beijing to continue her appeal, and met up with Liu Hua again beneath the overpass.

On November 25, Liu Hua went back to her home village, returning to Beijing with her husband on December 9. Liu Hua's husband's name is Yue Yongjin. He and Liu Hua had reported the former village committee's corruption and embezzlement of public funds, and as a result met with retaliation. In August 2002, even though Yue Yongjin was elected village chairman, the village committee refused to give him a letter of appointment or official seal, and as a result he was unable to perform his official duties. Liu Hua and her husband reported the problem to the higher authorities, but no one came to the village to hear them out. That's why Liu Hua finally decided to come to Beijing to file a petition.

Life beneath the overpass is full of hardship. "We have to limit our daily living expenses to three yuan," said the woman from Shaoguan.

There is an abandoned waste-disposal site near Yongding Meng, from which they salvage discarded doors, windows, or scrap wood to carry back for use as firewood. "Last time, before I went home I collected a pile of firewood and left it for them," said Liu Hua, adding that Meng Yanjun, the youngest of the petitioners, is still a child in her eyes.

Water is one of the biggest issues residents of the Bridge Home face. There are no standpipes for them to access, and they cannot use those of nearby residents. It is also impossible to take water from the frozen moat. Eventually, an old man who watches over a public toilet near the Beijing South Train Station took pity on them and let them fetch water there.

As for food, three yuan is not sufficient to keep one's stomach full. "We eat two meals a day every day. Sometimes we go to the market on the south side and pick up some cabbage." Liu Hua says people sometimes furtively give them rice and buns that they receive from a visitor's assistance stand.

There is no sense of security beneath the overpass. On November 5, when Beijing experienced its first heavy snow of the winter, at about ten o'clock in the evening, eight urban patrol officers armed with cudgels invaded the space and expelled the residents, confiscating scrap wood they had collected for fuel. On December 10, urban patrol officers returned to the space and destroyed all the residents' stoves, cooking utensils, stocked rice, and vegetables before leaving.

Only One Happy Ending So Far

Every Saturday since winter began, five Korean students have come to the Bridge Home at Majia Bao, distributing noodles, buns, and eggs to the residents. These visits have become the highlight of the week for the people beneath the overpass.

"So many people have been coming to Beijing to petition for so many years. They start out scattered all over the city, but gather here once it starts getting cold." Four members of eighteen-year-old Meng Yanjun's family—his father and mother, elder brother and younger brother—were robbed and murdered, but the murderer was not sentenced to death after being caught. Because of this, Meng has been petitioning since he was fourteen years old.

"I came to Beijing with a dictionary," Meng Yanjun says. He never finished secondary school, and needs to consult the dictionary when writing his petition and reporting materials. Over the years his new dictionary has become battered and torn. "I've spent a total of 470,000 yuan on my petitions and reports," Meng says.

His father ran a pharmaceutical company before he died, and the family's circumstances were comfortable, but over the past two years Meng has run through all of his family's money and has ended up living under the overpass.

"Since I first came to this place, only one person's problem has been solved. That person was from Guangxi." Meng Yanjun says very few cases reach a satisfactory resolution through the petitioning process, and the person from Guangxi seems to have just been lucky. He left the Bridge Home full of joy and with the hearty congratulations of the others. "Just to get some kind of response is considered pretty good," says Meng, observing that most people's petitions disappear like a pebble thrown into the sea.

Previously, Meng Yanjun had a job in a small hotel, and a colleague helped him write his petition materials. On November 1, Meng Yanjun quit his job at the hotel and began to live under an overpass in Kaiyang with his savings of several hundred yuan, but he was eventually expelled.

Meng Yanjun's efforts have not been entirely wasted. One of China's most influential television programs, China Central Television's *Interview Focus,* has featured him twice, and his family's murder case was sent back to the Supreme Court of Hebei Province for reexamination. On September 17, 2002, Meng and his elder sister went to Tiananmen Square, where Meng produced a piece of white cloth, spread it near the national flag, and knelt down on it with his sister. He slashed his palm with a knife, letting his fresh blood stain the white cloth. As he was about to go into shock, some policemen took him and his sister away. This incident was reported by quite a few news media, and was referred to in the Western press as the "Tiananmen Flag Incident."

"I don't know when I can stop living under the overpass. I'd like to go back to school." His harsh living conditions and the strain of years of petitioning have afflicted Meng with heart disease at this tender age. When reaching a particularly dramatic point in his story, Meng suddenly collapses in a faint, but then revives and continues to talk about his experiences as if nothing had happened.

As I was completing this article, I learned from a photographer I work with that one morning more than ten police cars surrounded the overpass near the Beijing South Train Station, and more than one hundred police officers and urban control personnel expelled all the residents of the Bridge Home. My photographer was present at the time, and said he saw many people arrested and loaded into police vehicles. He saw people screaming, crying, and swearing. The whole clearance process took more than an hour.

One day at the end of December, I visited the space under the overpass again. It was completely cleared from east to west, and not a single trace of people's lives remained. I felt as if everything I had seen before was a dream.

Translated by Akiko Kageyama

The original Chinese article was published in the February 5, 2004 edition of HRIC's Internet newsletter, *Huaxia Dianzi Bao.*

THE END OF THE ROPE

Zhang Lin

Crushing poverty has kept the people of Bengbu, Anhui Province struggling on the brink of survival. Now they're fighting back.

One hundred years ago, the area around Bengbu was little more than a sandy shoal where freshwater mussels flourished. Known in Chinese as *beng*, the bivalves gave the city its name, which means "mussel wharf."

A corruption incident gave birth to this city of migrants when the Qing Dynasty government was constructing China's first long-distance railway, running from Beijing to Nanjing's Pukou District. Known as the Jingpu Line, the railway had to cross the Huai River, and after detailed reconnaissance, the engineers decided to construct a bridge at Changhuaiwei, a populous town with firm ground.

What the engineers didn't consider was that they would have to traverse the ancestral burial ground of a distinguished local clan. The clan, fearing destruction of its feng shui, raised a large sum of money and bribed the Beijing officials in charge of the railway project to move the bridge. And so it was that Bengbu was born where the railway line crossed the Huai River. With the passage of a hundred years of development, Bengbu is now home to nearly 1 million people.

Bengbu is situated in the hinterland, and its economic development has relied on a pattern of environmental degradation at the expense of the health of the city's workers. Pollution has become so serious that it threatens the survival of local residents. On July 16, 2004, the Huai River flooded after torrential rains, forcing open local sewage outlets. More than 500 million tons of high-index waste turned the river into a 150 kilometer–long sewage canal; the river turned black and emitted an appalling stench, and algae rapidly bred on its surface. The sewage all converged at Bengbu, creating the worst pollution of the Huai River in history.

The Huai River is China's third largest tributary, and was the first to introduce large-scale management of sewer drainage. Under the aegis of China's State Council, 60 billion yuan was invested over the course of ten years in this sewage-management project. But as is the case with all Party policies, the project dealt with the symptoms rather than the illness, accomplishing little more than covering the problem with an expensive bandage. The polluting industries along the river adhered to the government's management policy largely by storing up their sewage, which gradually seeped into the ground and seriously polluted the groundwater, poisoning 170 million of the region's residents. The flooding in July finally brought the horror of the situation to the surface.

Investigations by environmental experts established that breweries, paper mills, and chemical factories were the main scourges of the Huai River. Several thousand polluting enterprises routinely dumped their waste directly into the river, ignoring sewage-management practices for the sake of maximizing profit. Ultimately, like the origins of Bengbu itself, this disaster was rooted in political corruption. It is well known that government officials at all levels are constantly on the watch for opportunities to extort money, and the well-funded polluting enterprises present easy pickings. The slightest objection can yield a pocket full of cash, and the Red Profiteers who run the enterprises readily collude with corrupt officials, distributing their profits to the detriment of the common good.

Corrupt officials have come up with amazing excuses for their protection of polluting industries. They say things like, "The businesses have to survive, the workers have to eat." This same logic could be applied to criminals: thieves have to eat, so they should be allowed to steal; hooligans have to eat, so they should be allowed to commit murder and arson. Almost any crime known to man can be rationalized by these officials when a red envelope is dangled before their eyes!

One example is Bengbu Fengyuan Group, which has been poisoning nearby residents with its pollutants for years. In Baliqiao Village, many healthy people in their forties with no history of disease have died of liver cancer. In many cases, siblings and married couples have succumbed simultaneously. According to my own research, dozens of healthy Baliqiao residents have died in the past few years. I discussed the possibility of a lawsuit with some of their surviving relatives, but they all shook their heads and said, "Fengyuan Group's main backer is a member of the Central Political Commission; who can win a lawsuit against them? Which court, which judge would even accept this case?"

Then they brought out a stack of photos showing people with blood and bruises all over their bodies, heads and faces, men and women, elderly and children, photos so dreadful that they made my skin crawl. Baliqiao residents painfully recounted how the Fengyuan Group had joined up with Bengbu officials to forcibly remove village residents in order to expand the polluting enterprise. For the sake of the health of their future generations, the villagers refused. The Fengyuan Group then organized hundreds of gangsters and fitted them with company security uniforms, and sent them in with several hundred uniformed military police to attack the villagers. Even an eighty-year-old woman was beaten bloody, her teeth scattered on the ground.

The villagers told me that after this incident they petitioned the provincial capital and Beijing many times, but all their entreaties for assistance were ignored. For this reason, they no longer placed any hopes of justice from the Communist Party, and felt that only if the Party fell from power they might receive some retribution.

My own family has suffered ill effects from the Fengyuan Group's pollution. The soil near our home has become so polluted that any vegetables grown on it are tainted, and I'm constantly worried that we'll contract an incurable illness from eating anything grown there. The Fengyuan Group also constantly spews dangerous pollutants into the air, especially at night, creating a smell like burnt soy sauce or something even worse. On windless days the stench permeates our home, but there is no escape, because outside it smells even worse. China has truly descended into chaos and darkness!

A City of Silent Tragedy

Bengbu was once Anhui's main industrial city, but under the economic reforms of the 1980s it gradually lost its importance, and since the June 4th massacre it has deteriorated yearly, with factories ceasing or reducing production and many small enterprises closing down altogether.

A tragic story circulated around Bengbu, illustrating the horrific circumstances of the city's unemployed. According to this story, husband and wife were both employed in communal enterprises, and both lost

their jobs. They had a ten-year-old daughter. The father was paid an unemployment allowance of a little more than 100 yuan per month, but
the mother's work unit went bankrupt, and she received nothing. The
family had no other assets, and the three of them had to make do on the
father's unemployment allowance. The father hurried nearly every day
to the Labor Bureau office to see if any new jobs were posted, but after
half a year of searching he still had nothing.

The mother's health had always been poor, and under the pressures of
their straitened circumstances she suffered a series of illnesses. As the
family had no money for medical fees, she had to bear her infirmities,
which became increasingly severe.

The daughter didn't understand what had happened. Previously the
family had always been able to enjoy some pork, some fish or chicken,
at least once a week. Now for months they'd had nothing but salted vegetables, maybe some cabbage or turnip, now and again some tofu and
greens. She felt she was starving, and clamored daily for some meat.

She had no way of knowing that the family's income was only
enough to buy their coal, some oil and salt, and to pay their rent and
utilities. There was simply nothing left over for food. Her mother went
out every day to the market with a basket and scrounged vegetables that
no one else wanted, or that could be bought for next to nothing, and
tried to fashion a meal out of those discards at home. The parents were
already fretting over the girl's school fees for the next semester, which
would be due at the New Year. Facing his daughter's entreaties, the father could only say, "Next week, my dear, next week I'll definitely buy
some meat for you to eat."

The next time the father picked up his unemployment allowance, he
brought it home to discuss with his wife how they should spend it. He
found his wife weeping alone, and anxiously asked her what was the
matter. His wife sobbed that she no longer wanted to live. "I was forced
to go to the countryside when I was fifteen years old, laboring myself to
exhaustion for more than ten years with never enough to eat. It was so
difficult for me to get back to the city, only to spend more than ten more
years of hard labor at the factory.

"Ai! I sacrificed my youth and everything else to Chairman Mao and
to Comrade Xiaoping and the Communist Party. Now my body is broken and my health is ruined and they don't even give me money
enough to eat. I don't know how to do anything but operate a textile

machine, and at my age how can I find work in a new occupation? By living I only remain a burden to my family. I've thought it over, and I think it's best for me to die."

The husband wanted to comfort his wife, but when he tried to speak he broke down in tears, recognizing that his own situation was no better. Even if he found another job after a few months, that would only bring in a little more than 200 yuan a month, still inadequate for a family of three. After working half his life, he didn't own a roof over his head or a parcel of land. New housing policies were being implemented, but they had no money for a new place. Would they be thrown out in the street? What hope could he give her?

So he said nothing, but turned and went out the door. The thought of his family's tragic circumstances, and the similar conditions faced by so many other unemployed workers, and his months of vain effort to find work, plunged him into despair. He didn't even care any more if others saw him weeping. Why should he care about anything more in this cruel society, in this cold world? Quietly, he reached a decision.

When his daughter came home for lunch at noon, she cried out with joy as she saw a big pot of stewed pork and turnip on the table, along with a bottle of wine. Her parents were sitting at the table waiting for her, and lovingly urged her to enjoy her meal. The father drank half a glass of wine, which he hadn't enjoyed for months, and then cut large chunks of pork for his wife, daughter, and himself to eat. At first his wife didn't want to eat any meat, preferring to leave more for her husband and daughter, but she was unable to resist her husband's warm entreaties, and, dabbing her tears, she ate some as well, all the while worrying about what had gotten into her husband to buy so much meat and not leave enough money even for rice the rest of the month.

For several days no one left the house. The neighbors began to wonder, and then to discuss among themselves. Finally the neighborhood committee broke down the door, and upon entering the house they found the family all dead, the husband clutching his wife in one arm and his daughter in the other. Subsequently the coroner determined that all three had died from rat poison, which was found in the remains of the stewed pork. The conclusion drawn was that the husband had been unable to bear the continued poverty of his wife and daughter, and seeing no other way out, had killed them and himself.

After the Communist Party seized power, sent-down educated

youths and laid-off workers such as this man and his wife effectively became bound to the Party in what amounted to decades-long indentured
servitude. After they had been squeezed dry of their blood and sweat,
they were kicked aside and ignored. Even in the slave societies of 2,000
years ago, only the cruelest master would cast away and ignore an old or
sick slave.

And yet this has occurred under a self-described worker's party that
claims to represent the interests of the mass majority of its people!

If such a thing were to take place in another country, it would certainly be widely reported in the media. But in China, where the news
media are subjected to complete control, there have been no reports of
thousands or millions of similar cases that have arisen in the past fifty
years. It's as if such a tragedy never occurred. This case is known only to
other residents of our city, who circulate it with a sigh, "This society is
really too cruel, too dark!"

Too cruel and dark to contemplate. Each person can only bow his
head like a lowly ant, foraging for food and eking out an ignoble
existence.

The Hidden Underclass

When we talk of Bengbu's worker issues, we must also discuss the half of
the city's working population made up of rural migrants who enjoy almost no basic protections or rights and face constant discrimination.
The manufacturing, construction, and service industries are now
manned largely by these migrants, who face even worse prejudice than
that experienced by blacks in America. At least American law prohibits
racial discrimination, while in China the government's administrative
and judicial systems are actually the source of discrimination against
migrants.

I remember when I was in middle school and high school, the children of farmers were all relegated to a corner of the classroom as if they
were an alien species. The teacher never called on them and seemed to
care nothing about them. In fact, they were separated from us by nothing more than a narrow road, but their accents were completely different from ours. Back then, the other students used to mimic the accents
of the peasant children, treating them like figures of fun. Recalling those
times upsets me now. How much needless suffering they endured!

This kind of discrimination results from the household registration system, which is effectively a modern form of serfdom. A person is tied to his place of origin for his whole life, as if he were a buffalo or horse owned by his master. China abandoned the serf system 2,000 years ago, and for several dynasties and generations Chinese enjoyed freedom of movement and labor to a great extent. It is only during the Communist era that China regressed 2,000 years through the violence and repression of Mao Zedong and his comrades-in-arms.

One night, while out on a walk in the small hours of the morning, I noticed more than twenty pedicabs along the road. The pedicabs were covered with quilts, in which workers were wrapped and sleeping. As it happened, there was a newsstand nearby. I went over and bought a newspaper, casually asking the proprietor what was going on.

The proprietor sighed, "Those are all migrant workers whose homes are miles away. If they drive their pedicabs home every day, they'll have no strength left to work. They make about 10 yuan a day pedaling those cabs, and out of that they have to pay for what they eat and drink. If they rent some place to stay the night, they'll have no money to take home to their wives and kids. So every night they curl up like dogs and sleep in their pedicabs.

"The worst is when it rains at night—even covered with their quilts they get as soaked as a stewed chicken. Any city dweller would be off to the hospital the next morning, but these country fellows, they just hop on their pedicabs the next day and get to work. It's a damned mule's existence—you'd hardly believe a human being could live like that."

For a long time now, migrant workers have not only had to contend with low pay, poor working conditions, and frequent workplace injuries, but also the almost complete lack of social services or protection. They not only take up the most offensive, dangerous, and heavy work, but are even deprived of the meager earnings they were promised. Across China, migrant workers are owed an estimated 100 billion yuan in unpaid wages. That's why an increasing number of workers have resorted to suicide threats as a means of forcing their employers to show some decency and pay them enough to eat. Some workers, while pressing for their unpaid wages, have even been subjected to violent beatings by gangsters collaborating with their employers.

At best, migrant workers are treated like the lowest caste of society and subjected to constant discrimination. Lacking an urban residential permit, they are refused medical treatment, insurance, pensions, and other social services, and are also subjected to all kinds of limitations in their training and occupational choices, as well as being deprived of what most people would consider basic human rights, such as the ability to live with their spouses, or for their children to receive an education. Homeless migrant workers sleeping in the streets have become a common sight.

In the vast majority of enterprises, workers' wages are only adequate to support their daily living expenses. If they encounter an employer who withholds their wages, they are forced to go hungry. In the first half of 2004, the living expenses of migrant workers increased precipitately, but their wages of a few hundred yuan did not follow suit. The government took no measures to assist them, but even tried to cover up the fact of this sharp increase in the cost of living. According to statistics presented by the economist Chen Huai, migrant wages have increased by only 68 yuan, or 0.8 percent per year, over the past twelve years, a period that has seen economic growth of around 9 percent per year. The rate of wage increase over the past twelve years is lower than the increase in the cost of foodstuffs in the first half of 2004 alone!

Most migrant workers live in accommodations no better than a stable. They have no source of entertainment; they can't even watch television. All they can do is labor at a fourteen-hour workday. The workers have a popular saying: "For five or six years you work overtime until 2 A.M., and all that's left at the end of the year is your bus fare home, not even enough for new clothes." Their wages are further eroded by the cost of various documentation inflicted on them by law enforcement and urban management officials—temporary residency permits, defense certificates, family planning certificates—and their related fines.

Given that migrants spend most of the money they earn, why do they bother to come to the cities to work at all? It's because poverty and ruin have made rural China intolerable to young people. That is also the reason for the explosive growth in the ranks of vice. An official can support a mistress on as little as 1,000 yuan, and a full-fledged prostitute typically earns a few thousand yuan a month.

Another consequence is rampant crime, the refuge of many migrants who encounter job loss or fraud. Under the leadership of the Communist Party, many Chinese people who see no way out lose all sense of shame and even compete to see who can be more ruthless. China has become a society of thieves and prostitutes.

Households on the outskirts of Bengbu cultivate an average of 1.4 *mu* of land each. According to China's present agricultural production technology, each agricultural worker should be capable of cultivating thirty *mu* of land. As Bengbu's urban unemployment rate now stands at 30 percent, adding in the agricultural workers brings total unemployment for greater Bengbu to something like 50 percent.

Such a high unemployment rate obviously indicates a problem with the social system. If it weren't for the barbarous authoritarianism of the power concentrated in the Communist Party, any other type of government would be unable to sustain such incompetent rule; the people would rise up and social order would disintegrate.

Scavenging for Survival

The Bengbu municipal government issues unemployment allowances of 120 yuan per month to only a tiny minority of the city's unemployed. So the vast majority of the unemployed, if they have no relatives to help them out, are left to work out their own means of survival. Scavenging in the rubbish has become a way of life for thousands of residents.

One cold day around noon I went out to buy something to eat. I was enticed by Xinjiang lamb shish kebab, and for two yuan I bought twelve skewers, which I ate next to the kebab stand. While standing there I noticed an old scavenger sheltering himself by a nearby building and gnawing on some hardtack. The man looked very old indeed, his face a mass of wrinkles—I thought he must be at least eighty. I bought another two yuan worth of mutton and took it over to the old man. He stared at me in surprise and did not extend his hand. Only after I insisted did he hesitantly accept the food. I noticed that his hands were black, possibly from frostbite.

I asked him, "Such an old man as you, why are you out scavenging on such a cold winter's day?"

He smiled bitterly and said, "I'm not even sixty. My fields only grow enough to pay the village government and keep them from knocking down my house. If I don't come out and find some scrap, how can

I keep my family from starving?" He went on to say, "Thank you. In all my life this is the first time I've eaten lamb shish kebab. Can you tell me if there's a water tap around here? I haven't been able to find one."

I was surprised that he couldn't get drinking water, but on further thought I realized that this impoverished district of ours did not in fact have a public water tap. The managers of the neighborhood's public toilets had wired the water faucets shut, possibly to keep migrant workers from sneaking in and drawing water from them, and even when paying to use a public toilet, I was usually unable to wash my hands.

I told him to come along with me, and we sat down among a row of stools at an open-air street stall, where I ordered him a bowl of vegetable soup for 1 yuan. I told him that I didn't know where there was a water tap, and suggested that he ask at a food stall for some water.

"I'm afraid of how people will react," he said miserably. "We scavengers are dirty from head to toe, how can I dare to ask someone for water?"

One day as I took my daughter out to the market to buy food, I encountered an obstruction. Standing nearby was a girl who attracted my notice because she was so filthy, black from head to toe. Even her face was black; she looked as if she'd been plucked out of a rubbish heap. The only thing that identified her as a girl was her long hair, tied into a braid, and her large, shiny black eyes.

I looked at her, stunned, until she slowly, carefully, picked up her bag of trash and moved it out of my way. After I returned home, I discussed the incident with my wife and a neighbor. They said they had both noticed this girl before. A few months ago she had appeared in the neighborhood scrounging food from the rubbish heaps, a truly wretched creature.

I provokingly asked the neighbor, who had taken in a stray dog, why she didn't take in this girl instead. Wouldn't that be an act of virtue even greater than taking in a stray dog? The neighbor protested that she received a retirement allowance of barely 300 yuan per month, which along with her husband's wages was just enough to support the two of them. How could she afford to raise a child? Her dog was old and blind in one eye, and she had only taken it because her friend didn't want it. If she took in a child, the school fees alone would cost her tens of thousands of yuan, and where was that money to come from?

When I said I wanted to help the child, my wife immediately brought up the experience of a businessman friend, Lao Ma. One day he had come across newborn twin girls who had been abandoned in the street. Moved with pity, he had picked the babies up and taken them to a welfare center. The welfare center told him that this required the permission of the Civil Administration. Too many live infants were left at the door of the welfare center every day, and the staff could only discard them as rubbish.

Lao Ma was in a quandary then. He had to go off to earn a living, and his wife was not at all pleased with his bringing this trouble upon them; eventually she divorced him. Three years later Lao Ma finally found a friend who was willing to take in one of the girls, reducing his burden. Eventually Lao Ma remarried, and fortunately his new wife was a very kind person who devoted her full effort to looking after the remaining child. Then Lao Ma could finally enjoy some peace of mind. But sending the child to school was very expensive. In order to formally enter the girl into their family register, the couple had to pay heavy bribes to Civil Administration and Public Security officials.

So my wife asked me, "What financial resources do you have to raise this girl?" There was nothing I could say in reply.

All the same, I remained uneasy, and was unable to concentrate on my writing projects. Out on a walk in the park, I once again ran into the scavenger girl, along with her mother. Like the girl, her mother was black with filth from head to toe, small and thin. I asked her why she took the child out scavenging instead of sending her to school.

The mother answered, "We don't even have money for food or a place to sleep—how can I afford to send her to school? We had three children, and couldn't afford the family-planning fines, so the neighborhood family-planning committee came and took away all of our belongings and demolished our house. We sent two of our kids off to family members, and brought this one along with us to scavenge. Even though she's only eight years old, she still manages to find a few yuan worth of items every day, enough to support herself, with some left over to send to her brother and sister."

I used to think that my elder daughter was greatly to be pitied because the government's long-term persecution of me as a political dissident had robbed her of her parents' care. But my encounter with the little scavenger girl made me realize that China has countless children

whose lives are more tragic and pitiful even than Anderson's Little
Match Girl.

The next day I discussed this matter with a friend, but he could only
sigh helplessly. In fact, if it were not for the government's pressure,
with my political-activism abilities I would certainly be able to collect
enough money to support this girl and provide her with a comfortable home and schooling. But the Communist Party monopolizes and
controls everything. In 2003 some house churches in Henan Province
established several welfare centers for abandoned infants and the elderly, including one welfare center specifically devoted to AIDS patients.
But the local government seized all of the premises or ordered them
destroyed.

That evening, I went back to the park in hopes of finding the
vagabond family and giving them some money and clothing, but I
couldn't find them. Gazing up at the sky, I could not hold back my tears,
wondering what small, dark corner they had found as refuge from the
cold.

Most major cities have hundreds or thousands of people scavenging
garbage. That would make a total of 10 million scavengers throughout
China's 10,000 cities and towns. Most of them have been left little alternative by their rapacious village governments, and choose this means of
supporting themselves rather than begging. It is a phenomenon that results from "socialism with Chinese characteristics," but the government
ignores their existence, and the news media seldom report their tragic
circumstances.

In Bengbu it is almost impossible for an unemployed person over
thirty to find a job. Employers are only interested in hiring young villagers in their twenties who are willing to work fourteen hours a day for
a few hundred yuan per month without a day off.

Older peasants who are fit and strong can take on construction work,
but others have little alternative but scavenging. Most city dwellers look
on them with disgust. Observing the filth on their bodies, smelling their
odor, thinking of them rummaging through trash for scrap paper, bot-
tles, and plastic bags and stuffing them into fertilizer bags, is enough to
turn one's stomach. But I sympathize with them. Although they are
dirty, they work for their living and harm no one. The way I look at it,
they are far cleaner than those well-dressed, overstuffed corrupt officials
and businessmen who pull out fat wallets to pay thousands of yuan for a

meal and complain about the taste. At least these people are not criminals; their souls are pristine. And if they should ultimately fall unconscious and die on top of a rubbish heap, I believe that God will have prepared a special place for them in Heaven, where they can be warm and clean, and where their souls can be comforted at last.

The Threat of Inflation

Cost-of-living increases that affect migrant workers and the unemployed likewise affect the populace at large. The price of steel and other such basic commodities at one point doubled, and the price of basic foodstuffs such as grains, oil, and eggs has also been steadily rising. Compared with the beginning of 2003, the price of essential consumer goods has already increased by more than 50 percent, and real estate prices have also risen at a similar rate.

During the same period, workers' income has not increased by so much as a cent. Apart from the roughly 10 percent of the population made up of corrupt officials and red capitalists, who rely on under-the-table income and have little need to concern themselves with rising costs, the vast majority of Chinese who rely on wages or other legal income have not seen any increase in their income. For these people, a 50 percent increase in the cost of living means an effective 33 percent drop in their standard of living. The vast majority of ordinary people have no savings to fall back on. Many still believe this is a temporary situation, not realizing that it is just the beginning of a full-scale crisis brought on by "socialism with Chinese characteristics."

The official banks, unable to attract savings deposits, are experiencing difficulties and have called on the government to raise interest rates. They allege that people not only earn next to nothing from their bank savings, but in effect actually lose money, and are therefore unwilling to put their money in the banks.

What is actually behind all of this is the central government's excessive issuing of new currency. Going back even further is the fact that China is already on the brink of an economic crisis; without profligately issuing currency to preserve financial balance, the CCP would probably plunge into bankruptcy. For that reason, fully aware of the terrible consequences of excessive currency issue, they can only recklessly forge ahead. This situation will progress all the way to collapse if the CCP refuses to alter its basic policies for management of the country, because the financial pressure the current government is facing is not the result of policy errors in recent years, but rather the cumulative effect of erroneous policies spanning decades.

The fact that all levels of government have been "eating their corn while it's still on the stalk," and that their accounts are awash in red ink, has long been concealed from the public. The vast majority of large state–owned enterprises depend on bank loans to pay for their continued operations, and banks and insurance companies are themselves massive financial black holes that stave off bankruptcy through a constant infusion of public funds.

So the present crisis is essentially one faced by society as a whole. Having exhausted all other methods, the CCP's excessive issue of currency is like drinking poison to quench thirst. It is quite possible that discontented people in the general population, who are finding survival difficult as their standard of living suffers the effects of the increasingly detrimental economic conditions, will be unable to tolerate the situation any more and will suddenly erupt.

That is why a crisis can break out so rapidly. The protest movement by retired workers in Bengbu in late 2004 reached a considerable scale, and had a huge impact on the local government. During the protests I made a point of visiting the protest areas to carry out my own observations and report them to media outside of China.

Bengbu's "Gray Panthers"

Beginning around seven o'clock on the morning of October 22, 2004, retired workers from all of Bengbu's work units gathered along Shengli Road, Bengbu's central thoroughfare. By 7:40 A.M., thousands of people had occupied the roadway, blocking traffic. At the height of the demonstration, a stretch of roadway one kilometer long, from Bengbu's Science and Culture Hall to the junction with Gongnong Road, was filled with an estimated 10,000 retired workers.

The Bengbu Textile factory was the city's manufacturing backbone, with nearly 10,000 retired employees, and female textile workers were the main force behind this protest. Operators of textile machinery typically suffer a variety of illnesses after long years in a horrendously noisy environment, but the authorities for a long time refused to recognize their infirmities as occupational illnesses, and denied them special medical treatment and safeguards.

Once these women had their youth squeezed out of them, they were usually too ill and weak for anything else. Their meager pensions of 300 to 500 yuan per month provided them with barely enough to get by, and were largely inadequate for them to obtain medical treatment. I saw at the protest that many demonstrators had to be physically supported by family members, or had stools brought for them to sit on while they protested.

Apparently, the pensioners had chosen this particular day because it was the date for the grand opening of Bengbu's Guangcai Grand Market, an event that Premier Wen Jiabao was rumored to be planning to attend. Many people considered Wen Jiabao relatively sympathetic to the people, and the protesters hoped that if Wen saw the situation, he would direct the local government to provide some benefits and compensation to the retired workers who had suffered long-term injury.

Some protesters said that in the preceding few days, tens of thousands of pensioners had staged a series of demonstrations in Hefei, and had succeeded in forcing the Hefei authorities to increase their pensions. Protesters generally believed that in the face of a malfeasant government, struggle was the only way to protect their personal interests.

During the Bengbu protest, several sedans were abandoned by officials who had apparently attempted to enter the protest area, but then lost their nerve in the midst of the angry crowd. But one elderly protester offered an alternative analysis: "I've been a member of the Communist Party for fifty years, and am well aware of the Party's subtle guile. You must all keep in mind that fifteen years ago, the central Party officials allowed PLA troops to abandon a large number of armored tanks on Beijing's Chang An Street. Then they sent agents to set fire to the tanks and blamed it on the students and other protesters, using it as an excuse to crush them. So it's quite possible that the authorities have left these vehicles here on purpose. You should by no means vandalize these vehicles, but rather make a point of protecting them."

The authorities did not carry out any suppressive action that day, and did not even send police to the scene. Perhaps because of the recent mass riots in Chongqing's Wanzhou District, local governments elsewhere were afraid of spurring another bloody altercation that would arouse the wrath of the masses. The scene of the protest was like that of

Beijing's Tiananmen Square before the June 4th crackdown, unusually calm and quiet, as if on a public holiday. Even the angriest protesters didn't carry out any radical action; people just sat in small groups discussing social problems and deploring corruption.

Because the government did not accede to demands for a pension increase, the retirees continued their protest a second day. They occupied an even larger area this time, but threats and obstruction by the authorities prevented some of the protesters from participating. Even so, at one point thousands of pensioners occupied a three-kilometer stretch of road between the Transport Bureau and Zhuyuan Road and the side streets in between.

During the morning, the authorities tried to thwart the protesters with two squadrons of anti-riot police, but the protesters were not intimidated, and refused to withdraw. With no orders on what to do next, most of the policemen stood around telling jokes and chatting to pass the time.

Because most of the protesters were elderly people around seventy years old, when the noonday sun began beating down on them, many went home to rest, but some came back again in the afternoon to resume their protest. I bought bottled tea for them to drink, concerned for their welfare in the heat that I myself found exhausting.

This was the largest protest Bengbu had experienced since the 1989 Democracy Movement. But these worker protesters had a number of disadvantages compared with the students in 1989. First, they paid no attention to publicity, and carried no more than a couple of banners. Second, they didn't organize subgroups (such as factory workers, automotive workers, etc.), so it was easy for protesters to just give up and leave. Third, they put little emphasis on organized speaking opportunities, so many onlookers had no idea what they were there for. Fourth, they devoted most of their effort to disrupting traffic, which resulted in their being cut off from the public and losing opportunities to gain public sympathy and awareness of their plight, which should have been their main goal.

With the protest expected to end the next day, the authorities saw no need to take further action to suppress the demonstrations. Having seriously weighed the consequences of violent suppression, the authorities do not lightly engage in bloodshed. Bengbu has around 70,000–80,000 pensioners, and their friends and relatives are spread throughout the city. If the police had come down harshly against the demonstrations, it could have caused the deaths of some of the already frail protesters, enraging the entire city and leading to calamitous consequences.

On the third day, I didn't go to the protest site until three o'clock in the afternoon, expecting the demonstration to be winding down by then. To my surprise, I found Bengbu's traffic nexus was still occupied by an ocean of protesters and onlookers. In the middle of the crowd were several hundred soldiers in helmets and brandishing arms, accompanied by hundreds of policemen.

The protesters told me this was just one of three zones they were now occupying, with pensioners from every factory and work unit in the city participating. They emphasized that this was a completely spontaneous protest by pensioners at the end of their rope.

Around 3:30 P.M., the police and soldiers took advantage of the restricted mobility of the elderly protesters and the lack of liaison between them to suddenly launch an offensive. With lightning swiftness, they arrested a protester who was distributing leaflets and quickly transported him to an ambulance in the restricted zone. When some protesters became aware of the situation and ran over to assist their comrade, they were deflected by police riot shields, and the ambulance sped away.

At this point the protesters became agitated, and the atmosphere grew tense. As I was carrying my child at the time, a police officer warned me that they were about to clear the scene by force; it was possible that people could be injured in the chaos, and especially that a child might be trampled. So I made my way out of the crowd and found an elevated position nearby from which I could observe the proceedings.

I suspect that officials closely monitoring the situation from within the official control center could also sense the tense atmosphere threatening to explode at a moment's notice; ultimately the police and soldiers were ordered to withdraw, so that an escalation of the situation was avoided.

As the soldiers and police returned to their vehicles and withdrew in the direction of the Chaoyang Huai Bridge, a shout of victory roared up from the protesters. The hapless soldiers, fearing attack, hurriedly raised their riot shields. In fact, the crowds were only providing them with a derisive sendoff.

Many protesters told me they would not withdraw until they had achieved their aim. It seemed the protest would continue for some time. And because there was no organization behind the protest, arresting a handful of people would clearly serve no purpose. As the authorities were refusing to negotiate, I was afraid that the situation would begin to turn ugly the next day.

The Communist Chinese government has never at any level recognized the people's right to protest, and has no concept of negotiations as a troubleshooting method, so the authorities tend to be at a loss when faced with mass protests. The people, for their part, normally resign themselves to adversity, but once they are aroused to resistance they are hard to control. Another difficulty with negotiation is that the government suppresses civic organizations, so there are no representatives of the people with whom they can negotiate and reach a mutually acceptable agreement.

My family members had warned me not to become too involved in the protests, as I was under constant monitoring. But I felt it was important to provide objective reports on the situation for the outside world. It was probably inevitable that early on the morning of the 25th, a telephone call from the Bengbu Municipal Public Security Bureau's Political Unit summoned me to appear at their office for interrogation.

The interrogator accused me of writing three articles about the protests and making Bengbu's situation known to the outside world. In particular, reports in the international media had had a negative impact. I insisted that my reports were factual, and that as a citizen I had a responsibility to report on the situation.

But the interrogator sternly insisted that in the past year I had written more than a hundred articles, and by the standards of recent years I should have been prosecuted long ago. They had been very lenient up to now, but I had ventured into a sensitive area, and I had to immediately stop my reporting. And in order to ameliorate the effect of what I'd already written, I could not accept any more interviews about the protest, or I would immediately be prosecuted. I could see that my situation was dangerous, and that if I wanted to continue my activities in the future, I would have to compromise, or I would lose my freedom once again.

After exiting the Public Security Bureau, I soon came up to the area formerly occupied by the protesters, and found traffic flowing normally. But at the entrance to the main thoroughfare, protesters were still standing alongside the road, and in the surrounding area, a large number of police officers and soldiers were awaiting orders. I estimated that thousands of soldiers and police officers were spread throughout the protest area.

Upon carefully reading the notices that the Bengbu Municipal PSB had posted all around, I noticed that the authorities were referring to the protests as "mass protests" but not insisting that they were an "illegal activity." The notice said that if the "mass protest obstructed traffic or surrounded government offices, it would be violating the 'Public Order Ordinance,' and would be subject to public order penalties." This indicated that the authorities had retreated from their traditional stance and were tolerating the right to mass protest.

Twenty-six years ago, the peasants of Anhui's Fengyang Village launched a major experiment that was the first step in China's reform of rural economics. After that, most of the peasants who had grown up under the bitter deprivations of the Mao era began to finally eat their fill. The significance of the Bengbu pensioners' protest movement should not be underestimated. Local authorities did not rashly use violence to suppress the protests as the authorities in Wanzhou had, but instead cautiously considered the situation, and on the one hand promised to expeditiously address the concerns raised by the workers while on the other hand doing their best to adjust the city's traffic flow so that the general population would not be too adversely affected. The authorities' enlightened response ultimately resolved an imminent crisis.

Other local authorities would do well to implement the "Bengbu model" as a means of conflict resolution and crisis intervention when facing mass protests in the future. But the authorities must first recognize the people's right to protest, and then take the lead in avoiding violence. Most important of all, the authorities must understand that mass protests are the necessary response to social conflicts that have already reached an extreme. Protests are not a threat to be feared; if met with a relaxed response, a protest by thousands or even by tens of thousands of pensioners will not cause the sky to fall.

The protest by the Bengbu pensioners ultimately enjoyed a degree of success, in that the Bengbu authorities increased pensions by 61 to 64 yuan, ending the dispute before it could spread to other workers.

But the success of this protest has also served as a revelation to workers in all fields; in defending their rights and interests, they cannot depend on anyone but themselves. And when it is necessary, they will have to take to the streets to fight for the rights that belong to them.

Postcript: On January 29, 2005, Zhang Lin was detained in Bengbu. A dozen policemen searched Zhang's home on February 6 and confiscated his computer, and on June 28 the Bengbu City Intermediate People's Court sentenced him to five years in prison on charges of endangering state security.

Translated by Stacy Mosher

THE POWER OF A RED ROSE:
A POETIC ORATION

Huang Xiang

3:50 P.M., November 22, 2003. For the Republic of Georgia, this is a
sacred moment, a moment of commencement. From this moment,
history alters its course in Georgia. Following in the footsteps of the
peaceful uprisings in Belgrade, Indonesia, Beirut, and Argentina, Georgia, too, has just completed a bloodless revolution. I am amazed, I am
enthralled, for I witness the universal awakening of democratic consciousness in the twenty-first century; I witness yet another amazing
success story of democratic reform! Within this significant historical
event in this tiny remote state, with awe and wonder I discover what I
have long worshipped—the latent power of individual lives and the ir-
repressible breakthrough of consciousness; a radical reordering and a
qualitative transformation of existential values; a cosmic explosion of
life and inexhaustible energy, contained in a red rose . . .

On this day, in Georgia, at Liberty Square in Tbilisi,
A multitude suddenly gathers beneath the winter sun,
Heads like lily pads spread across a pond in ceaseless undulation.
Against the backdrop of floating green, a sudden flash of red—
It is a rose, a red rose, a solitary red rose!
It is fated to appear at this moment, to appear in one hand;
It is fated at the same moment to be raised aloft.
The man with the rose, holding his red rose high,
Is the first to charge into the Town Hall as the newly founded
     Congress meets,
Toward President Shevardnadze as he delivers his speech.[1]
In the name of the red rose, the man declares to the president:
Please resign! Please step down! Please step aside! The people do not
     need you!
An explosion of cheers; the crowd surges around him,

The waves of sound from megaphones lifting him up, raising the red
     rose higher and higher.
In an instant the murky masses flood the hall,
Submerging the president and submerging the man with the rose.
A huge iron hammer is brought to the podium and smashes
     down—
The voting machine on the podium is shattered, a country and its
     power machine pulverized.
In shrieks and screams the Congress collapses, documents dancing in
     the air,
Shevardnadze spirited out the back door by his bodyguards.
And so the people regain their right to support and
Their right to oppose,
To demolish what they wish to demolish, to elect whom they really
     wish to elect.
The president is forced to resign, deposed from power; Georgia takes
     new leaders, and the people achieve a bloodless revolution, a red
     rose revolution!
A red rose is a Liu Di, a Du Daobin,
A Huang Qi, an An Jun, a Yang Zili, a Tao Haidong, a Li Dawei, a
     Zhao Changqing,
An Ouyang Yi, a Yan Jun, a Luo Yongzhong, a Zheng Enchong, a He
     Depu,
A Ren Bumei, a Yu Jie, a Liao Yiwu, a Yu Shicun, a Wang Yi, a Fan
     Baihua,
A Donghai Yixiao, a Yang Chunguang, a Liu Xiaobo, a Mo Lihua![2]
One red rose is hundreds and thousands of red roses; it is millions of
     acutely silent Chinese people!
A red rose is a bomb, a grenade, a machine gun, a ballot, a pen, a torch
     of enlightenment and self-awakening; a spaceship cruising through
     the universe; the all-conquering and unconquerable power of
     collective humanity.
A red rose can ward off the Siberian cold front.
A red rose can proclaim the Georgian spring.
If a dictator dares to trample the people underfoot and tolerates
     allegiance to none but himself,
The people will rise as one and tower above him.

If a dictator dares to shoot a bullet into the crowd,
The people in their collective authority will declare him on public
    trial.
Raise the red rose! Raise the red rose! Raise the red rose!

This world does not answer to one man, but to each and every
    person.
This world does not allow anyone to dictate to others,
And the people, made up of individuals, can reply with 10 million
    cries of "No!"
Everyone has an equal right to participate in elections,
Everyone is subject to the same conditions and rules of power.
The people can give you power, and the people can strip you of
    power.
The people can put you in office, and the people can remove you
    from office.
This world answers to each person, and to the will of all combined.
It does not answer to bullies, bandits, hoodlums, rascals, and other
    human scum, or to ruffians and mobs who cry "revolution," or to
    those "public servants" who bare their hairy chests and spit in the
    faces of millions.
The people want democracy, not oligarchy. The people want respect
    for life and self, not worship of some idol, or worship of violence,
    or worship of a corpse.
In the name of the red rose, I declare:
Remove the rotten carcass from the Square! Cast it from its artificial
    shrine![3]
Tiananmen is China's Liberty Square, not some enormous crypt,
    nor some torture chamber for flesh and spirit, nor liberty's
    slaughterhouse.
Pull the icon down from walls of soul and brick! Each man is his own
    god.
If anyone presents himself as the people's god, the people have
    a thousand holy reasons to unzip their trousers and piss on
    his head.
Let's cleanse our memories of the shame of badges, red books, and
    thunderous rallies.

The people have not chosen to live in historical repetition and
   vicious cycles, have not chosen to be trapped in the shadow of the
   Cultural Revolution and Mao Zedong, but rather have chosen
   liberty and sunlight.
Raise the red rose, Chinese people of the twenty-first century!

You who have been forced from your jobs or homes, you who worship
   in house churches, who are confined to bed with AIDS; you who
   have been forced to have abortions, and whose unborn flesh and
   blood are served as a nourishing delicacy; you who have narrowly
   escaped death in floods and collapsing coal mines, you who have
   vanished mysteriously on the Internet;
You who are deprived of your right to freely associate and form
   parties; you who have lost your right to freely express yourselves in
   public; you who have been molested and persecuted for asserting
   the rights of the public and the media;
You who have been senselessly and relentlessly shadowed; you who
   have been put on a blacklist or condemned to a life sentence; you
   whose independent natures have repeatedly subjected you to
   atrocities in prison and virtual incarceration upon release . . .
Raise the red rose! Raise the red rose! Raise the red rose!
One person is a red rose, petals unfurling free beneath the blue sky;
   independent petals, democratic petals.
Raise the red rose on Tiananmen Square, on Tiananmen Tower;
Across the vast landscape of China, raise the red rose!

Let's turn the thousand years' ocean of blood into an ocean of flowers,
   into a heaving, howling ocean of sunlight!
A red rose is a kind of power. Ten million red roses are 10 million
   people living under 10 million free choices.
People of China, raise the red roses of your lives! For as long as you
   raise the courage,
Brute force will falter, tyranny will shrivel, darkness will blanch and
   retreat.
As long as you can raise the faith, this world will not fall to the
   bayonets and lies of dictators.
There is no representative or core that can impose itself upon millions
   of lives;

If you acknowledge the king of cocks, you might as well drop your
    pants and present your buttocks for rape;

There is no exclusive command center for the world;

If you allow yourself to be gagged, you will drown in the spittle of
    others.

Why is there dictatorship in this world? Because you consent to it and
    become its accomplice.

Why is there totalitarianism in this world? Because you recognize it
    and become its co-conspirator.

When you should howl, you twitter; when you should roar, you
    murmur; when you should charge, you cringe.

You're a broken-legged sparrow, a befuddled chicken, a mute owl.

You're anemic, you're calcium deficient, you're impotent, you're
    nothing but a myopic, muddleheaded, lethargic, apathetic
    cynic!

Your elders left you some scattered bones from a shameful death;

You inherited a submissive, slavish, living corpse.

O how strange! Throughout the vast land of China there is not a
    single red rose, the red rose of life, the red rose that dares to be held
    high, the red rose that dares to be smashed into a pulp beneath the
    trampling wheel, the red rose that dares to thrust its prickly self
    at others, the red rose that dares to light the world with the
    self-immolation of its liberated soul.

Raise the red rose! Raise the red rose! Raise the red rose!

While living, let's live in the spirit of the red rose.

Bow to the red rose, pay homage to the red rose.

Whoever draws near to the red rose draws nearest to God.

Whoever believes in the red rose believes in love and kindness.

Whoever raises the red rose raises the sword of justice, raises the
    scepter of human conscience, and becomes a pillar supporting the
    paradise to which mankind has aspired throughout the ages.

The red rose blooms in our hearts;

It is the smile of God in our hearts, the opening of the Gospel in our
    bodies.

Each one of us is a red rose, a red rose bursting through flesh and
    blood.

Each one of us is a living Washington, Lincoln, Jefferson;

A living Homer, Dante, Goethe; a living Jesus, a living Siddhartha
　　Gautama,
A living Mohammed.
Those who respect others will be respected.
No one can claim ultimate superiority, dominance, honor, or
　　power.
He who is worshiped in life
Waits for incense and candles after death.
As to those who should not be on the altar, let's pull them down—
　　let's pluck off their crowns, extinguish their halos, strip their
　　stinking bodies of their saffron robes, and return them to mere
　　flesh and blood, just like you and me.
No one is more special than anyone else,
Even if he resides in a secluded palace in life and lies in a royal
　　mausoleum in death, or reigns over a desolate temple, or is displayed
　　in a memorial hall before thousands.
The people of China are so damned pathetic, nobody dares to publicly
　　shout:
Who should sit on high? Who should grovel below?
Life is an amusement park—it is not for the enjoyment of one but
　　for all.
There is no solitaire in life.
Life is also a casino—for those who dare to come and go, win and lose,
　　there is nothing but wild adventure,
Nothing but mad gambling, and no eternal winner.
Life is even more like a prison; no one escapes the bounds of life and
　　death or the imprisonment of existence; no one is born to be jailer,
　　guard, or cell bully!
Raise the red rose! Raise the red rose! Raise the red rose!
A red rose is a tender and peaceful power;
It is a fragrant rejection, resistance, and destruction;
It is beauty's contempt and transcendence of darkness; it is the eternal
　　blue dream of humanity that floats between the sea, the sky, and the
　　vast land . . .

Translated by Yunshan Ye with Stacy Mosher

Notes

1. The man with the red rose was Mikhail Saakashvili, who on January 4, 2004, was elected president of Georgia in a landslide victory.
2. All the persons mentioned are active political dissidents or well-known independent writers. Some have been imprisoned for expressing their opinions and some remain in custody.
3. The poet here is referring to the mausoleum housing Mao Zedong's preserved corpse at Tiananmen Square.

PART FOUR

White Nights: Personal Reflections

Our daylight dissolved into your midnight
To become a white night enmeshed in nightmares
As twilight descended upon your shoulders
Dawn's light slowly ascended

from **To the Students at Tiananmen**
by Wang Yu

Composed June 3, 1989

"Without a multiparty system, free elections, and separation of powers, any political reform is fraudulent." On the basis of this apparently obvious statement and others like it disseminated through electronic journals and Web sites, Internet dissident Wang Xiaoning was sentenced to ten years in prison for "incitement to subvert state power." The imprisonment of critical voices like his has served as an effective means for the Chinese government to maintain political control and contain debates for needed change. Many other Internet dissidents, along with journalists, lawyers, labor activists, and others have been detained, charged, and harshly sentenced in an effort to remove their perceived threat to control and stability. Prisons, reeducation-through-labor camps, and detention centers hold thousands of political prisoners, though the exact number is not known.

The Chinese authorities continue to deny the disastrous errors of the turbulent years of the Cultural Revolution or the violence against unarmed protesters in Tiananmen Square in 1989, because admitting the depths of these errors would expose the basic flaws at the root of the entire structure of political and social control. Other countries, through their governments and civil society, have chosen to grapple with questions of when and how to deal with past abuses in ways that enable a way forward. In China, attempts to address these social wounds through open discussion, articles, personal reflections, and other expressions are often met with censorship, detention, intimidation, or other sanctions. This official refusal to address claims for accountability and redress of past wrongs is an obstacle to China's moving forward towards a democratic rule of law system.

The writings in this section, echoing a theme throughout this volume, either directly or obliquely reference individual challenges to the control of information, dissent, and the critical role of accounting for past abuses. Zeng Linlin's recollection of her experiences as a child during the Cultural Revolution exposes the shadow that the events of those years still casts over the present. The interview with Wang Youqin, who has painstakingly recorded the stories of victims of the Cultural Revolution, demonstrates one individual's efforts to preserve a history of a past that remains officially taboo. Two personal reflections by Ren Bumei and Gao Ertai illustrate the lengths to which the Chinese authorities have gone to silence any voice of dissent. A poem by Wang Yu closes the section with a reflection on the very personal impact that state control has had, even beyond China's national boundaries.

The sense of loss that permeates these pieces powerfully demonstrates the force that state control in China has had on its society and on individuals. The power of these writings, however, is not only in the loss that they convey, but also in the perseverance that they demonstrate, of preserving individual memory and resilience in the face of that loss.

DEATH-ROW STUDY SESSION

Zeng Linlin

Zhang Zhixin, a cadre in the Liaoning provincial government, was arrested in September 1969 after voicing her disenchantment with the Cultural Revolution's violent factional struggles. She gained immortality in Liu Binyan's A Higher Kind of Loyalty, *which reported that when Zhang was executed in April 1975, her throat was cut to prevent her from shouting slogans with her last breath. In the following essay, Zhang's daughter, who was not yet 18 when her mother died, recalls her family's ordeal.*

In the early spring of 1975 there was a fierce blizzard. That day, two Shenyang court officials came to my house to notify my father, myself, and my younger brother to attend a meeting in town. Father and I carried my brother, and braving the blizzard we arrived at the town guest house. Upon pushing open the door, we were met with a blast of hot air, as the room had indoor heating. In spite of the heat, my heart trembled and I felt colder than outside in the storm.

The Shenyang court officials told us to sit down, that we would be having a "study session." One of the officials produced a copy of *Chairman Mao's Quotations,* opened the book, and began to recite from it. I don't remember the content completely, but the gist was a passage about class struggle and another about the need to resolutely crush all counterrevolutionaries. Then they mentioned my mother, and proceeded to ask my father some questions. Father said that he had divorced my mother several years earlier, and had been given custody of us children.

The court official asked me: "Do you know about your mother's behavior in prison?" I nodded my head, even though I had no idea about my mother's situation. I had heard people say that she was a counterrevolutionary. After Mother went to prison, Father visited with clothing and other items, but he was not allowed to see her. Even her brother, who came all the way from Beijing, was not allowed to see her. From the time Mother was arrested, all contact with us was cut off, and we had no news of her at all.

The Shenyang court official said loudly: "Your mother is very reactionary and will not reform herself. She is stubborn, opposes the Great Helmsman Chairman Mao, opposes Mao Zedong Thought, opposes the revolutionary proletarian line and piles offense upon offense. The government is considering adding to her punishment. If she is given the death penalty, how would you feel?"

I stared blankly, not knowing how to respond. My heart was shattered, but I remained outwardly calm and suppressed my tears. Father had told me never to cry in front of others, or it would mean that I had not drawn a clear line between myself and my mother. Father answered for me: "If this is the case, whatever the government does is fine."

The court official then asked: "If she is executed, will you bury the body? Do you want her belongings back?"

I stared at the ground and remained silent. Father again answered for me: "We do not want anything."

They did not ask anything further. The court officials conferred for a short time; one wrote something down, and the other instructed me, telling me that I was a well-educated girl, that the Party emphasized an individual's attitude and behavior and that I should draw a clear line between myself and my mother. He wanted me to say what I thought about my mother's crimes. I repeated the rote political phrases that my teacher had taught us. But my heart was confused, and I cannot now remember exactly what I said.

One official showed the other what he had written, after which they again whispered to each other and wrote some more. Then they required me to sign and affix my fingerprint to the document. The "study session" was over. During the encounter, my brother was so scared that he clung silently to my father the whole time.

Afterward Father led us from the guest house, staggering through the howling blizzard. He did not make dinner when we got home, but split a steamed corn bun into two pieces, which he gave to me and my brother, saying, "Eat this and go to bed."

I lay quietly in bed. Father sat alone, staring at the light as if in a trance. He then looked over at the bed, and thinking that my brother and I were asleep, he slowly stood up and began rummaging through a box of belongings, looking at pictures of Mother. Father could not control himself and began to cry. I climbed down from bed, jumped into his arms, and began sobbing. Father comforted me, and said, "Don't cry, we can't let the neighbors hear us." Hearing our cries, my brother woke up as well and climbed into Father's arms. I don't know how many tears we cried that night.

This is a very painful memory, almost too painful to recall. The document that Linlin was required by the court officials to sign and fingerprint is excerpted below:

Linlin: After hearing that Zhang Zhixin was convicted of a counterrevolutionary crime, I thought that it would hinder my progress. But after studying and raising my political awareness, I realized that even a mother-daughter relationship has a class nature. Even though she gave birth to me and is my mother, she is a counterrevolutionary and is my enemy. She opposes the Party and Chairman Mao, and we must continue to struggle against her. As a result of education by my teachers and family, I recognize that she is a counterrevolutionary, and I have drawn a clear line between myself and her so that my progress is not hindered.

Questioner: Zhang Zhixin clings to her erroneous views, and her crimes are very heinous. What is your opinion?

Linlin, Tongtong: We resolutely oppose her, and agree she should be put to death to rid the people of this poison. We don't even want her body. We support whatever the government does. We don't want her belongings. We don't want anything. The government can do as it sees fit.

That year Tongtong was not yet ten years old, and Linlin was not yet eighteen. Even if this "record" is not just the creation of a court official, under the circumstances of that time Linlin and Tongtong had no other choice but to say what was required of them.

Translated by a friend of HRIC

The original Chinese article has been posted on numerous Web sites, but originated as part of a longer article published in the Guangzhou-based Nanfang Zhoumo *(Southern Weekend)*. The full article can be accessed at: http://www.southern.com/news/com munity/shzt/party/first/200206271778.htm.

THE PAST IS NOT ANOTHER COUNTRY

An Interview with Wang Youqin

In 1966, Mao Zedong launched the Cultural Revolution as a means of eliminating political opposition and securing "Marxism-Leninism–Mao Zedong Thought" as China's dominant ideology. Mao's main revolutionary tools were students (known as Red Guards) and workers, whom he organized against intellectuals and other figures of authority. In the ensuing ten years, an estimated 100 million Chinese lives were destroyed through persecution, detention, and torture, with at least 1 million believed to have met unnatural deaths. The Chinese government continues to actively discourage in-depth examination of the period, which remains an open wound in the psyche of many Chinese people.

In October of 2000, Wang Youqin launched a Web site recognizing those who died from persecution during the Cultural Revolution. The Web site, www.chinese-memorial.org, bears the slogan, "We will never forget you." A little more than a year after the Web site was launched, Chinese authorities blocked access from the mainland.

China Rights Forum: Why is it important to confront the Cultural Revolution rather than just to treat it as a matter of history?

Wang Youqin: The Cultural Revolution ended only 29 years ago. Almost half of the population of China today experienced the ten years of the Cultural Revolution or grew up during that time.

As far as the development of China's economy in recent years is concerned, it is clear that the Chinese authorities have changed Mao's policies to a great extent. First, they discontinued the cultural revolutionary practice of long-term, large-scale, and systematic persecution. Second, they started adopting new economic policies that gradually released Chinese people from the trap of poverty of Mao's time. In this context, the Cultural Revolution is not merely the past but is closely related to the present.

CRF: In the case of many atrocities in other parts of the world, the per-secutors manage to dehumanize their victims through ethnic or cultural differences. How were the lines drawn in the Cultural Revolution?

WY: In China, the persecutions were planned and arranged in advance. The leaders of the persecutions issued directives regarding what kinds of people would be targeted and how to attack them in detail, step by step. They defined categories of "enemies" and created new phrases in the Chinese language to label them. In my book *Victims of the Cultural Revolution,*[1] I describe the backgrounds of 659 victims who died not for particular things they did, but simply because they belonged to a cate-gory of "enemies."

Teachers were a major target of the Cultural Revolution, as Mao clearly explained to the American journalist Edgar Snow. The result of this decision was obvious and serious. At the Girls' Middle School at-tached to Beijing Normal University, one vice-principal was beaten to death by Red Guard students, and four teachers committed suicide after being attacked. At Beijing Kuanjie Elementary School, the principal and dean were killed by their students. At Peking University, sixty-three people died from persecution. It is painful to list the number of deaths in more than 200 schools that I was able to include in my investigations. I also regret that Mr. Snow did not mention the death of any teachers in his writings.

In my opinion, the boundary between the persecutors and victims was clear up to a certain point. But it often happened that some people who had previously been persecutors became victims as the Cultural Revolution targeted more and more "enemies." For example, Jiang Longji and Lu Ping, two top cadres at Peking University, labeled more than 700 professors and students as "Rightists," a category of "enemy," in 1957 and 1958. Many of the "Rightists" of Peking University were sent to jail or labor camps, and six of them were sentenced to death and executed. In 1966, both Jiang and Lu were attacked as "counterrevolu-tionary revisionists." Both of them were brutally tortured, and Jiang committed suicide.

If we place two photographic negatives together, one on top of an-other, we will see a blurred picture. After the Cultural Revolution, some people wanted to emphasize that they were persecuted and denied that they had persecuted others earlier. Their double standard has caused moral and historical confusion.

CRF: You have read Solzhenitsyn extensively and are very familiar with persecutions in the Soviet Union during the Communist era. Do you feel Russia has been able to confront its violent past more effectively than China?

WY: It is true that Chinese have produced much less writing on their violent past than Russians. There are many reasons for this. I will just raise one of them here: the persecution in China was more serious than in Russia in some respects. In Russia, Stalin had "show trials" for the enemies he purged, but in China, Mao did not even bother with trials. Many teachers and principals were beaten to death by their Red Guard students, in their own schools, and without any verdict.

The nature of this greater terror caused even deeper fear and psychological scars. Many survivors don't want to describe what they suffered during the Cultural Revolution, and some have even suffered a kind of amnesia.

There was a song entitled "Song of Ox-Ghosts and Snake-Demons" that was composed by high school students who were Red Guards. They forced educators to sing it with a macabre melody while condemning them. This song spread from Beijing throughout the whole country. The lyrics went as fellows:

I am an ox-ghost and snake-demon.
I am an ox-ghost and snake-demon.
I am guilty. I am guilty.
I committed crimes against the people,
So the people take me as the object of the dictatorship.
I have to lower my head and admit my guilt.
I must be obedient.
I am not allowed to speak or act incorrectly.
If I speak or act incorrectly,
May you beat me and smash me,
Beat me and smash me.

It is interesting that none of the teachers I interviewed could recall all ten lines of these lyrics, despite the fact that many teachers were forced to sing it several times a day throughout 1966. It was a former student, also a Red Guard, who sent me the entire song when I put out a request over the Internet. For the teachers, psychological trauma destroyed their memory of such details. This can be considered a typical example of the selective memory of victims.

However, feelings of terror should not become an excuse for forgetting the past. China has a long tradition of written history, and Chinese scholars should make more effort to record recent history.

CRF: In your essay "Repentance for the Death of Li Jie,"[2] you write about a teacher named Guan Qiulan who still felt guilty because she failed to intervene on behalf of someone who was later persecuted to death. Do you think this kind of "survivor guilt" is also an impediment, along with the large number of participants?

WY: In my paper entitled "63 Victims and the Cultural Revolution at Peking University," I pointed out that only one of the sixty-three victims died in prison; the others were simply killed or committed suicide after being tortured on campus or nearby. During the Cultural Revolution, Mao Zedong specifically ordered the implementation of what he called "mass dictatorship," which meant letting ordinary people carry out most of the persecution rather than the prisons and police force.

After the revolution started, targeted persons were referred to as "ox-ghosts" and "snake-demons," and eventually every work unit established jails that came to be known as "ox shacks." In one of the "ox shacks" at Peking University, more than 200 people were locked up for 10 months.

One result of the "mass dictatorship" was that a great many people participated in the persecution to a greater or lesser degree for a variety of reasons. But if they are not willing to express their regrets now, it will be hard for them to face up to the facts in the past.

The Cultural Revolution destroyed not only so many people's lives, but also the moral standards of society generally. In this context, I was deeply touched when I interviewed Guan Qiulan, and I wrote her into the story of Li Jie, a victim.

The introduction to my Internet memorial includes a true story that has drawn a strong reaction from many readers. I interviewed a teacher who spent many years in a so-called "labor-reform" camp during the Cultural Revolution. His job was to tend cattle and chickens, and one day they killed a cow that had become too old to work. They killed the cow near a willow tree, where green grass always grew abundantly. After the killing, when the teacher tried to drive cattle to the willow tree to feed, they resisted and moaned, bellowing as if in protest. But he found that chickens were different. When you slaughtered a chicken and threw its intestines on the ground, all the other chickens would rush over and fight over those intestines.

I raised a question in my introduction: Which attitude should people adopt—that of the cattle or of the chickens? A reader in China e-mailed me a message with the subject line: "I don't want to be a chicken any more." From this kind of response, I feel the survival of a strong sense of morality such as I saw in Guan Qiulan.

CRF: A French journalist recently published a book, *Machete Season,* in which he interviews some perpetrators of the Rwanda genocide about what they did and why they took part in the slaughter. Do you see any value in someone undertaking a similar project regarding the persecutors of the Cultural Revolution?

WY: I have not seen any projects regarding persecutors in the Cultural Revolution. If we want to understand how the Cultural Revolution occurred and prevent it from happening again, we need to understand how the persecutors were produced and how they gained the power to do what they did.

Because of the lack of knowledge of victims in public memory, many of China's persecutors are not forced to admit or apologize for what they did. Some of these persecutors have even threatened those who want to tell the truth.

CRF: What methods adopted overseas might help expose the truth of what happened in China?

WY: I would like to see some organizations involved in working on the Cultural Revolution. In 2004 a Russian human rights group published two CD-Roms with the names of 1,345,796 victims. More than 25,000 Cambodian victims of the Khmer Rouge have been documented. In contrast, I have only 1,000 names on my Web memorial, even though I have worked very hard to collect the names of Chinese victims over the last twenty years.

An individual's efforts are limited, and what I have uncovered is just a very small portion of the brutality that occurred. Some people take the cynical view that Chinese victims' lives are cheaper than those of other nations because of the large population.

Lacking organizational support, we have to rely on individual volunteers. Five years ago, a person who helped me with the Web memorial called himself a *yi gong* in Chinese, which means a "volunteer worker for justice." Many people have helped with my project, and I consider myself to be one of the yi gongs.

CRF: Ideally, what results would you like to see from confronting the Cultural Revolution and its lingering effect on Chinese society?

WY: Confronting the Cultural Revolution has a lot to do with China's current social system and moral standards. Monetary compensation should be paid to the victims, even if it's just a symbolic amount. But I don't see the possibility of that happening in the near future. In fact, victims' families never mention compensation to me. Many of them simply send me information about their loved ones to put on the Internet, and they expect no more than that.

CRF: Why do you think the Chinese authorities block your Web site, when the government has officially acknowledged that mistakes were made during the Cultural Revolution?

WY: During the Cultural Revolution, the Chinese media never mentioned a word about the victims. Newspapers and films of that period show Red Guards marching through Tiananmen Square, waving red flags and Mao's little red book, yelling the slogan, "May Chairman Mao live for 10 thousand years." The victims were considered enemies, pieces of trash that were beneath mention. The families of most victims were not even allowed to keep their loved one's ashes after cremation.

I have tried to find a corner in cyberspace for the victims, but even that is not allowed. Beijing authorities blocked my Web memorial after sixteen months on the Internet. In his book *1984,* George Orwell wrote this slogan of the Party: "Who controls the past controls the future. Who controls the present controls the past." The book that Orwell wrote fifty years ago realistically describes what happened to my Web memorial in the year 2002. It was not a surprise, but I still felt very sad.

CRF: Can we hope that the Cultural Revolution experience was so exceptionally horrendous that it will never happen again?

WY: "Never Again" is a great slogan, and we need to realize it through education of the younger generation. I am glad to see my work play a small role in this respect. I have put my e-mail address on the Web memorial and in my book so readers can send me their feedback. I have received letters not only from people who experienced the Revolution, but also from young students. Months ago I received a letter that went like this:

> Hello! My name is Katie, and I am sixteen years old. I am doing a presentation on Mao Zedong for English class. I was looking for the effects of the Cultural Revolution on the people of China, and I found your article, it brought tears to my eyes.

Several days later, I received another letter from her:

> Actually, I am simulating a Chinese classroom during the Cultural Revolution, and I am the teacher. I have made thirty-one red wristbands, and a scarf for myself; I even have two people from my class who have agreed to be a red guard and a student who unfortunately must be informed of her parents being taken to a struggle meeting. My "students" are going to recite Mao's quotes, and I have a Chinese friend teaching me how to actually say one of his poster slogans. The class is going to learn the strictness of such an atmosphere, and hopefully will understand the scary power [Mao] had over China.

Katie's letters show that the lessons from the Cultural Revolution can reach beyond nations and eras. Her ideas brought me great encouragement, and I will continue my project on the Cultural Revolution for the sake of our younger generation and the bright future we deserve.

Notes

1. Wang Youqin, *Victims of the Cultural Revolution: An Investigative Account of Persecution, Imprisonment, and Murder (Wenge Shounanzhe),* Hong Kong: Open Magazine Publishing, 2004. Wang plans to publish a second volume.
2. This essay, entitled "Wei Li Jie Zhi Si Chanhui," was translated into English in *China Rights Forum,* 4, (2005): 45.

A MIGRATION OF SOULS

Ren Bumei

The publication of a memoir by an exiled Tiananmen veteran inspires a dissident Internet essayist to reflect on the experience of exile within his own country.

What are June 4th and its "children" to Beijing? In his novel *Resurrection,* Tolstoy makes repeated mention of a bird in Nekhlyudov's game bag—a bird that was wounded but not dead, and which continued to flap about inside the bag, causing the initial shame of the bag's owner to change to anger, and that anger into hate. Beijing, too, has its birds—a flock of birds that have migrated throughout the world, but which every spring and summer journey in their dreams to Tiananmen Square, filling the air with their mournful cries. The year 2004 saw the fifteenth such spring and summer.

There is a writer in Vancouver, Canada, named An Tian—an exile who perhaps could be described as one of those birds who are wounded but not dead, and who embarked on a spiritual homecoming this spring. We encountered each other in passing, each clutching in his claws a sheaf of essays to drop on the bald heads of Zhongnanhai.

We "met" through An Tian's novel, *Tiananmen Lover,*[1] in a sort of trans-Pacific conversation. Our common concern over the past fifteen years for Tiananmen—our shared "lover"—makes me an accomplice of this Calypso. At one point the novel's female protagonist writes in a letter to her son, "Your mother can't wait so long; a human life is limited." At the end the writer sighs, "Always remember, the endless expanse of the past empties over time, and the emotions that stirred us dissipate like smoke!" These words express a depressing truth: we are already old, while our memories only grow younger.

As the fifteenth anniversary of June 4th approached, countless refugees scattered across the globe raised graying heads in hopes of seeing Tiananmen one last time. There our youth and love is buried; we are nothing more than kites set loose above Tiananmen, with a single string tethering our souls and tugging on our heartstrings every night for the past fifteen years. Tiananmen is our cross; it has determined our paths and choices, our sorrows and joys, partings and meetings over these past fifteen years; all those who have abandoned their native places can find their roots here. Tiananmen is a lover that inspires a passion all the more desperate for being unrequited; even after fifteen long years, even as memories fade and hopes are relinquished, it remains the profound expression of the hardship and frustrations of a disillusioned generation.

Tiananmen is our shame, our "Wailing Wall," transforming the entire world into a city of refuge, making a portion of our own people into "wandering Jews" who face the world as people without a country. Tiananmen is the execution ground of conscience, the crematorium of our race and our cemetery, guarded by bayonets for fifteen years. No flowers can be laid there, where our lovers, friends, flag, and tents are buried, where our last dreams of the honor of China are buried. Tiananmen is a commode down which are flushed the vain displays of false nobility, a political farce staged in a cabaret built over corpses. . . .

Tiananmen is our destiny. I can imagine that we Tiananmen exiles, including An Tian and myself, will utter long sighs at this fifteen-year milestone in our journey, and then lapse into prolonged silence. The earthly powers have utterly defeated God, and we have nothing left to give. The written word is our last recourse, our genuine escape. But I would like to draw a distinction between my escape and that of An Tian, or rather between internal and foreign exile. Recently I've wanted to recall in detail my experiences in China over the past fifteen years; I think a lot has already been written by overseas exiles, but there may be a need for testimony from those living in exile within China as well.

The overseas exiles have lost their country, but those inside China have lost this and more; they have become people without legal protection. The pain of the overseas exile is that of cultural alienation, while the pain of the internal exile is largely that of police abuse. But every time I've raised my pen to write of this, I've set it down again. I lack the literary skill and the courage to review the past. So I'm grateful for the opportunity presented by this "book review," which encourages me to reexamine the "turbulent fifteen years" through the emotions aroused by *Tiananmen Lover.*

The tragedy did not end on June 4, 1989, nor did it stop at any national border. In fact, it is still ongoing. The "aftermath of June 4th" has become part of, and has perpetuated, the "tragedy of June 4th." Due to selfish interests, and the culprits' dread of the enormous change that has taken place in Russia and Eastern Europe, over the past fifteen years "stability" has become China's only genuine ideology. Since 1989 China has become a virtual police state, with police replacing Red Guards and martial-law troops in controlling daily life, accompanied by a steady and unrelenting clampdown on political activities.

This is the latest black period in Chinese political history since the Cultural Revolution's "ten years of chaos," and could be called the "fifteen years of chaos," a period in which political persecution has been carried out through police power rather than through mass popular movements. "June 4th activists" were the initial targets of persecution, with a large number imprisoned, some executed, and some dying in the course of lengthy custodial terms. An even larger number lost their employment, and those who have followed the dictates of conscience have been marginalized. The marketization of the economy has accelerated the extent of this marginalization, while luring some activists to partake in the division of the spoils.

This is an era of rule by an authoritarian leadership through the police and the capitalist class, in which conscience has become a crime against the State, while at the same time developing into a financial rationale for the existence of police departments and their demands for funds.

I'm one of the lucky ones; I have never been imprisoned. In 1990 I went to Hainan to earn a living and had my first run-in with the police during a "drifter cleanup" campaign. Rounded up by the border police along with others who lacked temporary residency permits, I won my freedom with a monetary exchange. But another friend, who was from the law faculty of Wuhan University and had participated in the Students Autonomous Union in 1989, was detained, along with his girlfriend, for fifteen days on charges of "sex peddling."

My first encounter with the police in relation to political activities was in 1997, during the days surrounding the death of Deng Xiaoping. After that I was a "marked man." In late February 1997, the authorities confiscated my car, my cell phone, and documents and took me to the local dispatch station for questioning. Three days later I was allowed to reclaim my belongings, but my security was gone for good. This was entirely unprovoked, because I had ceased all political activity begin-

ning in 1990. Looking back, I suspect I was caught up in a countrywide
roundup of "sensitive people" around the time of Deng's death, which
also gave the authorities an opportunity to discover new targets, especially those presenting a financial incentive.

A few weeks later my driver was detained. The local authorities, representing "the motherland and the people," assigned him a "glorious
task": to monitor and report on the activities of Ren Bumei.

My driver was still in his teens and he was very afraid. We had a good
relationship, so he asked me what he should do. I told him to resign and
I would continue to pay him, but when the police found out two
days later, they gave him a good scolding and told him to "refuse to resign"; otherwise he would be "sent up the hill" (Reeducation Through
Labor). When he came to me again, I said, "You're fired," and wrote out
the necessary documents of dismissal. The police officer he gave them
to ripped them into pieces and threw them in his face: "Tell Ren Bumei
that we don't believe we can't deal with him!"

The work of "dealing with" me had well and truly begun. About a
week later, my local dispatch center called me in for seven or eight
hours of interrogation. Police searched my home, dumping out all my
books, papers, and photographs, and leeringly read the love letters my
wife and I had exchanged while courting. In the end they found nothing, because I simply didn't possess any "reactionary materials." When I
protested, they detained me again. I remember looking up from the entrance of our building and seeing my wife weeping on the balcony.

After I was released late that night, my young daughters asked me,
"Daddy, why did Mr. Policeman come for you?" The question aroused
a flood of feeling in me, and I simply held them close without replying.
I often found it difficult to answer my daughters' questions. One day
around that time, their nursery had conducted a memorial service for
Deng Xiaoping, and one of my daughters asked, "Daddy, will Grandpa
Deng go to Heaven?"

From then on it was impossible for me to continue my business. But
the greatest change in my life came when I agreed to my wife's plan to
emigrate with our daughters. Over the next two years, my family lived a
fearful existence. My wife would wake up in the middle of the night,
certain that she had felt a pair of eyes staring at us from the dark outside.
One day she told me, "There's someone watching us from a room in the
building across the street." I began paying attention, and after a few days

discovered that there was never a light on in that room, but there was always someone smoking. We soon became used to this kind of life.

Later I gained a deeper understanding of such surveillance by reading two books by Soviet writers, *Testimony: The Memoirs of Dmitri Shostakovich,*[2] and *Memoirs of the Last Chairman of the KGB.*[3] No one knows how costly surveillance is, and to what extent it is carried out. Former Soviet leader Nikita Khrushchev said, "They are wasting taxpayers' money to listen to someone farting." But the cost seems outweighed by the advantage of power.

Our minders didn't seem overly concerned about concealing their activities, and sometimes they even seemed to flaunt their special privilege and detailed knowledge. Once a police officer "assigned" to me telephoned my wife and asked her for my new cell phone number. Even more blatantly, whenever we encountered the police from then on, they would warn me, "We know every move you make!"

Even now I still have not gained a firm understanding of why my country turned me into an exile. It is an entirely counterproductive tactic: the state regards everyone as criminals because it lacks a feeling of security; the surveillance forces people to recall June 4th, and even turns them into genuine dissidents; and the persecuted become a financial resource for the monitoring organization. This retrograde political process escalates as the persecution continues and intensifies.

Even as an "innocent victim," I still felt guilty before my family. Constant police harassment led even my wife to doubt me: "If you really haven't done anything, why do the police keep coming for you?!" All I could do was hold my tongue.

I recall an incident toward the end of 1989 when a fellow student who had just come out of detention asked me accusingly, "We all went in, why didn't you?" In recent years, while I have been operating my Sleepless Nights Forum Web site,[4] I am constantly asked, "Why doesn't anything happen to you?" The meaning behind the words is, "Why haven't you 'gone inside'?" A writer of some small fame insisted I was lying: "He has absolutely never experienced police harassment, he's just bragging; if the police were keeping an eye on him, why was his wife allowed to emigrate?" At this point I will answer all these questions at once: "Go ask the police. I don't know."

The tenth anniversary of June 4th fell in 1999, and as I anticipated, this gave the authorities a new opportunity to "deal with" me. Around the middle of April the authorities caused me to lose my job with Guangzhou's *Southern Exposure (Nanfeng Chang)* magazine after I moderated an economic symposium attended by some elderly intellectual Party members such as Li Rui, Li Shenzhi, Wu Xiang, Wu Mingyu, and Sun Changjiang.[5] Around the time of the U.S. bombing of the Chinese Embassy in Belgrade in May, police burst into my room while I was staying in a dormitory at Peking University. Then in August, while I was attending a writers' conference in Inner Mongolia, several friends saw police force their way into my hotel room while I was out. The scholar Song Yongyi, who was also attending the conference, was arrested and imprisoned soon after returning to Beijing.[6]

But the most frightening incident in 1999 was at Beijing Capital Airport on June 5. Around two in the morning on June 4, the police broke into my home in southern China on the pretext of "checking my household registration." They searched every corner but found nothing. Then they took me to the local dispatch station to once again take down the same old information: name, age, sex, etc.

By the time I left the dispatch station, dawn had broken. I couldn't even feel indignant any more; I just laughed bitterly to myself. I hurried off to the airport because I was expected in Beijing on June 5 to take part in a business conference. As it turned out, the police were already waiting for me at the airport. They took me to the airport police station and searched me and my luggage thoroughly. They even made me take off my shoes. They were very disappointed. Eventually I boarded the plane and breathed a sigh of relief. I was too optimistic.

A little more than three hours later, the plane touched down at Beijing Capital Airport. After the plane came to a halt, a flight attendant suddenly announced that "all travelers should take out their identification documents for inspection upon leaving the plane." I immediately understood. I said, "They're looking for me, let me off first."

Several police officers were waiting as I descended the stairs, and they quickly grabbed me and loaded me into their vehicle as the other passengers stared out of the aircraft windows. It was like a scene from a movie, and I had a hard time seeing myself as the protagonist.

As I looked at the earnest expressions of my police escorts, I could hardly keep from laughing, and longed to ask how I could be worth all this, but they ordered me to "stop smirking." I was taken to a meeting room in the waiting area of the airport, where an incredibly hostile inquisition began, but after several hours they still had nothing, because there actually *was* nothing. At the same time, they constantly used "very professional" methods to interrogate me about my reasons for coming to Beijing, and kept telephoning the southern police department that had "opened" my case.

After several hours, their attitude began to change—a classic method—from "frankness and lenience," to "we're just doing our job," to "let's be friends." I was allowed to adjust my physical position accordingly, from standing at attention to leaning against the wall, to finally being allowed to sit or stand at will. It was clear they realized they'd made a mistake, also clear that someone down south had filed a false report, but they still needed to find something worth reporting back to justify their effort. They made me write a "confession" that they could hand to their superiors. My natural sense of humor came to my aid, and I wrote out part of a "confession" from an article I'd planned to publish on the tenth anniversary of June 4th and gave it to them. In fact, over the past ten years I had been feeling a genuinely deep regret over how my negligible role in the June 4th tragedy had been inappropriately elevated through this repeated questioning, and felt a need to confess. I had just become acquainted with Christian beliefs, and I felt God had arranged this incident to teach me a lesson.

Afterward I enjoyed their hospitality overnight at the airport. Two young police officers slept with me and watched over me that night; one was full of hostility, and reminded me of the pathological vigilance and self-assurance of a little Red Guard. I felt there was an aesthetic incompatibility between his physical beauty and his cruelty, or perhaps it was the national education system that bred this strange combination. The other had just recently become a father; he had a kind face and was very friendly toward me.

I felt a great longing for my daughters. The distance between fathers in China can be so great—the two policemen chatted about grocery shopping and home repairs. I was left alone, as if I weren't even part of the same human race. The Russian dissident Aleksandr Solzhenitsyn wrote, "Such people have no blood in their veins; their bodies contain only a thin liquid, and they possess not even a shred of human sympathy. People are being destroyed, and the people being investigated are seen as aliens or things; and the investigators, because they have narrowly survived or escaped a similar fate, and especially because they are deciding the fates of these pitiful bugs, have degenerated into an arrogant heartlessness."

The next day, they took money out of my pocket, bought a plane ticket for me, and escorted me onto a plane. I was given a three-point warning: 1) I was not to tell the southern police what had happened at Capital Airport (they were afraid of being ridiculed by their colleagues); 2) I was not to visit Beijing again in the near future—"We'll be keeping an eye on you"; 3) I was not to protest, as it would serve no purpose.

I very much wanted to return home and see my daughters, so I boarded the plane without protest. Then something even more ridiculous occurred: I was handed over to the "care" of an air marshal, but because of exhaustion (I had scarcely slept for three days) I experienced heart problems, and the air marshal eyed me closely, at the same time asking me accusingly, "Why do you insist on practicing Falun Gong?!" Clearly, that was the "crime" that the Beijing police had told him I was guilty of—it was the one rationale they could get away with for almost anything.

This wasn't the first time the police falsely accused me of being a Falun Gong practitioner (the reader should understand that on the basis of human rights I fully sympathize with and respect these practitioners). On a previous occasion, someone told my friends that I was a Falun Gong practitioner, causing them to distance themselves from me. As a Christian I thanked God that these petty dirty tricks had not developed into genuine persecution. Perhaps God was using these trials to remind me of those pitiful souls whose circumstances were even more unfortunate than mine. I was to receive more such reminders.

After 1999 I began to write and carry out scholarly research in earnest. In fact, it was the authorities who helped me return to my literary endeavors. I had no political inclinations by nature, and only aspired to be a good writer. Since 1989 I had abandoned my reading and writing temporarily in order to make a living, but constant surveillance made it impossible for me to continue my commercial work. Everyone knows that anyone who has "political problems" in China is deprived of virtually all opportunity for social or economic participation. Even if the police aren't minding you, others will still keep their distance.

In all honesty, I now had reason to be grateful for this change. I had long felt the education policies of the last ten years were seriously flawed. The anti-American protests in Beijing in May 1999 shocked me greatly and spurred me to develop a new set of language course books. I completed this project in 2002 and began to develop my Sleepless Nights Forum Web site. A previous Web site called Frontiers of Thought (sixiang de jingjie) had been shut down. Now I planned to demonstrate an even more heroic effort for the freedom of the Internet. Sleepless Nights Forum caused me to be targeted once again for the sake of "stability," but it also attracted a circle of faithful supporters.

In the spring of 2002, the Internet police shut down Sleepless Nights Forum for the first time. Police broke down the door of my Beijing office and took me and a friend to the local dispatch station for interrogation. As I left my home, I took along a quilt and some personal necessities, but the police officer assured me, "This won't take long."

During this "conversation" I immediately admitted to being Ren Bumei, the Web master of Sleepless Nights Forum. This greatly improved the efficiency of the conversation. Then they asked whether Sleepless Nights Forum wasn't illegal. I answered, "Not at all." They asked, "Why did you criticize Premier Zhu Rongji?" I answered, "Why can't I criticize Premier Zhu Rongji?" They asked, "Do you believe that we have the power to deny you the opportunity to visit your family?" I answered, "I believe it." They asked, "Do you know how we're going to deal with you?" I answered, "I don't know." After about six hours I was granted my liberty, but my identification documents were retained, and they notified me that I was not allowed to leave Beijing while under investigation. But the worst was yet to come.

That same night I was detained while visiting a businessman friend who was taken in for questioning over a matter in Tianjin. When the police ascertained I was not connected with that case, they allowed me to sit down, but refused to release me. One police officer picked up a Falun Gong pamphlet from the floor and insisted that I had brought it in, but after they confirmed my identity with the Beijing Political Defense Squad, they dropped this ploy, although still clearly seeking an excuse for my erroneous arrest.

I spent that night in the waiting room of the dispatch station. I was the only one there at the time who enjoyed relatively free and "favorable" treatment. There were thirty-odd other people there who looked like workers, all handcuffed to their seats. Who knew how many had been falsely arrested? The young guard enjoyed his power to allow or deny others the opportunity to go to the bathroom. I became aware once again of the darker aspects of Chinese society. This episode occurred around Good Friday. In my heart I thanked God for calling me through these means to participate in His suffering. In the depths of night I prayed over and over again, "Do not allow the hearts of the police to harden further, let China soon repent of its evil ways. . . ."

When I left the dispatch station around noon the next day, the police were somewhat apologetic but warned me not to discuss this experience with others. A few days later the Internet police began investigating Sleepless Nights Forum, then came back with their conclusion: "The essays on Sleepless Nights Forum do not break the law, but could you please stop writing them?" The police also said, "We agree with a lot of what you write, but you can express your views to the National People's Congress and the Chinese People's Political Consultative Conference."

The matter seemed to end there. But a couple of days later my landlord asked me to move out (my lease had not yet expired), and the property management office chased me continuously. They said, "Someone told us you're a spy from Canada, so we can't let you live here." This new lie almost scared even me. I could understand their terror, so I moved out as soon as I could.

I was homeless once again. Ever since my wife and daughters had emigrated at the end of 2000, I had felt rootless and alone. Whenever I thought of my children I regretted sending them off, but whenever I found myself in another dark place, I was glad that they had left China at last—this was no longer a place fit for human habitation, and was especially unfit for children. In fact, ever since 1997, I had avoided spending the June 1st Children's Day with my daughters, because I was afraid that its proximity to June 4th would give the police an excuse to harass me in front of them. Up to now, I have not been able to explain to my daughters why we must be apart, or why I have not yet been able to leave China.

Over these last three years the Chinese authorities have consistently refused to issue me a passport, citing my participation in the Tiananmen incident as a reason.[8] I remember once, when talking with a police officer about the pain of being separated from my family, I became somewhat emotional, and he very patiently listened to my complaint, then quietly asked me, "What is the point of telling me this?" I believe I can understand this paragraph written by An Tian: "Child, your mother doesn't want you to hate anyone. What you should hate is this system, this culture that grinds to smithereens any morsel of human decency."

But I think the problem is more complicated than this. How did all of this darkness come about? At one time we occupied the Square, and in revenge the government has occupied our homes for the past fifteen years. It's impossible to deny that the police, like us, are victims of the policy of "stability above all." I believe, and indeed the lack of callous abuse in my personal contact with individual police officers has shown, that this country has made progress in some areas. But this progress has all along been accompanied by huge regressions, and the progress falls far too short of what we would hope.

I respect the exploration of this question by An Tian and others, but we should not be satisfied by the answers put forward in these works. The reader may discover that my essay has digressed somewhat from a discussion of *Tiananmen Lover*. In fact, I would like to add two items to this kind of overseas "June 4th literature": 1) the aftermath of June 4th, and 2) internal exile.

The aftermath of June 4th is a continuation of the Tiananmen Incident, but it has not been adequately explored in literature. The aftermath of June 4th is the real tragedy of June 4th; it transformed a political incident into a cultural incident, and led the human spirit from anger to despair, from verbal attack to self-reflection. At the same time, security concerns have prevented an adequate revelation and study of the problem of internal exile, and I believe internal exile even more definitively demonstrates the root of China's problems. I would in no way wish to downplay the pain expressed in overseas exile literature such as *Tiananmen Lover;* I only want to remind everyone that it is not enough.

An Tian writes, "Remember the experience of your father and mother, child; in the name of a participant in June 4th, indict those tyrannical authorities and the bestiality of those who carried out the massacre! Don't forgive them, even in the name of Christ!" But An Tian also writes, "I myself am guilty, the lover is not pure." God has used the June 4th tragedy to reveal His mysteries and His blessings here on earth. We should submit ourselves to this guidance.

Translated by Stacy Mosher

This article was posted in Chinese on the Web site of New Century Net: http://www.ncn.org/asp/zwginfo/da.Asp?ID=57695 &ad=5/13/2004

Notes

1. *Tiananmen Lover (Tiananmen Qingren)* can be read in Chinese among the selection of An Tian's essays posted on the Boxun Web site: http://boxun.com/my-cgi/post/display_all.cgi?cat=antian.
2. *Testimony: The Memoirs of Dmitri Shostakovich,* HarperCollins Publishers, 1979, Chinese translation information unavailable.
3. Vadim Viktorovich Bakatin, *Breaking Out: Memoirs of the Last Chairman of the KGB,* published in Russia by Novosti, 1992, no apparent English translation. Chinese translation published as *Baituo kegebo—Kegebo zuihou yiren zhuxi huiyilu,* Xinhua Publishing, 1998. An army general, Bakatin was in 1991 appointed to dismantle the dreaded intelligence service following the disbanding of the Soviet Union.
4. Bume Ziye, www.bmzy005.com, eventually permanently blocked.
5. Li Rui was once personal secretary to Mao Zedong. Li Shenzhi, who died in April 2003, was one of China's most important campaigners for political reform and democracy. Wu Mingyu, as Vice-Minister of the State Science and Technology Commission, was charged with heading up China's science reform in the 1980s, but subsequently fell out of favor. Sun Changjiang was a political reformer under the late Communist Party chief, Hu Yaobang. The translator was unable to find further information on Wu Xiang.
6. A librarian at Dickinson College, Song was in China researching the Cultural Revolution when he was arrested in his Beijing hotel on August 7, 1999, and eventually charged with "purchasing and illegally providing intelligence to parties outside of China." He was finally released on January 28, 2000 and allowed to return to the U.S.
7. Yu Jie is a dissident Chinese writer. Lu Kun is the wife of jailed dissident Yang Zhili.
8. Ren Bumei was finally allowed to emigrate to Canada at the end of 2004.

ADDRESS UNKNOWN

Gao Ertai

Dissident artist and writer Gao Ertai wrote this tribute to the persevering spirit of his twenty-five-year-old daughter, Gao Lin, who died three months after the writer fled China in 1992.

My child, I'm talking to you, can you hear me? I hope you can, but I'm afraid you cannot.

Do you remember? The day after we buried your mother, late at night, I gathered you in my arms and took you to her grave at the edge of the desert. We waited a long time, but she didn't return.

I understood her. I believed that as long as her soul remained, she was certain to return to us. The fact that she didn't proves that human life is extinguished like a candle. There is no soul, there is no reincarnation; physical movement and the ebb and flow of nature are all there is.

That's why I'm afraid.

You were only three years old then, but your eyes held a solemnity and melancholy beyond your years. I remember the expression in them even now. I'm certain that like me, you also remember that silvery moonlight and its boundless desolation.

I had rushed home from staging an exhibition in Jiuquan, and after everything was taken care of I had to go back. We hitched a ride from Dunhuang, through Anxi, Yumen, and the Jiayuguan Pass back to Jiuquan, the bleakness of the Gobi and Chuanyuan stretching before us. The bus jolted terribly, shaking you until your head ached. You were nauseous and sleepless the whole way.

We spent a period of time in the noise and chaos of the exhibition, then arrived at the No. 57 Cadre School, where adults went to have their thinking reformed. Everything was done in groups. There was no one to play with you, there were no toys or picture books, there were no nice things to eat and no fun places to go to. All you could do was fol-low me around all day long. When we were sent out to work, you went along and sat at the edge of the field playing with sand and stones, so covered in dirt that you looked as if you were made of clay. When we had our meetings, you spun around in the meeting room, inhaling the secondhand smoke of our cigarettes. . . . You were like a tiny blade of grass sprouting from a tin roof.

At meal times you went with us to the canteen. If you were lucky you got a bite of meat and vegetables once or twice a month. Sometimes I gave you a piece of meat from my bowl, but you always said, "Don't, Papa, you eat it." People sitting nearby praised your good attitude.

When night fell you would wait for me by the roadside. I could always see you searching for me among the groups of workers, your little frame motionless in the impenetrable darkness. When I drew near, you would run over to me and raise your face and lift your arms for me to pick you up.

Once, I discovered you with a piece of meat in your mouth. I thought you had stolen it, and without asking for an explanation I immediately yelled at you and told you to spit it out. You watched me quietly all the while, then you said that the meat was some I had given you at lunch time, and you had kept the last piece to enjoy the flavor a little longer.

I begged your forgiveness, and you cried till your lips turned blue. Carrying you in one arm, with the other I pounded myself on the head and said, "Papa was bad. You should hit Papa." Still weeping, you said over and over again, "I won't hit you."

I felt I was a total bastard.

Eventually the leaders of the cadre school were good enough to give me a simple room with a table, a bench, and a stove. In your words, this was now our home. Although it was very basic, we could make toys, tell stories, draw comics, and enjoy some happiness. Unfortunately, our walls were made of clay, so we had no place to pin up our pictures. Unfortunately, we had to go out early and come back late, so our time at home was too limited.

One autumn day, as we were walking home, we caught a little hedgehog, just the size of a fist. It had a pink face and legs, bright, shiny eyes, and a twitching nose. An adorable creature, it would eat whatever we fed it. After growing rapidly for about two months, it suddenly disappeared. Our window hadn't been broken, and there were no holes in the walls or floor. We couldn't understand what had happened to it. You thought some invisible creature in the house must have eaten it, and from then on you were afraid to be at home alone.

At the end of that year, the cadre school arranged a song-and-dance performance, putting up posters and decorating the halls to celebrate the New Year. No one else knew how to draw, so I had to help out, sometimes until very late at night. You wouldn't sleep without me, but the scene was chaotic. One night, when it got too late, I brought you home, and you refused to go to bed unless I promised not to go back. Still dressed, I lay down and patted you, and you asked me, "Why don't you get undressed? Are you waiting for me to fall asleep so you can go out again?" I said I wouldn't do that, I was just waiting for you to go to sleep and then I would sleep, too. You believed me, and after a while you fell asleep. I quietly got up, quietly closed the stove, and put out the lamp, and made my way through the two courtyards to the meeting room.

The windows of the meeting room were webbed with frost. Although the lamp was bright and the babble of voices loud, with two coal stoves burning red hot and the chimney howling, we still felt the night wind piercing the cracks in the door like the blade of a knife. Suddenly the door burst open, and you charged in through the mist, crying, completely naked. Everyone in the room gasped in astonishment. I was shocked, then grabbed you furiously and thrashed you, yelling, "Are you trying to kill yourself?" You wept until your lips were swollen, and it was a long time before you could get your breath back.

Several women who were there came over and complained that my temper was too fierce. I said nothing, but wrapped you in my coat and held you by the stove. You insisted on pushing your hand out and grasped one of my fingers. I could feel you shivering through the thick sheepskin. Finally you fell asleep, your little hand still gripping my finger. Looking at your face, still blue with cold, and your tiny, trembling fingers, I felt I really was a bastard. It occurred to me that for a little girl to come running out into the icy weather in the middle of the night, her body naked beneath the stars, she must have been terribly afraid.

Fortunately you didn't get sick after that episode. When you awoke the next day, you were chattering and smiling as if you remembered nothing. I still felt repentant and pained, and said I was a bad father. You replied, "No, that's not true. Papa is good. Papa is wonderful."

For some reason my eyes filled with tears.

Your mother and I married in March 1966 at the Dunhuang Cultural Relics Research Center. When the horrors of the Cultural Revolution began that June, I was one of the first affected. Your mother took my writings and went to stay with your grandparents. Your grandfather, a well-known physician, was soon labeled a counterrevolutionary, and Red Guards streamed in and out of the house day and night, ransacking and beating. There was no way to escape, only to endure.

You were born in January of 1967, at the height of the turmoil. At the time I believed the government had reached the peak of its tyranny and couldn't continue much longer this way. So even though I could not yet see light, I felt we were approaching the end of the tunnel. We named you Gao Lin, from a stanza of "Harsh Winter," a poem by the Song Dynasty poet Lu You that reads, "I see a green glimpse of forest" (*yi jian wei lü sheng gao lin*). I believed we would soon see buds pushing out of the bare tree branches in the spring breeze. History is the convergence of many coincidental factors, impossible to predict. Subjective wishes affect objective judgment, and self-deception is inevitable.

I wonder if you felt your mother's depression and terror while you were still in her womb. Did you hear the screaming and shouting outside? Newly descended into this chaos, did you retain an impression of the nightmarish scenes, the maniacal laughter, the gleeful beatings, the scarlet streaks of blood caught in the beam of a flashlight at night, the vision of faces in gas masks whenever atomic bombs were tested, the antichemical warfare corps spraying foam in the streets? When I think back on these scenes, I recall the expression in your eyes, so serious and so melancholy, not that of a child. I don't know if this is merely a reconstruction of my own memories.

We had planned to send you back to my home village in Jiangnan,[1] where my mother and sister could look after you, where you would have cousins to play with and could live more comfortably. But as soon as you arrived there, you became ill. Scabies, kidney infection, sinusitis, headaches, one after another. Your grandmother and aunt rushed you by long-distance bus to a hospital in Nanjing every day and prepared nourishing food for you to eat. Because you were sick, you received more attention than your cousins, but for the same reason you couldn't be as happy as they were. Whenever the time came for our annual family visits, I returned to Gaochun and took you all to the countryside to play. When I saw your cousins running and shouting, and you following slowly behind, I felt very sad.

On top of your illness, my second marriage brought a huge amount of confusion and conflict. We thought this was just an adult tragedy, and it never occurred to me how much all this was hurting you. Finding it impossible to deal with so many difficulties, your grandmother and aunt took you and your cousins away from Gaochun to the countryside. It was a time of hardship and confusion, but by the time you reached school age you had recovered from most of your illnesses apart from an occasional headache.

For our family visit that year, we rented two bicycles in the city and rode them to the countryside. You and your cousins clamored to be taught to ride, but the bicycles were too large for young children, and when you sat on the seat your feet dangled in the air. You took the bicycles out to the yard every day and practiced with some neighbor children. At the end of the day you were covered with bruises and scrapes from head to toe, and your New Year's clothes were soon in tatters.

After five or six days you had learned to ride. I went out to the yard and watched as you grasped the handlebars, stood on one pedal, raised one leg, and swung it over to the other pedal. Then you were off, pumping wildly as you spun around the yard. The other children hadn't learned to ride, and could only stand along the perimeter and watch. I felt your success was the result of not being afraid of pain or falling. Your grandmother and I and your aunts really admired your pluck and determination, but your grandmother warned us not to praise you, or you might lose all your inhibitions. So I said nothing, but in my heart I was glad.

What made me even happier was that in spite of your headaches, you did very well in school, and always came out at the top of your class. At the end of the 1970s your second aunt and I were both "rehabilitated," and had our reputations and employment restored. You accompanied me wherever I went, constantly changing schools and getting used to new cities and people.

Beijing No. 11 School, Lanzhou University Attached School, Gansu

University Attached School, Sichuan University Attached School, these were all top secondary schools, but you always gained admission to them. I was really proud of you.

In those days you often said that you always dreamed of flying, that you dreamed you were flying like a bird in the sky. You were always watching the birds, your little arms spread like wings. When I was a young boy I never had this kind of experience. While I was a young man, the most beautiful vision I had was of the light at the end of the tunnel. I'm sure you never knew how much your innocent words and spontaneous movements transported me to the realm of lyric poetry.

You were still suffering from headaches, and we looked everywhere for treatment, but we could never determine the cause. Beijing Tianqiao Hospital was said to be the best in all of China for neurological studies, and Dr. X the best neurologist. They could find no organic illness and believed it was psychosomatic, but the lengthy treatment without results raised doubts. When you finally succumbed to schizophrenia, your headaches got better. I wonder if the two were related.

One sultry evening in the summer of 1985, Guoguo came over to repair our electric stove. You stood alongside watching the whole time, chatting and joking with him. After he left, you said you thought he was handsome. It gave me a shock to realize suddenly that you had grown up.

That year you were eighteen, a senior at the Sichuan Normal University Attached Secondary School. Guoguo's father, Professor Su Heng, was a friend of mine. I knew that their family liked you very much, and asked if you wanted me to drop some hints on your behalf.

You said, "No, no, no! I don't like him! If I liked him I would tell him myself." You said a man's value was not in his looks but in his brain. It had never occurred to me that you would know how to speak of a man's value.

You liked *Jean-Christophe* and *Jane Eyre*. I recommended an excellent article discussing these books, written by a friend of mine at the Beijing Academy of Social Sciences. He was over forty, balding, short, and plump. When he came to visit I paid no particular notice. It never occurred to me that you would fall in love with him because of this article.

I told you that he had a girlfriend in Beijing. I said, "Even if he didn't, and even if he loved you, a good essay doesn't make a good man." You paid me no mind, but continued to write letters to him right up until he married someone else, at which time you gave way to heartbroken despair. I felt very bad, but there was nothing I could do to help.

Fortunately, you were just graduating from secondary school at that time, preparing to go to Nankai University in Tianjin to study, and the shadow of your sorrow faded in the brightness of your prospects. As the time for your departure approached, and you washed and mended your clothes and packed your personal belongings, a smile gradually returned to your face.

I had no way of knowing that during the "antiliberalism" movement, someone found some information on me and made a report to the State Education Board. Just before the school term began, the Nankai committee head, Wang Kun, and the head of the Chinese Studies office, Liu Fuyou, both contacted me to say that Nankai had come under criticism for admitting you, and that they had been forced to rescind your enrollment. You refused to accept the truth and insisted on attending classes. A few days later you disappeared. When I found you at the bus station, your eyes were dull and expressionless and your speech abnormal. I took you to the hospital for examination and they diagnosed you with schizophrenia.

The first time I went to visit you at the psychiatric hospital, you were conscious. Your face was a bit swollen, your eyes were melancholy, your reactions delayed. Both of your heels were injured, the flesh mangled.

I asked you how your feet had come to be injured, and you said you didn't know. I asked the doctor, and he said you had tried to rush out of the hospital, and they had caught you and given you an injection and pulled you back into your room, and that your heels had scraped against the floor and stairs.

I gritted my teeth and said nothing.

I remember that year when your mother died in the countryside, and I took you away from the village at Dunhuang, the local officials wouldn't transfer your meal ration or household registration, because they said a child eventually became a pair of working hands. I had to fight hard to finally manage the transfer. On the "residential transfer card," where the reason for transfer had to be filled in, scrawled in faded ink are the words, "joining father." Although it's just a bureaucratic document, it still moves me to read it.

I never guessed that the result of joining your father would be this.

From the time you joined me, I never properly took care of you. Even though I was able to keep you with me after I was rehabilitated, you were at school and I was writing or teaching, each of us busy with our own activities. Having just emerged from the abyss, I was under pressure from all sides. On top of that I had a belly full of rage and sorrow that made me constantly want to cry out, to argue, to stir up rebellious thoughts in others; I spent my days and nights in a frenzy of writing. This brought on another string of persecutions that disrupted our lives. The divorce proceedings from my second wife took years, and you were dragged into the unpleasantness.

You were a good girl; you bore up well under hardship and made outstanding achievements, and I was proud of you. But I had no idea what might be bothering or worrying you, and it never occurred to me that I should know. Our home life was substandard. I never learned how to cook, and when you came home from school we'd simply have our meal in the school canteen. I never asked if you liked eating that food. I remember you once told me you were tired of eating *mantou,* but I paid no real attention.

I remember that when I was at Lanzhou University, we learned that Lanzhou Normal's attached secondary school had a higher rate of college admission than the attached secondary school of Lanzhou University, and you insisted that I find a way to transfer you. The Normal University was far away. The night before you left, you examined my clothing piece by piece. You darned all the holes and replaced all the missing buttons. You mended frayed spots in the elbows, knees, collars, and cuffs with matching thread. Watching you sewing away in your chair by the window, I was deeply moved. But it never occurred to me to thank you.

So many years have passed since then.

Even when you came back from the hospital, to my deepest regret, I often forgot to ensure that you took your medication on time. The doctor advised that it would not be good for you to stay at home, that you needed to be distracted by some occupation. The work quota that the Sichuan Normal University personnel department had obtained for you from the Labor Bureau was given to someone else. I didn't learn of this until I went to Nanjing University. At Nanjing University they agreed to arrange work for you, but because I was detained and imprisoned they didn't make good on their promise. I learned about this after I left prison.

Even after I learned of it, there was nothing I could do but blame my own impotence. I could only come before you with true repentance and say, "My child, I'm sorry."

At one point there seemed to be some hope that you could be completely cured.

In the summer of 1987, after a delay of seven years, the court granted my divorce. At the end of that year, your Auntie Bao and I married in Chengdu, and she obtained a transfer to live there. Seventeen years after your mother's death we were a complete family once again. Your intuition was extremely good, in spite of your short life experience. The first time you met Auntie Bao in Beijing, when we were still only ordinary friends, you said to me, "This is someone you can trust." When you had a problem you sometimes telephoned her rather than me. I was glad to see that you got along.

After you left the hospital, you required medication to control your condition and help you stay alert. The medication included antidepressants and tranquilizers, all with side effects. Extended use could cause liver damage and a drop in intellectual ability. You were afraid, and kept lowering the dosage on your own, so it was hard to keep your condition stable. I was also afraid that you would lose your mental abilities, and didn't know which way to turn, so I left it to you to decide your dosage; there were times when there was too much going on at home and the confusion overwhelmed us all, and I would criticize you for this and that, forgetting that you were ill.

When you knew that Auntie Bao was coming, you were very happy. When I brought her home that day, as soon as we came in the door we saw taped on the white wall the words, "A Warm Welcome to Auntie Bao." Each word was a different color and tacked up at different angles, creating a crazy, merry effect. I was completely surprised, and Auntie Bao was so pleased that she leaped into your arms.

Three times each day she made sure you took your medication on time. Your emotions became more stable. Our home returned to a semblance of order and tidiness. When I came home there was warm food to eat, and you had someone to talk to. You loved pouring your heart out, and after she finished teaching her art classes she would come home and talk with you while doing her housework. It seemed that for the first time in many years you had someone to whom you could express feelings you'd kept bottled up inside. Memories that struck like lightning bolts in the darkness; the congestion of your stream of consciousness; the disembodied voices; the psychic torment; the spiritual hell of your suppressed dreams and abyss of despair; all these, with exposure, faded and lost their power.

Gradually you became willing to resume your studies. You were still very smart, and although it was hard for you to concentrate, you retained what you learned. Gradually you were able to continue for longer periods of time and showed an increasing interest in your subjects; we were very happy.

Once, we talked about what you would do in the future, and your answer astonished me. You said that once you had recovered, you wished to study medicine and become a psychiatrist who treated schizophrenia. You said that it was only after you became ill that you understood how painful and frightening this illness was, and only after recovering did you know how to escape it. You said you were determined to help other sick people so they would experience less pain and recover more quickly. You said Freud, Jung, and Adler were all brilliant, but that they lacked direct personal experience and sometimes contradicted themselves, and you wanted to write a book to fill in the gaps they left.

This was the second time I felt proud of you.

These were happy days. We would go out for a walk every evening. In the wooded paths outside the university the three of us would march along to the rhythm of the songs we sung. Some of the songs we made up as we went along, and if we liked them we kept singing them for days afterward. Unfortunately, after we moved to Nanjing University, there were no such wooded paths outside the campus.

In 1989 there was an arrest campaign nationwide, and everyone on campus was in constant fear. In order to spare you the anxiety, I sent you to your aunt's home in Gaochun for a while.

After I was detained, police searched our home at Nanjing University. I was sent first to Nanjing's Wawaqiao Prison, and subsequently escorted to a detention center in Chengdu. In order to be near me in prison, Auntie Bao had to hurry from Nanjing to Chengdu.

The crime with which I was charged was "counterrevolutionary propaganda and subversion." In spite of the articles I'd written, my remarks in private conversation, and speeches in public forums, the authorities were ultimately unable to convict me, and in the spring of the second year of my detention I was released. But it wasn't "release on acquittal," but rather "completion of investigation." I was liable to be arrested at any false step. Auntie Bao was in poor health and found it hard to bear up under this tumult; as soon as I was released from prison, she fell ill. After three months in the hospital she was reduced to skin and bones.

During this period, under pressure from the State Education Commission, Nanjing University no longer wanted me around and took back our apartment, which was still in chaos from the police search. When we returned to Nanjing we had no home, and all we could do was sell off our books and furniture and return temporarily to Sichuan Normal University.

My personnel file was at Nanjing University, but my food ration, household registration, and personal connections were at Sichuan Normal University. I wasn't allowed to lift a finger; I couldn't teach or publish articles or books. My book *Selected Essays of Gao Ertai*, published by Bashu Publishing House, was withdrawn after two attempts to distribute it. Fortunately I also knew how to draw, so I still had outlets for expression. By the time Auntie Bao's health improved I had already found work teaching in the Fine Arts faculty. With our life resuming some measure of stability, I brought you back to Chengdu from Gaochun so you could return to your old life and studies, and to our evening walks.

We never guessed that fate would knock at our door again.

Two dissidents on the wanted list, Bei Ming and Zheng Yi,[2] turned up unexpectedly. They were being pursued by police and had exhausted all their resources and all routes of escape. Zheng was ill and needed an operation. We had to help them.

This matter should have been kept secret, but in order to raise some money for them and find safe shelter and medical treatment, it was necessary for me to ride around the city on my bicycle approaching people for help, and I was rebuffed many times. So after everything was arranged, and they were sent safely on their way, we lost our own sense of security. It's not that we didn't trust our friends, but I remembered very clearly that when the police questioned me in prison, they had a lot of information that only our friends would have known. If I were sent back to prison, there was no way of knowing when I would be released, and this time Auntie Bao was implicated along with me. When I thought of her health situation, and recalled what Xiao Xuehui[3] had told us about the women's prison after her release, fear chilled me to the bone. I decided we had to escape.

Attempting to escape would be dangerous, but waiting was even more dangerous. Casting ourselves to an unknown fate seemed preferable to the thought of spending aimless, tenuous days at the mercy of the carelessness of our enemies and the loyalty of our friends.

Auntie Bao was afraid, and kept delaying our departure. Bei Ming and Zheng Yi eventually escaped to Hong Kong and told people there of our situation. People came over to help us, and that gave us the courage to set out.

Although we'd been thinking of it constantly, the moment of our departure seemed to arrive very suddenly. I asked your third aunt to look after you. She was my youngest sister, and I knew you were safe with her. The main problem was that both she and her husband had to work, and there was no one home to keep you company during the day. So I also sent a telegram to your second aunt in Gaochun, and she came to Chengdu to stay with you. During this vital juncture, your only thought was for our safety, and you repeatedly urged us to be careful on the trip, and repeatedly told us to write to you as soon as we got out so you could stop worrying.

I regretted deeply my inability to look after you, and hearing your entreaties I felt even more deeply saddened. Facing the perils ahead, I could only urge you to take care of yourself, and hope that once we were out and settled we could arrange for you to join us, and start a new life together.

Our route of escape was entirely in the hands of our rescuers. When your aunt received the telegram, she set off immediately, but she wouldn't arrive for three days, and we couldn't wait that long. Our future was already in progress; our tickets had been purchased. Without even time to put our home in order, we hurriedly embarked on our journey, led by someone we'd never met.

On the day of our departure, Auntie Bao prepared our belongings and I took you to your third aunt's home. On the way there I was afraid you would keep looking around and reveal your nervousness. On the bus we ran into several people we knew, and you laughed and chatted with them as if everything were normal. When we got off the bus you criticized me for my unnatural smile and tense manner, and worried that I'd run into trouble while in flight. When I saw how serious you were, I was less worried.

We disembarked at the terminus on 38th Road and changed to another bus, after which we had to walk the rest of the way to Niushikau. You were carrying a bag of your belongings, and I said, "I'm stronger, let me carry it." You refused, so we carried it together.

There were no shops on that street, and the houses presented a wall of dreary and unrelenting gray; passing cars sprayed muddy water all around, making it difficult for pedestrians. As we walked along you suddenly said, "Papa, if you live through this, the rest of your life will be very happy."

I said I hoped you were right.

You said, "Your greatest happiness is Auntie Bao."

I said that was true.

I said you could put your mind entirely at rest. As soon as I said it, a sense of foreboding overcame me.

I hoisted your bag onto my shoulder and said, "As soon as we get out, I'll write to you."

You said, "I'll be waiting."

Those three words, "I'll be waiting," continue to echo in my ears even now.

The walk on that out-of-the-way road always revisits me in my dreams. I had ventured to that place only occasionally before, and felt entirely alien there. But since that day it has become deeply familiar; even that soul-piercing grayness has instilled in me an unfathomable nostalgia, as if the essence of the word "home" was concentrated in that small place.

That day was June 28, 1992.

We arrived in Hong Kong late at night on July 11. The boat came to rest along a beach, not a pier. The man in charge of the rescue mission, Pastor X, a devout Christian, drove his car to meet us and arranged for us to stay at the home of Legislative Councilor Cheung Man-kwong. We met with an extremely warm reception. Cheung and his wife gave up their own bedroom for us and slept on a sofa in their living room for two weeks. To find such warm friendship among total strangers filled us with boundless wonder and gratitude.

We didn't write to you or to anyone else. Our hosts instructed us not to leave the apartment or to have any contact with the outside world. The rescue mission had to be kept secret, because it hadn't been approved by the Hong Kong British authorities; we were illegal immigrants, and could not expose ourselves.

In order to change our identities, we had to first surrender ourselves to the authorities and undergo investigation. Pastor X assured us that the authorities would process our case quickly. In that way, Auntie Bao and I were sent to a prison in Hong Kong's northern hinterland. It seemed it was my fate to be imprisoned again, to escape from one prison only to enter another. It was the first time for Auntie Bao, and the third time for me. There were great differences between my first time and the last, and many interesting experiences.

We were released after a couple of weeks with official identification cards in our hands. Pastor X picked us up and took us to a resort village near the water. He said that because Hong Kong was near the mainland, the situation remained complicated, and we wouldn't be genuinely safe until we obtained political asylum in the United States. Even though we were now legal residents of Hong Kong, we should still keep a low profile. We should have no contact with anyone but him and his assistant, and in particular we should not contact anyone on the mainland. We wanted to send a brief letter home, but he said, "You can't do that. It's for the sake of your own safety and that of your family members."

Our quarters were far from the city, so we spent most of the time walking along the beach, and we talked constantly about you. Auntie Bao felt especially moved and emotional when I told her of our conversation on the way from Xiangqiaozi to Niushikou. She felt we had wronged you and said, "I keep thinking, if she had been my own child, would I have been willing to leave her behind and go so far away?"

We gazed out onto a ridge of green hills, silently wishing that everything would work out, and that we would soon be reunited.

In early October we went into town for some shopping and ran into Wang Chengyi, whom we'd met previously on the mainland. He was the son of a teacher I'd deeply respected, and I asked him to telephone you using his own name. A few days later he arrived at our secret home and told us you were no longer among the living.

For three months you had stayed at home, waiting every day for a letter from us, becoming more agitated as each day passed. You relapsed into your old illness, and before you could be taken to the hospital, you suddenly disappeared. The next day in a wooded area outside of town they found the mortal shell that you had given back to nature.

That year you were twenty-five years old, the same age as your mother when she died.

You had no flowers at your funeral, no music, no parents, and no grave. Your aunt placed your memorial tablet beside the Buddha on Jiu-huashan.[4]

Time passed. It's now been five years since we arrived in America. During these five years we've moved several times, but every place we live, we place your photo on the table. Auntie Bao regularly polishes the glass and frame so they shine. There are always fresh flowers in the vase beside your photo. Every year at the Qing Ming festival she lights incense for you to express our gratitude for all the love you gave us, our guilt over our failure to properly care for you, our deep regret, and our fathomless longing.

In accordance with the ancient customs of our country, on Qing Ming we also light incense for your mother, Auntie Bao's mother, and my father and mother. Directly and indirectly, all of them were also victims of the tyrannical regime. We remember their kindness, but have no way to repay it; we remember their suffering, but have no way to avenge it. "The past was foreordained, the future will pass like a dream."[5] It is the impotence of the ordinary individual in the face of historic events.

When I was still in China, I wanted to alter the course of history. That heedless enthusiasm was a search for meaning. Since leaving China I have lost that meaning.

In order to maintain independent political thought, in order to truthfully face life, we retreated to the hills and cut ourselves off from social life, purchasing an old village house, a computer, books, and some paintings, accompanied only by a boundless expanse of forest and the ocean's long horizon. Seagulls swoop in the lower stratosphere, while higher up eagles soar. Looking at them, I think of you, recalling your thin arms like wings spread in flight. Sometimes I suddenly have a feeling that you are at my side, or perhaps among them.

Modern physics states that in the chaos of the universe, the direction of time's arrow is dependent on fluctuations in entropy, and is therefore reversible. I believe that if time is reversible, it is possible to conceive of reincarnation. The rise and fall of the solar system and human culture is the result of a combination of random and unpredictable factors. I wonder if reincarnated beings maintain a resemblance. I wonder if in the world beyond our senses there is some kind of order. I wonder if there is a so-called "underworld." I believe that if there is, there must be some passage to another world from which one can return to this world. Perhaps someday we will encounter each other again.

Strolling in the shade of the trees, singing the songs we made up.

At least we can cherish that hope.

Translated by Stacy Mosher

The original Chinese article was posted on the Internet at http://www.blogbus.com/blogbus/blog/diary.php?diaryid=397502.

Notes

1. Jiangnan is the region south of the Yangtze River, known for its scenic beauty, which encompasses Shanghai, Nanjing, and Suzhou, among other cities.
2. Zheng Yi, author of the famous novel *The Old Well,* fled China because of his involvement in the 1989 Democracy Movement. Bei Ming is Zheng Yi's wife. The couple now lives in the United States.
3. Xiao Xuehui is a Chengdu-based philosopher and social and political commentator.
4. Mt. Jiuhua, in Anhui Province, is a sacred place for Buddhist pilgrims.
5. This line comes from the poem "Farewell to a Japanese Buddhist Priest Bound Homeward" by the Tang Dynasty poet Qian Qi (722–780).

SOMEONE OUTSIDE THE DOOR

Wang Yu

There are doors all over the world
You are the one who collects what others have lost
Then you generously throw them out
On the long journey

Though you are wildly arrogant
And want to rush into the thundering storm
To search for the future
As you would search for poems in the sleepless midnight
You cannot help but admire
The unhurried clouds on their way across the sky
We are travelers on a trip of little distance
But we never reach our destination on time even when we hurry

You were formed before you
You will be yourself after
Your life is an endless whistle
The echo of your footsteps will be heard through time

You are no more the childish fool
Drawing portraits for others on the water
And leaving the ripples to yourself
You have already begun your journey
Looking to the future
Looking for a shooting star
Your mother once told you
It was your twin brother

PART FIVE

The Shepherd's Song: Voices of the Spirit

Please give me back the door that never locked
    even without a room, still I want it back, please!
Please give me back the rooster that wakes me mornings
    even if you've eaten it
    still I want the bones back, please!
Please give me back the shepherd's hilltop song
    even if you've recorded it
    still I want the flute back, please!
Please give me back
    a relationship to my brothers and sisters
    even if just for half a year, still I want it back, please!
Please give me back the space I love
    even if you've sullied it
    still give me back the right to preserve it, please!
Please give me back the whole of the globe
    even divided into thousands of nations
    hundreds of millions of villages
    still I want it back, please!

Give It Back to Me
By Yan Li

Adapted from a translation by John Chow

On February 2, 2005, Uyghur author Nurmemet Yasin was sentenced to ten years in prison for "inciting separatism." Yasin was arrested one month after publishing his story "The Wild Pigeon" in the Kashgar Literature Journal. The story described a wild blue pigeon that had traveled far from home, only to be locked in a bird cage by tame pigeons when it returned. Although the other pigeons fed him, the wild pigeon opted to commit suicide rather than remain imprisoned in his own home. In part because pro-independence Uyghurs use a blue flag, the Chinese authorities interpreted the story as a form of dissent. Yasin was tried in closed hearings and denied access to a lawyer.

The PRC's Communist authorities have suppressed independent spiritual, artistic, cultural, and religious expression since assuming power in 1949. While some of the most extreme examples of this suppression were seen during the Cultural Revolution, even during less politically fraught periods, control over spiritual and cultural expression has been strongly maintained. In recent years the government has made efforts at rebuilding cultural sites that were previously destroyed, and religion within an officially delineated space has also grown tremendously. The size and relative freedom for religious practice, however, varies dramatically region by region and group by group. Falun Gong practices in particular have been outlawed and even demonized, and thousands of practitioners detained and tortured. Religious practice and other assertions of cultural identity in the Xinjiang Uyghur Autonomous Region, Inner Mongolia, and Tibet are still considered threats to state security, on the basis of which many people have been imprisoned.

The writings in this section represent some of the voices speaking out for spiritual freedom and integrity of the human spirit. The section opens with a poem by Yan Li calling for the return of all that has been lost. Jin Yanming's essay describes the efforts of a dissident's family to maintain their bonds of love and loyalty under official oppression. Hu Ping's essay on the Falun Gong explores the significance of the movement in modern China, as well as the reasons behind the government's virulent suppression of its followers. Ka Lun Leung explores the scholarly interest that China's intellectuals have taken in Christianity, and the impediments they face if they wish to make a leap of faith. Wang Ai's essay follows the work of artist Yan Zhengxue and the unique and difficult conditions under which he continued to create his art in labor camps. Finally, Yu Jie's open letter to the police who detained him is a personal reflection on pain, suppression, and forgiveness.

As the final section in this collection of writings, the stories here demonstrate a fierce perseverance in the face of relentless suppression and control. These voices are evidence that the macro economic success touted by the Chinese government does not tell the whole story. Despite recent official acknowledgment of the growing social and economic inequalities undermining social stability, a truly harmonious society will require respect for the human spirit. The voices in this volume provide insights and hope for the difficult work that remains.

A MOTHER'S STORY

Jin Yanming

Liu Jingsheng, a political and labor activist, was detained in May 1992 and sentenced to fifteen years in prison. Liu's wife here describes her efforts to make a life for herself and her son following Liu's imprisonment.

"What crime did Papa commit?" My child began asking this difficult question at the age of nine. As he grew older, this question became the proverbial Gordian Knot, and even now I am not able to answer it.

May 28, 1992 is a day I will never forget. On this day my family's life was changed forever, and my son Liu Xiaoguang's childhood became veiled in darkness. That evening, Liu Jingsheng did not return home as usual. As the night wore on, I began to feel that some misfortune had befallen him. The next day I went looking for him at the homes of his friends, but they had similarly disappeared without a trace. I knew what had happened, but it was not until half a month later, when several policemen came to my house with a search warrant, that Liu Jingsheng's fate was confirmed.

At that time, my first instinct was to protect my child. I could not allow him to see our house being ransacked, so I immediately called my in-laws and told them not to let Xiaoguang return home.

When my son asked for his papa, I lied and said that he had gone away on business. But the clever child saw my distress, and I saw a dark cloud cover his innocent face. After consulting Liu Jingsheng's parents, I decided to tell the boy the truth about his father.

Upon hearing that his papa had been arrested, Xiaoguang cried bitterly. Like most boys, Xiaoguang had a lofty ambition: he wanted to become a policeman so that he could rid society of bad people. He couldn't understand how his own papa could have suddenly turned into a bad person.

With no way to explain it, I hid my emotions as best as I could and told him that his papa had just encountered a bit of trouble, and that he would come home very soon.

We waited until the end of the year, but Liu Jingsheng still did not return home; and we waited until May 28, 1993 and May 28, 1994, and Liu Jingsheng still did not return home. Finally, after more than two-and-a-half years of detention, Liu Jingsheng was tried on December 14, 1994, for his role as a co-founder of the China Freedom and Democracy Party. As a family member, I was allowed to attend the proceedings, during which he was sentenced to fifteen years in prison on charges of "organizing and leading a counterrevolutionary organization" and "inciting counterrevolutionary subversion."

At that time, Xiaoguang was nine years old. Upon hearing my husband's sentence, my first thought was for my child, because the experiences of our generation had shown that having a father convicted of a counterrevolutionary crime would mean that he would be unable to live the same kind of life as other children his age. Xiaoguang was in the third grade at that time. He was clever and lively and loved to draw. I hardly dared to contemplate whether he could be the same boy from now on.

My Life with Liu Jingsheng

In 1982 I was sent to work at the Beijing Public Transportation Company, where I met Liu Jingsheng, a bus driver on the No. 27 bus line. I was twenty-five years old at the time. Liu Jingsheng was a generous person with a wonderful sense of humor, intelligent and hardworking. He was more than six feet tall, with a thin, strong face. He was the kind of man who gave a woman a sense of security, and I gained a very favorable impression of him. In 1984 we married, and the following year I gave birth to our son.

In fact, when I think about it now I realize that I barely knew my husband when I married him. I had no idea how committed to politics he was, and didn't even know about the role he had played in the Democracy Wall Movement. It was only later that I learned of the important role Liu Jingsheng had played in founding the underground magazine *Exploration (Tansuo)* and of his work with Wei Jingsheng, and began to reflect on "democracy" and "human rights," concepts that were very foreign and rarely discussed in China at that time.

Liu Jingsheng opened my eyes to a whole new way of looking at the world. In fact, it was not that I had no interest in politics, but rather that I avoided the subject as a means of self-protection.

I was born in Beijing in 1957 to a Manchurian family descended from Qing Dynasty nobility. Our family had been forced to sinicize our surname as a means of self-preservation. I knew little of the hardships suffered by my forebears, but from as early as I can remember, I was aware that I was different from my schoolmates. When the Cultural Revolution broke out, I was nine years old. In my childhood and early teenage years, the very word "politics" filled me with terror, and for many years I would have nothing to do with any political organization. When it came time to join the Communist Youth League, I was one of the few students in my school who would not even fill out an application. The best description of my attitude was "aversion to politics."

But fate plays jokes on people, and I ended up marrying a man whose blood boiled with political conviction and commitment.

Unlike me, Liu Jingsheng enjoyed a happy and carefree childhood. His parents were political cadres at the Chinese Academy of Sciences; he lived in comfort, and all of life's opportunities were open to him. The political advantages he enjoyed from childhood made him optimistic, energetic, and plainspoken. But because he didn't understand that the world he lived in was not actually so bright and tolerant, he didn't realize the hardships he would face in the political life he eventually chose.

Fifteen years: the prime of life was snatched from us. To this day I don't know what thoughts ran through Liu Jingsheng's head when he heard his sentence in court. For me, it struck like a thunderbolt.

After the trial, many friends came to comfort me, and some who were uninvolved in politics quietly advised me to divorce my husband.

Yes, fifteen years is a long time in a human life, and for a woman with no political convictions, it's a torment. I understood people's good intentions and society's conventions, and on many a long, lonely night I gazed at the dark sky, the bright moonlight, the desolate stars, and wondered what Liu Jingsheng was doing, what he was thinking and feeling. . . .

A Child's Heavy Heart

All of this was hard for Xiaoguang to comprehend. He often picked up a photograph of his father and stared at it for long periods, then asked me, "What crime did Papa commit? Is Papa a bad man? Why did the police take him away?"

He had no understanding of politics, and couldn't understand that it wasn't a simple matter of good people versus bad people. But I firmly responded, "Your papa is not a bad man, he's a good man. You'll understand the rest when you grow up."

Because of his father's absence, I feared that my son would develop psychological problems, so I redoubled my efforts to protect and nurture him. I regularly took him to group activities so he wouldn't feel that he was different from other children. In October 1992, the China Youth Cultural Palace organized a toy exchange event, and when I heard of it, I took him over so he could see what it was like to play with so many other children. We didn't have anything worth giving to anyone else, so we just watched. Seeing that some people were buying and selling toys, Xiaoguang asked me, "Look, aren't they hawking toys over there?"

I didn't respond at first, because I didn't understand where this strange observation had come from. But then he went on to say, "My papa wasn't a hawker. Why did he get arrested while nothing is happening to these people?"

This made me aware how every small event must remind him of his suffering and loss. It turned out that he was thinking of a small business that Liu Jingsheng operated years ago, and he thought his father's arrest was related to that.

I told him, "Your father wasn't a hawker."

"So why was he arrested?" the boy persisted.

I said, "You'll understand when you grow up."

But Xiaoguang would not let up on this question, and after we returned home, he told his grandmother, "Today I saw a lot of people hawking toys. Why don't the police arrest them like they arrested my father?"

His grandmother was perplexed, but after I whispered to her where this notion had come from, she answered: "Yes, your mother is right, when you grow up you'll understand."

One day, a neighbor came over and told me that China's president had died. The news had not yet been made public, so she had to be very secretive while telling me. All of a sudden, Xiaoguang sat up in his bed and shouted, "Who died? Who died?"

I impatiently replied, "It's none of your business, be good and go back to sleep."

Xiaoguang began to sob loudly and asked, "Is it my papa who died? My papa is dead, isn't he!"

My heart sank as I realized what an important place his father occupied in this boy's mind, and how troubled he was. I reassured him that it was President Li Xianlian who had died, not his father. Only then was he able to calm down.

After Liu Jingsheng was imprisoned, I had been unwilling to bring our son along to visit him in prison, because I worried about the shadow it would cast over him psychologically. But at Liu Jingsheng's repeated request, I finally brought the boy along one day during the summer holiday.

We didn't exchange a word on the entire journey to the prison. In the prison's visiting room we sat silently behind the thick Plexiglas. When Liu Jingsheng was brought in, Xiaoguang let out a gasp and snatched up the telephone. Liu Jingsheng stared blankly for a moment, then sat down behind the Plexiglas and slowly picked up the telephone. Before either could say a word, both broke down in tears.

Finally they began a stilted conversation. I noticed that Xiaoguang was staring at his father's prison uniform and gnawing his lip. Liu Jingsheng would ask a question, and Xiaoguang would answer it. I reminded Xiaoguang, "Didn't you bring something nice to show your father, and lots of good news to tell him?" But he just stared at the prison uniform and stayed silent.

Finally, he simply asked, "Papa, are you okay?"

The expression in Xiaoguang's eyes pierced me to the core. I understood the deep connection between a father and his son, and I blamed myself for not letting him come to see his father before.

On the way home my son still said nothing. But as we got off the bus, he suddenly blurted out, "Mama, I don't want to be a policeman anymore."

"Why?" I asked.

"Because the police don't just arrest bad people. They arrest good people, too. And I don't want to be a lawyer either, because lawyers aren't able to protect good people."

Winter vacation quickly arrived, and I decided to take him again to see his father. Again we set off on that road we'd traveled before, and entered that familiar door. And we sat down in that familiar visitor's room. And in the same way, Liu Jingsheng came out, and Xiaoguang picked up the telephone, and Liu Jingsheng smiled at his son and asked questions nonstop. But what surprised me was the dull expression on Xiaoguang's face. There were no tears; he just passively answered the questions Liu Jingsheng asked. After a short time, Xiaoguang passed the telephone to me.

On the way home he stared silently out of the bus window. I asked, "Xiaoguang, what are you thinking?"

He turned his head and coolly said to me, "Mama, I don't want to go next time. You go by yourself."

"Why?" I asked. I instinctively grasped his hand, and a tear sprang out of the corner of his eye.

Boiling Resentment

Before Liu Jingsheng was arrested, when he and his friends would start talking about politics I would shoo them out of the house, because I didn't want the boy to overhear. After Liu Jingsheng was arrested, friends often came to our house to comfort me and give legal advice, and their conversation inevitably turned to politics. When this happened I would take them outside, because I was afraid of the effect this kind of talk would have on my son. I didn't want him to hear about society's darkness and cruelty, or to be psychologically burdened on his father's account; I wanted my son to grow up happy and innocent like other children.

When my husband was arrested, Xiaoguang was still in primary school. His teacher knew about the situation and sympathized with us. She tried her best to protect my son; she never raised the subject of Xiaoguang's father, and didn't let the other students know about it.

In 1995 Xiaoguang entered middle school. His teacher there somehow found out about Liu Jingsheng, and began treating Xiaoguang with prejudice. Xiaoguang loved to draw, and in primary school he had taken part in children's art exhibitions in China and Spain. But this teacher didn't allow Xiaoguang to participate in group art activities, and often said wounding and belittling things to him.

My son began to lose his self-confidence, and built up resentment against the teacher. When the teacher prohibited throwing objects out of the classroom window, Xiaoguang threw a cup out the window. When the teacher criticized him in class, after class he went up to the teacher's lectern, and pretending to stumble, kicked a hole in it. One time he became so angry with the teacher that he smashed his fist through the window in the classroom door, injuring his hand.

I became extremely anxious, because hatred and enmity harms not only others, but also the one who harbors those feelings.

When my son graduated from middle school in 1998, I decided that he should attend a high school far from where we lived, where others didn't know the details of our family background. I had no control over the political path my husband had taken, but I was not going to let my child be harmed by it, or worse yet, let him follow the same path. I sent my son to the Wenquan boarding school in the suburbs of Beijing, where there was no political discrimination and no political influence. Later that year I transferred him to a high school in Li County, near the prison, where a relative taught and where Xiaoguang would be completely insulated from Beijing's political climate.

For the Sake of My Child

My son was gone. Alone in our small house, I felt terribly lonely. Every day after work I would return home and sit under the fluorescent light, my heart as empty as the room. Seeing husbands and wives chatting amicably, or happy reunions between mothers and children, my heart ached. I had only one thought to sustain me: anything for the sake of my child.

I knew that society was supposed to distribute resources fairly, and that the law was supposed to be administered with justice. But I didn't feel that the judgment against Liu Jingsheng was just, or that my family had been treated fairly.

There was nothing I could do about Liu Jingsheng's circumstances, but I could still do all in my power to take care of my child. Working as a ticket-taker for the Beijing Transportation Company, I bore frigid winds in the winter and sweltering heat in the summer for the sake of earning a little more for Liu Jingsheng in prison, and for our son. In 1997 I began working in a friend's bookstore. For more than a year, I rose at six o'clock every morning to go to work at the bus company, then rushed off at four o'clock to the bookstore, where I'd work until 9 P.M. After work I would return home and fall into bed, too tired even to wash my face. Xiaoguang and I endured this hardship and destitution for ten years.

Xiaoguang grew by leaps and bounds and surpassed me in height. Looking at this six-foot-tall boy, I felt happy and gratified—in spite of everything, my son had grown to manhood! At Li County High School he learned how to take care of himself and how to interact with people, and he came to understand his mother and father.

In 2001, Xiaoguang sat his college entrance exam, and was admitted into the Public Policy and Management Department of Beijing's University of Science and Engineering. When I conveyed this happy news to Liu Jingsheng during my next prison visit, he smiled so broadly that tears trickled out of his eyes.

I didn't say anything, and just allowed the hint of a smile to cross my face, but my heart was racing. Yes, our child had grown up, and had made all my effort and hardship worthwhile. I, an ordinary woman with no interest in politics, a woman with no preparation against political persecution, a woman with romantic ideals, a woman who harbored high hopes for her family's future, had managed to withstand such heavy political oppression.

I had not abandoned Liu Jingsheng's expectations, I had not failed to live up to a mother's obligations, I had not obstructed my child's future prospects, I had not surrendered to the pressures of life. For ten years I had shouldered all of life's burdens alone, almost completely suppressing my own needs and missing out on so many of life's pleasures. For ten years my life was dedicated to one thing—protecting my child.

Postscript: Liu Jingsheng was released from prison early, on November 27, 2004. In April 2005 he attempted to open a public-interest consultancy in Beijing, but it was immediately closed down.

Translated by a friend of HRIC

The original Chinese article was posted on the tenth anniversary of Liu Jingsheng's detention on the Web site of Renminbao.com: http://renminbao.com/rmb/articles/2002/5/21/21003.html.

THE FALUN GONG PHENOMENON

Hu Ping

The Chinese government has been particularly virulent in its suppression of Falun Gong, a peaceful quasi-religious movement that proliferated rapidly in the 1990s. Hu Ping examines the popular appeal of Falun Gong, and the reasons why the Chinese government has chosen to treat it as a threat.

The Significance and the Origins of Falun Gong

The Falun Gong phenomenon has undeniably been one of the most important developments in China's transition to the new century. Although it set out with no such intention, Falun Gong now represents a serious challenge to the Chinese Communist government. Some people have gone so far as to declare that Falun Gong will be the Chinese government's Waterloo, or perhaps its Moscow.

Jiang Zemin once said, "I don't believe Falun Gong cannot be controlled." It appears that before Jiang ordered the suppression of the Falun Gong in 1999, some of the more clear-sighted people around him had advised against it. There was a tacit acknowledgment that mowing the grass would not destroy the roots, and many officials were content to turn a blind eye to activities that didn't take place right under their noses. But some Falun Gong practitioners insisted on continuing their public activities, spurring the authorities to take action. Jiang Zemin himself may have sensed that he had blundered into a trap, and that having climbed onto the tiger's back, he would find it difficult to dismount. Many people who had initially disregarded Falun Gong were amazed at how events transpired.

Regardless of how one might judge Falun Gong, I believe it is important to gain a full understanding of the group, not only, and perhaps not even primarily, from the political angle.

WHAT ACCOUNTS FOR FALUN GONG'S RAPID GROWTH?

In the few years following 1989, Falun Gong grew from nothing into a massive movement involving tens of millions of people. The causes should be sought in Chinese society after 1989.

In post-1989 China, the Communist Party found itself ideologically bankrupt. Others have pointed out that communist ideology is itself a kind of religion, which originally served to suppress other ideologies and religions while at the same time taking their place. For that reason it is not surprising that when communism became morally bankrupt, other forms of religion sprang up to fill the vacuum.

Likewise, the 1989 Democracy Movement had lifted high the flag of rationalism, and its failure was the failure of rationalism. For that reason it was followed by a wave of irrationalism, and the sudden invasion of all manner of strange events and miraculous beings.

The atheistic authorities instinctively detested these supernatural elements, but in the years of chaos immediately following Tiananmen, it is possible that at some level they were willing to tolerate religion as a relatively harmless outlet for popular frustrations: "If the people believe in gods or demons or *qigong* or mysterious powers, it's still better than if they believe in the democracy movement." Another factor was the popularity of Falun Gong among the increasingly superannuated proletarian revolutionaries. Like many an elderly monarch of yore, many of them became enraptured with mysticism and admitted various practitioners of special powers into their halls, bestowing official recognition and even a certain amount of publicity through official channels. In such a social environment it is by no means surprising that Falun Gong was able to develop so rapidly.

Falun Gong incorporates elements of both qigong and religion, incorporating more health-related elements than traditional religion, and more religious and moral elements than typical qigong schools. Available information suggests that many followers were introduced to Falun Gong as a result of their desire to improve their health, and once they learned more about Falun Gong, they became immersed in its moral teachings; on learning more about the moral teachings, they were introduced to its mystical and religious roots, which excited or awakened their latent religious yearnings; and thus they converted from mere exercise to devout faith.

Falun Gong has been able to develop so rapidly because it satisfies so many human needs. One of the most important of these is the need for interaction and belonging. During the Mao Zedong era, traditional social and popular groupings were destroyed, and people were forced into official groupings in which individuals were treated as undifferentiated elements; subsequent reforms disbanded these official groups and dispersed the people like sand. Since the authorities prohibit free association, people who are not members of formal authorized groups are easily pulled into less organized group activities.

Falun Gong provides regular collective activities, as well as a belief system. One follower describes Falun Gong as providing structure to daily life, as well as an opportunity to make friends and develop channels for mutual assistance, spiritual support, and encouragement. Falun Gong provides a sense of meaning and belonging to people who feel frustrated, lost, lonely, and impotent in a society roiling with change, suffused with materialism and devoid of morality. Indeed, religions in general gain much of their following from precisely these qualities.

THE POLITICAL NATURE OF FALUN GONG

Strictly speaking, Falun Gong is not political, and up to now has not involved itself in politics.

Falun Gong deals only with purifying the individual through exercise, and does not touch on social or national concerns. It has not suggested or even intimated a model for social change. Many religions or quasi-religious organizations pursue social reform to some extent, and for that reason may become part of a political movement, but there is no such tendency evident in Falun Gong.

From what we have been able to observe up to now, a significant proportion of Falun Gong practitioners consists of relatively unassertive middle-aged or elderly people, and a large proportion are women. The peaceful nature of Falun Gong's petitioning activities is attributable, I think, not to strict law enforcement, but to the humble honesty of its members. It is hard to imagine such people instigating a Taiping Rebellion.

Falun Gong founder Li Hongzhi has indeed attracted a huge number of followers, but that doesn't mean he could win an election. Some religions, such as Islam, make a point of involvement in politics and become political powers, and that is how a Khomeini arises. Given that Falun Gong is not political in nature, we can rest assured that in a modern democracy with freedom of religion and separation of church and state, Falun Gong would not become a political power.

Does the persistent petitioning of Falun Gong members against government suppression constitute political participation? No. Everything Falun Gong members have been doing is aimed at resisting the intrusion of politics onto Falun Gong turf. It takes the perverse logic of the CCP to accuse people of opposing the Party merely because they deny opposing it.

In October 2004, the *Epoch Times* Web site published a series of essays entitled "Nine Commentaries on the Communist Party," and not long afterward, the Web site embarked on a campaign calling on members of the Chinese Communist Party to resign [from the Party]. It is generally believed that most of the Web site's employees are Falun Gong practitioners, and people consider *Epoch Times* a Falun Gong Web site, so the Party resignation campaign is typically seen as a Falun Gong activity. As a result, people have begun to suggest that Falun Gong has effectively become a political organization, or will in the near future.

However, commenting on politics is not the same as participating in politics. In April 2005, Li Hongzhi said at a Falun Gong assembly, "There is nothing shameful about politics, but Falun Gong is not involved in politics."

In the same way, many of the students and scholars who took part in the 1989 Democracy Movement insist that they were only calling for freedom of expression, freedom of assembly, and other such basic human rights, and deny that they were engaged in politics. There is nothing unreasonable in that claim.

It is true that the Nine Commentaries and the Party resignation campaign indicate that the struggle of Falun Gong practitioners has advanced to a new level, but this was a logical progression.

The CCP has been persecuting Falun Gong ever since the Zhongnanhai incident of April 25, 1999. The official designation of Falun Gong has escalated from "superstition" and "pseudoscience" to "evil cult," and most recently to "reactionary political organization" that is "in collusion with Western forces hostile to China" and is a "tool of the forces for Taiwanese independence." I will not go into the factual

inconsistencies in these accusations (for example, Falun Gong supporters in Taiwan include people who are pro-unification as well as those
who are pro-independence), but it should be pointed out that this
pronouncement infers that originally Falun Gong was not reactionary or political, and was not in league with Western hostile forces or
forces for Taiwanese independence. It is the CCP itself that has identified a completely apolitical Falun Gong with these outside hostile
forces, and which has created for itself a huge "enemy" that only grows
more "hostile."

Under the pervasive and incessant persecution of the CCP Falun
Gong practitioners have had little alternative but to increase the
strength of their opposition. In the beginning, many Falun Gong practitioners would only fight for their own rights, and maintained silence
concerning the persecution of other groups. Eventually more and more
Falun Gong practitioners began to take a stand in defense of human
rights generally. Originally Falun Gong aimed the brunt of its criticisms
at Jiang Zemin, but after Jiang left office and the new Hu Jintao regime
refused to rehabilitate Falun Gong and continued to persecute practitioners, Falun Gong broadened its aim to include the entire regime and
the Communist Party that was at the root of the persecution. This
change, if not exactly natural, must surely be considered reasonable. If
some people insist on regarding Falun Gong as political, it can only be
in the sense that Vaclav Havel described, as "antipolitical politics."[1]

A Falun Gong practitioner might choose to participate in politics
and establish a political party in the name of Falun Gong, but it stands to
reason that other Falun Gong practitioners might participate in worldly
politics through a variety of other political persuasions and political parties, just as in Germany not all Christians endorse the Christian Democratic Party. For that reason, there is scant likelihood of Falun Gong
establishing itself as a state religion in China—it is much less likely to do
so, in fact, than Christianity, Confucianism, or Daoism. In my opinion,
even after Communist Party rule comes to an end, China will not develop a state religion of any kind.

IS FALUN GONG AN ORGANIZED MOVEMENT?
Early on, in the course of a confidential discussion, Jiang Zemin is reported to have compared the threat posed by Falun Gong with that
posed by Poland's Solidarity movement. This remark makes it clear that

the CCP objects to Falun Gong not as a "heretical cult," but as an organizational force that could rival the Party itself. This raises the question of whether Falun Gong is actually organized. Available information suggests that it is not.

If Falun Gong is organized, then where is its constitution? Where is its membership list? What are the procedures for becoming a member? What are the rights and duties of members? What is the organizational structure? How are leaders chosen, and how are their responsibilities divided? The authorities have arrested many Falun Gong practitioners since the suppression began in 1999, and surely by this point at least one of them would have been persuaded to "come clean" with information on how Falun Gong is organized so the authorities could infiltrate it. This has not happened, so it is safe to conclude that it cannot be done.

According to *A Critical Biography of Li Hongzhi (Li Hongzhi Ping Zhuan),* at the outset Falun Gong intended to register with the Civil Affairs Bureau as a "civil society group," but according to official requirements the group would have had to produce a constitution, a membership list, sources of funding, and so on; lacking those items, it was never able to register. In a letter to Beijing followers in late 1998, Li Hongzhi emphasized once again, "It would be best if we could register as an independent organization, so we could unify under that registration instead of each branch having to register individually. If we can't register, we'll just have to continue as before, with each group carrying out its own instruction and exercise without organizing, and maintaining its own special qualities and purity." And so, Falun Gong has remained an unorganized and unregulated group.

None of its local offices accepts donations of goods or money; there are no membership lists or even regular meeting places. All participants are free to come and go as they please; there is no induction ceremony and no constitution or other documentation. From all of the above it is clear that Falun Gong is not organized.

There are still quite a few people who believe that Falun Gong has a secret organizational structure because of its ability to arrange large mass activities. But there have been many instances of mass demonstrations in communist countries, and most have been spontaneous and unorganized.

Falun Gong drew particular attention with its mass petitioning movement, in Beijing on April 25, 1999. But closer examination shows

how this incident could have easily occurred without any formal organizational efforts.

As far as can be determined, the mass petitioning on April 25 was the
result of an incident that developed in Tianjin from April 19 to April
24, when the number of Falun Gong petitioners snowballed from fifty-
odd people to estimates of more than 10,000. The Tianjin authorities
responded in a way that could not satisfy the petitioners, but which also
did not instill terror in them, and as a result the petitioners felt encouraged to hope for a better outcome from a stronger petitioning drive.
Under these conditions it is not surprising that Falun Gong followers
were able to use their existing networks and communications channels,
including word of mouth, telephone, and the Internet, to rally so many
followers to Zhongnanhai.

The huge petitioning drive at Zhongnanhai on April 25 aroused
great suspicion because the Chinese authorities seemed to have known
nothing about it in advance, which suggests the existence of a secret organization. However, a friend who was visiting Beijing at the time heard
in advance that Falun Gong members would petition the State Security
Council, even though he had no connections with Falun Gong or
China's security apparatus. This suggests that there was no great secrecy
attached to the plans for the mass petition.

Various explanations have been offered for the authorities' lack of
preparation. One is that the authorities hoped to learn more about the
organization by letting its members and leaders come out in the open;
another is that the security forces underestimated the extent to which
the situation would develop.

In fact, just from the point of view of common sense there is little
likelihood of Falun Gong being a secret organization. Falun Gong was
tolerated for many years, even after it abandoned plans to register as an
organization, and practitioners engaged in public exercise sessions without ever feeling a need for secrecy.

After the government imposed its ban on Falun Gong, some of its activities had to go underground, and some members established methods
of communication that could be concealed from the authorities, as well
as overseas spokespersons to deal with the international community's
concern over official suppression of the group. Even now, however, it
cannot be said that Falun Gong has a genuine systematic structure.

What, then, is the source of Falun Gong's ability to rally group gatherings larger than those of many organized groups? We know that the purpose of establishing an organization is first of all to bring together people who share a common philosophy, interests, or needs. Falun Gong declares that only public group exercise can bring about the desired health benefits, so those who wish to take part in these group activities naturally seem organized in spite of the lack of a formal structure.

Falun Gong has developed a degree of organized group activity through its practice of daily exercise sessions, during which practitioners have an opportunity to discuss family matters and world affairs and offer each other mutual support. This promotes mutual trust, empathy, and shared views, and also facilitates fast and efficient communication.

Other comparable organizations, for example groups involved in the overseas democracy movement, can be said to have a high caliber of membership, a genuine organizational structure, and a system of constitutions and rules, but they suffer from a lack of regular organized activities. The fact is, democracy activists do not necessarily have much in common beyond their interest in the movement, and the hardships of life in exile compound the difficulties of sustaining enthusiasm and participation.

The problem boils down to the separation of ends and means. Falun Gong has managed to solve this problem by making the means an end in themselves. If a person does not maintain regular exercise, he will not derive the full health benefits; consequently, official prohibition of these exercises is detrimental to an individual's health. Similarly, if he exercises only in private he will receive the health benefits much more gradually. Of course he can choose to await the outcome of others' protests against government suppression, but in the meantime he loses health benefits.

It is true that if you defy the government ban and continue to take part in public group exercise, you may have to suffer consequences, but this will require you to exercise your *ren,* variously translated as forbearance, endurance, or tolerance. Ren is not only a moral imperative, it is also one of the rules of Falun Gong exercise. The more you exercise your ren by enduring suffering for the sake of Falun Gong, the more you gain, the stronger you become, and the more hope you have of accomplishing your goal.

Falun Gong and the Concept of Ren

The concept of ren has long been part of Chinese culture, but philosophy scholar Chen Kuide has pointed out that "Falun Gong makes ren a
central tenet, and in China's present social environment this effectively
satisfies the spiritual needs of a large proportion of the Chinese people."

Practitioners of Falun Gong do in fact display a stronger spirit of ren
than most other people. I see a number of reasons for this:

First of all, most people who practice Falun Gong are the kind of
honest, simple people who are most capable of ren. Conversely, this is
also the type of person most easily attracted to Falun Gong, and participation reinforces their innate temperament and disposition.

Secondly, there is the temperament-molding effect of Falun Gong
exercise. Ren can be put into practice through cultivating a serene mentality, and as Western anger-management methods have demonstrated, a
serene mentality can be achieved through certain physical exercises, including the type of qigong practiced in Falun Gong.

Thirdly, apart from engaging in physical exercise, Falun Gong practitioners engage in spiritual cleansing by channeling the Dafa and practicing meditation, similar to the Christian practice of regular prayer and
worship, the Confucian practice of physical and mental cultivation, and
maybe even the practice in the Cultural Revolution of daily readings
and struggle sessions.

Finally, morality is a practice and not a theory; it relies on willpower
and resolve, not reason. The authoritative tone of Li Hongzhi's *Zhuan
Falun* may be able to influence the willpower and the moral behavior of
those who hunger for strong guidance, encouragement, and discipline.

THE COMFORT OF REN

In a society with no justice and an era with no moral compass, the
source of greatest frustration to honest, dutiful people is not the fact that
they lose out and suffer abuse more than others. Rather, it is the discov-
ery that their honest and dutiful nature is not considered praiseworthy,
but rather a sign of stupidity and foolishness that subjects them to
ridicule and isolation. For this reason, they need, more than the average
person, the recognition and support of like-minded people. Because
they cannot receive encouragement in practical matters, they need,
more than other people, the solace of illusion; that is to say, they need

myths and they need religion. Falun Gong joins such people under a common myth so that they no longer feel alone and insignificant, and also enjoy access to reliable spiritual resources. For that reason they are able to persevere with their moral philosophy even more resolutely and heroically.

Many interpretations of the concept of ren recognize that people practice ren in pursuit of other greater goals. Common sense tells us that the sacrifice of short-term pleasures is necessary to achieve a greater and more lasting happiness. Traditional religion's encouragement of people to practice virtue uses a similar rationale, but bases its motivation on the reward for sacrifice to be found in the next life, not in the present one.

Likewise, Li Hongzhi says, "The rewards of the Buddha are gained through suffering," and, "He who suffers in this life will become a Buddha when he leaves it." Followers of Falun Gong believe that endurance of suffering is a small price to pay for the eternal rewards to come.

Ren is one of the three basic virtues promoted by Falun Gong, the others being truthfulness and benevolence. Truthfulness and benevolence are relatively easy to understand and accept, but ren is more complicated. In her detailed exploration of ren, writer and scholar Gong Xiaoxia observes, "Ren is not just a matter of holding back, but rather becomes a means of overcoming. The passive ren becomes an active ren, and gives spiritual strength to the weak."

Falun Gong forfeits the option of resentment and vengeance by employing ren to accomplish a reversal or creation of value in which an insult is no longer insulting, an injury is no longer an injury, being cheated is no longer being cheated. I have observed that many people who initially looked down on Falun Gong have been deeply impressed after observing the courage of practitioners in the face of pressure from the authorities.

The CCP has never been satisfied with physical persecution, but has always insisted that the oppressed "confess his errors." The CCP recognizes that refusal by the oppressed to concede moral superiority in spite of overwhelming physical torment means the Party will not have genuinely prevailed.

A common criticism of the Falun Gong goes: "You advocate ren, tolerance, so why not tolerate the authorities' criticism and prohibitions rather than going to Tiananmen Square and 'surrounding' Zhongnanhai?" But ren does not involve capitulation or retreat, but rather perseverance. Using public exercises and peaceful petitioning as an expression of perseverance is not in any way contradictory to ren.

It is in this sense that ren transcends passivity to become a kind of achievement. Marx criticized religion for using imaginary comforts as a substitute for practical struggle. What Marx did not consider was that when religion encourages one to persevere in holding to one's personal values against the coercive logic of the oppressor, this can also be considered a form of struggle.

The teachings of Falun Gong state, "In this universe there is a principle, 'In losing you win, and in winning you lose. If you fight your loss, you lose even more.'"

Falun Gong followers take joy from suffering, regard persecution as a test, and treat sacrifice as the ultimate goal. For that reason the usual tactics are not only ineffective against them, but actually spur them to greater resolve.

Falun Gong and the Search for the Meaning of Life

Many Falun Gong practitioners, when explaining the motivation behind their unyielding struggle, do not refer to a particular spiritual reward, but say they are defending the truth, or preserving morality or seeking the meaning of life. To seek the meaning of life is to seek a way to transcend the impermanence of physical existence by establishing either a mystical relationship with something that is unlimited or eternal such as God, the spirit of the universe or the universal Dafa, or a secular relationship with other human beings in which one is transformed into a larger self through the memory and history of humanity.

A little reflection makes clear the limitations of the nonreligious, secular form of immortality: 1) it can only be enjoyed by a small minority of great people who enter the historical record; 2) it requires a witness to record it or tell it to others, which is difficult under authoritarian control; and 3) it requires stability and continuity in history itself, and in prevailing social values.

One of the reasons that modern Chinese live so much in the present is the radical change in society and in values that they have experienced. As history has proven unreliable, immortality has come to be seen as unattainable, and many people have given up the notion in favor of living for the moment.

In comparison, a person choosing religious means of seeking immortality avoids these limitations. Before God, or before the law of the Buddha, there is no difference between the great and the humble, only a difference between those who are devout and those who are not. In addition, the believer gains a feeling of meaning in life through establishing a relationship with God or the spirit of the universe, and therefore doesn't require someone else to witness or record his actions. A jailed dissident's greatest fear is to be forgotten by the outside world, because that would eliminate the meaning of his existence and his suffering; but a believer has less fear of being alone because he believes God is always with him. Finally, the believer sees the values he pursues as originating with God or the spirit of the universe, which transcend the boundaries of history and are not subject to the vagaries of social values.

THE SPIRITUAL INADEQUACY OF MARXISM

Not many Chinese people are religious, but the Chinese attitude toward history has strong religious overtones. We maintain that history is progressive and meaningful and that as long as we choose to stand on the side of historical correctness, we need not fear whatever sufferings or hardships we encounter, because "history is just." And if we have to sacrifice our lives, we hold that "the annals will devote a page to our loyalty," and our name and our spirit will continue to live on after us. Is this not similar to the way that religion leads people to suffer hardship in the present for the sake of a reward in the next life?

There are two points we need to clarify here. First, the average person believes that to at least some extent virtue is its own reward. Second, the average person hopes that goodness will be rewarded, not because of a desire for personal benefit, but out of an innate longing for justice. Religion tells us that, however imperceptibly, what we do counts and that good and evil will be appropriately rewarded. This gives immeasurable spiritual support to the disadvantaged in an unjust and pragmatic society.

In speaking of religion, CCP authorities probably only remember Marx's famous statement, "Religion is the opium of the people"; but if we look back at the statement in its original context, what Marx said was, "Religion is the sigh of the oppressed creature, the heart of the heartless world, just as it is the spirit of the spiritless situation. It is the opium of the people."

What Marx meant was that in a world without feeling or justice, people need comfort and hope, just as a person should not have to endure the amputation of a limb without anesthetic.

It is true that Marx opposed religion, because he believed that religion trapped people in illusion and made them resigned to their fate so that they were unwilling to struggle for social progress. Marx advocated attaining an ideal society in which the illusion of religion was no longer necessary. But human society cannot possibly reach a perfect situation, and as a result it is an illusion to believe that human beings can live without illusion.

Marx's materialistic concept of history and its deterministic nature have their own religious quality, which captured the interest of Western intellectuals as traditional religion declined in influence. But the heaven on earth promised by Marx could only appear in the last stage of human history, in an era of great proletarian revolution and victory, at a stage when moral and historical determinism were reunited under the proletarian class. What reward does this earthly paradise provide to the multitudes who sacrifice their lives for its realization? As a substitute for religion, Marxism's narcotic effect is vastly inferior.

The Official Attack on Falun Gong

Given that religion resigns people to their fate, it's not surprising that the revolutionary Chinese Communist Party had little use for religion. But now that the Communist Party has become the ruling power in China, it favors religion as a means of helping them maintain order. Even so, when Party official and Falun Gong practitioner Wang Youqun in May 1999 wrote a letter to Zhu Rongji and Jiang Zemin explaining that Falun Gong was not involved in politics and respected public order and even benefited stability and unity, he ended up provoking the authorities. Why?

In fact, this is not surprising. What gave Wang the right to give credit to Li Hongzhi rather than the Communist Party? Christians assert that they submit to the government because Christ told them to submit to the higher authorities. This means they serve two powers, Christ and the government, but Christ takes precedence. This second-class submission cannot satisfy a dictatorial government. If Jiang Zemin had been clever, he would have swallowed his pride and declared that whether it's a black cat or a white cat, as long as it doesn't cause trouble it's a good cat. But Jiang Zemin was not clever.

History shows us that intelligent rulers have manipulated religion rather than suppressed it. But there are exceptions. Religious persecution in Europe in the Middle Ages arose from a system under which rulers were endorsed by a single religious group, and any reformers or alternative religions were perceived as a challenge to the legitimacy of those rulers. Communist Party rule similarly unifies government and religion (in the form of communism), and makes no allowance for reform or heresy.

Just as a dead pig no longer fears boiling water, the ideological bankruptcy following June 4th partially inured the government to the threat of nonpolitical ideologies, and along with other spiritual beliefs, Falun Gong enjoyed official tolerance for a time. But this situation could not last for long. Out of a wish to reestablish and rejuvenate ideological control, Jiang Zemin mobilized the entire Party machinery to suppress Falun Gong, and at the same time to wipe out Zhong Gong, Xiang Gong, and other religious groups. But Jiang underestimated the sincerity and tenacity of Falun Gong practitioners and through his harsh tactics ultimately unleashed a power that originally posed no threat.

Historians have noted that religious movements tend to thrive in the face of persecution. In fact many more religions have been wiped out through persecution, but it is true that when persecution fails to destroy a religion, it serves to establish it. Many an ordinary person, demonstrating extraordinary spiritual strength because of his beliefs, has served as an inspiration to those with religious inclinations, who become convinced that these teachings must be "true." Even for nonbelievers, the heroic moral integrity and spiritual strength of believers can inspire enormous respect even if the teachings themselves are not accepted. A religion that presents itself as truth must be made public; you cannot say to the light, "Shine only on me." In a similar manner, genuine political dissidents make their views public as a matter of course; otherwise, how many people in China today would not be considered dissidents?

FALUN GONG, SCIENCE AND SUPERSTITION

The Falun Gong has been criticized as antiscientific and as superstition. The modern understanding of "scientific" is a systematic knowledge or research of the various manifestations of the natural world or human society. Broadly put, science must be observable, measurable, replicable, testable, and nonspecific.

Two things must be said here. Firstly, science is not necessarily accurate. Given that one of the qualities of science is testability or refutability, this suggests that science can also be in error. Secondly, science is not necessarily truth. Many truths and values lie outside of science, and just as we cannot say everything that is scientific is true, we also cannot say that everything that is not scientific is in error or without value.

Using the above qualities as standards, it is clear that Falun Gong is nonscientific. For example, when Falun Gong states that there is a distinct physical difference between white matter and black matter, or when it states that a person's abdomen contains a wheel, these things cannot be observed or measured, and scientific rationality has the right to question such claims.

However, the CCP's attack on the Falun Gong, carried out in the name of and on the basis of science, is actually suppressing freedom of expression and freedom of religion. Just as religion and ideology have been used in the past to kill, the CCP is using science to kill, and thus defiles the name of science.

Superstition, unlike science, has never been properly defined. To a nonreligious person, all religion is superstition. For the believer, all religions that worship a god different from his own are a form of superstition. Superstition usually refers to content, for example, belief in supernormal powers, or in a mysterious connection between the natural world and the affairs of men (e.g., astrology). Sometimes it refers to an attitude, such as the unquestioning faith Red Guards placed in Mao Zedong, or that children place in their parents. One thing can be said for certain about superstition: it is an irrational belief that arises out of awe or fear toward something unknown.

Falun Gong requires its followers to improve themselves physically and spiritually through a course of exercises and by being good people, activities that no reasonable person would condemn. Like many successful religions, one of the strengths of Falun Gong is that what it requires of its followers is something that has value in itself in terms of normal human desires and aspirations. In addition, Falun Gong doesn't require its members to pay dues or offer sacrifices, nor does it offer up images for worship.

Is there any element of superstition in Falun Gong teachings? Yes, for instance, in attributing suffering and happiness to the interaction between virtue and karma. But while some people claim that Falun Gong advises those who are ill not to see a doctor, the charge is untrue. The Falun Gong scriptures state, "Can a hospital cure illness? Of course it can. . . . It is only that their cures are carried out through normal methods." Falun Gong believes that human illness is the result of karma, and while a doctor can cure the superficial manifestation, only exercise can cure the root cause. While some people may take this to an extreme and forgo medical treatment in favor of exercise only, most people do both.

In any case, superstition cannot be regarded as harmful from the standpoint of morality and social ramifications. The anthropologist James G. Frazer once observed that superstition benefited human society by providing a motivation for correct behavior, and that it was much better for society if people behaved correctly with the wrong motivation than if they did what was wrong for all the best of reasons.

Of course, harmful superstitious practices such as offering children as human sacrifices or requiring widows to burn themselves to death must be banned because they violate basic human rights. The crux of the matter is to oppose coercion—coercive imposition of superstition and coercive elimination of superstition. That obliges us to separate church and state, guarantee human rights, and protect freedom of speech and religion and rule of law.

The Power of Falun Gong Resistance

Several years ago some friends and I got together and discussed whether China would produce a new religion. All of us were deeply depressed over the moral chaos in present-day China. None of us accepted for a moment that Maoist China was a moral and rational nation, because morality requires genuine free choice, which Mao eliminated, and is based on confirming basic human rights and interests, which Mao denied. Reestablishing morality would require first of all reestablishing freedom and guarantees of human rights, and then on this basis promoting a more equitable moral viewpoint.

At the same time, we also knew that any attempt to establish enforceable rules of behavior based on worldly moral reason or viewpoints was unlikely to serve as an effective substitute for religion. During the decades that the CCP has been in power, it has managed to eradicate the sparse religious tradition that might open a historical opportunity for a new religion to develop. But we also suspected that under modern conditions a new religion was unlikely to become established.

The strength of Falun Gong is in its mixture of new and old. By incorporating elements of Buddhism and some Taoism, Falun Gong benefits from at least some of the strength of traditional religion, which was suppressed to the point of near extinction, while also creating new elements. Li Hongzhi says, "Do something that has never been openly expressed" and "What was spread throughout humanity in prehistoric times I am revealing again in the final stages. That is why it is precious."

This made people think, "No wonder those things of the past were not effective, it turns out that Buddhism's most valuable things were never revealed, and now they are being revealed for the first time!"

Something that is created out of thin air, with no prior history or tradition, will not be easily accepted nowadays. On the other hand, if it is only part of old tradition, it is also unlikely to impress people. By putting old slogans on a new signboard, Falun Gong benefits from both history and lack of precedent.

The writer Dai Qing knows quite a few Falun Gong followers. She says they worship Li Hongzhi as people once worshiped Mao Zedong, and are willing to die for him.[2] Given that Li Hongzhi does not aspire to any worldly power, the willingness of Falun Gong followers to give up all worldly welfare reveals much about the character of their religion and testifies to their spiritual strength.

From press reports, especially from photographs, we can see that Falun Gong practitioners who practice openly in public and do not conceal their faces are predominantly middle-aged, female, and average working-class people. This contrasts strikingly with the typical image of the oppositionist as a gentleman warrior, an elite intellectual, or a long-haired, bare-knuckled rowdy. No wonder some people have observed that in the Falun Gong "the old revolutionaries have encountered a new problem."

Falun Gong followers are quite different from democracy activists, who are well aware of the danger they face.

While individuals who are psychologically prepared may be stronger in the face of oppression, psychological preparation in groups may give rise to apprehension that, if not managed effectively, can result in people scattering like hares. Falun Gong followers had no intention of challenging the authorities, and once they were attacked, they were simply incredulous. Believing that they were innocent and undeserving of this treatment, they felt obliged to object and petition, and this was interpreted by the foolish and unreasonable authorities as protest and challenge. In this way people who never intended to challenge the authorities became the authorities' biggest challenge.

In its suppression of the masses, the CCP's typical tactic has been to disperse the gang by destroying the leader, or killing one to frighten a hundred, with the aim of disbanding a movement. But Falun Gong is not a typical group. Its public practice sessions and its petitioning drives are initiated by its ordinary members. There is no effective way for the iron fist of the proletarian dictatorship to deal with these harmless, ordinary, and predominantly elderly people. If the tactic is too mild, it won't have any effect. If it's too harsh, it will seem unjustified.

It has been said that quite a few officials and police officers "on the ground" confide that the typical Falun Gong practitioner is not in any sense a "public enemy," and object to being involved in suppressing them.

MARTYRDOM AND SUICIDE

Reports of self-immolation in Tiananmen Square by Falun Gong practitioners raised considerable alarm in 2001. The CCP used these incidents as further justification for its suppression, saying that Falun Gong teachings harmed followers by driving them to suicide. This claim requires a detailed exploration.

First of all, there was from the outset considerable controversy over whether the people who committed suicide were indeed followers of Falun Gong. It is known that in recent years there have been many suicides in China, especially among women, and in particular among rural women. A report in the Western media stated that Chinese women have the highest suicide rate in the world. These suicides have included many instances of self-immolation in public places.[3]

The official Falun Gong Web site had for more than a year been dealing with rumors of impending Falun Gong suicides, even mass suicides,
and there were worries that Chinese officials would use any suicide to
implicate Falun Gong. For that reason, immediately after the self-
immolations in Tiananmen Square, the first response by Falun Gong's
overseas spokesman was to deny that the suicides were Falun Gong followers. In fact, there is no way to ascertain this point, given the lack of
Falun Gong membership lists and the unreliability of official reports.
However, the *Epoch Times* in January 2006 published an article referring
to the incident as a "deadly hoax."[4]

Even if we assume that the people who committed suicide were
Falun Gong practitioners, the next question is, does Falun Gong encourage its followers to commit suicide? Many religions teach the existence of an afterlife superior to the present one, but expressly forbid
suicide. Contrary to the secular view that a person's life is his own to do
with as he wishes, religion teaches that a person's life is a gift from God,
and that by taking the initiative to terminate this life a person goes
against the will of God. Likewise, Li Hongzhi designates suicide a sin
because "As human life has a plan, you are breaking the comprehensive order. . . . God will not let you off for this, and that is why suicide
is a sin." (It is interesting to note that the Communist Party forbids
suicide on similar grounds, claiming that a communist's life belongs to
the Party, and therefore committing suicide is an act of opposition to the
Party.)

The belief in a superior afterlife and in God's plan for one's life tends
to equip religious believers with an ability to face hardship and misery
in the present life with greater fortitude. Whether we're talking about
people in Nazi concentration camps, in the Soviet gulag, or in China's
forced labor camps, the suicide rate among religious believers is consistently much lower than that of nonbelievers. Quite a number of religious friends have told me that without their faith they would have
been unable to survive to the present.

On a purely objective basis, if we examine reported suicide rates
among followers of Falun Gong compared with suicide rates among the
Chinese population in general and in other countries, we see that the
incidence of suicide is actually very low. Through extensive efforts,
the CCP identified 136 incidents of Falun Gong followers who committed suicide during the period from 1993 to July 1999, when the of-

ficial ban was imposed. Based on the official figure of 2.3 million followers during that period (and some have estimated a vastly larger following), that makes a rate of 0.84 suicides per 100,000 persons per year. Officially reported statistics for China as a whole in the years 1990–1994 show an average suicide rate of 16.7 per 100,000 persons per year. Even if we allow for the figure of 2.3 million Falun Gong members as a maximum over the seven-year period, and halve it to an average of 1.65 million, that still makes a suicide rate of only 1.7 per 100,000, one tenth of the rate among the Chinese population as a whole. If we allow for the possibility that all 136 suicides occurred in one year, we come up with a rate of only 5.9 per 100,000, still far below that of the population as a whole.

The conclusion to be drawn is clear: no matter how the calculation is carried out, the suicide rate among Falun Gong followers is low, which is especially notable when taking into account the large percentage of members who are advanced in age and in relatively poor physical health, groups among which suicide rates in China are traditionally very high. If anything, it should be said that practicing Falun Gong prevents suicide rather than promoting it.

The CCP has attempted to equate the Tiananmen self-immolations to the mass suicide by followers of Jim Jones' People's Temple cult in November 1978. However, this comparison is unjustified for the following reasons:

1) the People's Temple aspired to creating a utopian community, while Falun Gong only aims for individual healing;
2) the People's Temple used violent physical coercion to keep followers from leaving the fold, while Falun Gong participation is strictly voluntary;
3) the People's Temple isolated its followers in closed communities cut off from the rest of society, whereas Falun Gong practitioners retain their normal roles and activities in the wider community;
4) the People's Temple was an apocalyptic cult predicting the imminent end of the world, but neither Falun Gong scripture nor the writings of Li Hongzhi contain any such claims;
5) genuine mass suicide requires a fast and irreversible mode of death, such as the poison and firearms employed by the People's Temple. Public self-immolation is a painful and drawn-out form of suicide,

which may be thwarted by the lifesaving efforts of onlookers at any time; and ·

6) the People's Temple had prepared itself for violence through the stockpiling of weapons, but no weapon of any kind has ever been discovered among followers of Falun Gong.

The CCP's accusations that Falun Gong exercises "mind control" over its followers are similarly unfounded. Effective mind control requires a controlled and insulated environment, and physical coercion and punishment, all of which were employed by the People's Temple. It is clear that the conditions do not exist for Li Hongzhi to exercise mind control over Falun Gong followers, even if he wished to do so.

While the self-immolations in Tiananmen Square do not in any way resemble the mass suicides induced by apocalyptic cults such as the People's Temple, they strongly resemble protest-type suicides. Indeed, public self-immolation is the most common form of protest suicide, as exemplified by the suicide of Buddhist nun Pham Thi Mai in calling for the withdrawal of U.S. military forces from Vietnam in 1967, and the 1969 suicide of university student Jan Palach protesting the Soviet invasion of Czechoslovakia.

Religious teachings, while forbidding suicide, can nevertheless help a person more bravely face death when it is inevitable and make him willing to sacrifice his life for the sake of standing up for his values. In this context the Tiananmen suicides, if they were indeed followers of Falun Gong, should be seen as protecting and fighting for their religious freedom, and protesting the persecution of Falun Gong.

We may have our personal reservations about acts of martyrdom, and in particular we cannot agree to the murder of children in acts of mass martyrdom. At the same time, can it be right to criticize the "insanity" of those who choose death over oppression or injustice, but say nothing about those whose cruel treatment drives people to such acts of desperation?

Edward Gibbon devotes a considerable portion of his classic *Decline and Fall of the Roman Empire* to the Roman persecution of Christians. Gibbon notes that the Romans were mystified by the willingness of Christians to sacrifice their lives. Some of the oppressors saw their actions as a means of turning Christians from their erroneous beliefs, which they sincerely regarded as a dangerous threat to their own religion. There was no concept of freedom of religious beliefs in ancient times, unlike our present age, where freedom of religion is enshrined in the Universal Declaration of Human Rights. On that basis the persecution perpetrated by the Romans is more excusable than that of Jiang Zemin, who cannot claim similar ignorance.

The CCP's suppression of Falun Gong (and other "cults" such as Xiang Gong and Zhong Gong) is not based on any genuine threat that the group poses to the people as a harmful cult, and is not even because of the threat posed by followers surrounding Zhongnanhai, but rather because the huge public followings of these groups constituted a civic power outside of the Party. However, fear of this power could not be publicly voiced, hence the need for inventing some supposed "crime" committed by these groups.

In the present, with separation of church and state, the destructive potential of religion is effectively limited, while the development of an increasingly worldly society makes religion's positive relevance more evident. We should demonstrate a more open and enthusiastic attitude toward all religion, whether traditional or new, and remember what Francis Bacon said: "Some cures are worse than the disease." Some situations are not good, but forcibly suppressing them is even worse. Protecting all human rights, including freedom of religion, takes precedence over all else.

Historically, martyrdom has typically led to a political power softening its oppression of a religious group. There seem to be no previous examples in history similar to the Chinese government's stance in using religious protest suicide as an excuse to impose even greater suppression on a religious group. It is yet another historical precedent that brings shame upon the Chinese race.

Falun Gong as a Seed of Political Crisis

In July 1999, the twelfth session of the ninth National People's Congress passed a resolution on heretical sects. It is clear that this was Jiang Zemin's attempt to suppress Falun Gong, and the NPC simply served as a rubber stamp. But not everyone performed his desired role in the machinery: Tian Jiyun cast an abstaining vote and Ding Shisun declined to vote as a means of showing opposition.

Ding Shisun stated, "In the beliefs of any religion there are elements that are antiscientific and separated from the reality of society, bordering on superstition and illusion. The people have the right to believe or not to believe in religion. A religion cannot be judged as a heretical sect on the basis of being antiscientific. Millions of people believe in Falun Gong and it has been around for quite a long time, in a relatively organized form, indicating that they are meeting a spiritual need in society. Apart from taking legal action against perpetrators of illegal acts, we should use nothing but education and propaganda to deal with religion, superstition, or antiscientific teachings. We should not use oppression. We should advise and discourage but not forcibly eliminate or attack." Tian Jiyun likewise warned that eliminating Falun Gong was too extreme and risky, and not conducive to social stability and unity, and might well have undesirable repercussions.

It could be that Jiang Zemin himself early on recognized his mistake in taking things so far right from the outset. But Jiang is not the kind of person to admit and correct his mistakes. Originally Falun Gong was different from the democracy movement; retracting the decision to suppress the group would not necessarily have caused a crisis for the CCP's one-party rule. But Jiang Zemin would not retract the decision, because it could have caused a crisis for his position in the core leadership.

The communist system is the most unsystematic form of oligarchy. The power of the top leadership of the Communist Party is enormous but also fragile. A king can admit a sin or an error without losing his throne, because his position is established through bloodline or the mandate of heaven. The president of a democracy can admit error because his position is established through election, through the public mandate. But a Communist Party leader cannot survive a mistake; he cannot admit error because he is presented as the embodiment of truth and the representative of what is right. In the history of the Communist Party, as soon as a top leader admits error he falls from power, taking his close confederates with him. In China we've seen this in examples ranging from Chen Duxiu and Qu Qiubai to Wang Ming and Hua Guofeng.[5]

Jiang Zemin knew that if he openly admitted error he would no longer be able to retain his position in the inner circle. The more aware he became of his error, the more he needed to protect the myth of his infallibility, and the more he needed to perpetuate the error by suppressing those within the party who disagreed. In fact, one of the reasons Jiang issued the order to suppress the Falun Gong in the first place was to attack sympathizers within the Party and consolidate his own strength.

The CCP has maintained unrelenting repression of Falun Gong since the official ban was imposed in 1999. According to reports compiled by the Falun Gong and human rights organizations, up to the present more than 1,000 Falun Gong practitioners have been killed as a result of abusive treatment by the authorities, hundreds of thousands have been arbitrarily detained, more than 100,000 have been sent to Reeducation Through Labor camps, more than 500 have been sentenced to prison terms of up to eighteen years, and more than 1,000 have been forcibly committed to psychiatric institutions. While some of these figures are difficult to verify, enough Falun Gong practitioners have been arrested and beaten by police officers at Tiananmen Square in broad daylight and in the presence of tourists and other witnesses that it is easy to imagine even more numerous atrocities being committed behind the scenes.

When answering inquiries from parties outside China, senior CCP officials never categorically deny that Falun Gong practitioners have been brutally beaten, but attribute these instances to "low professional standards" among some law enforcement officers. This is completely false. A number of analysts have pointed out that, as with the firing on unarmed protesters on June 4, 1989, the torture of Falun Gong practitioners could only result from orders given from the highest levels of the leadership (granted, the command could be merely implied). Because there are too many Falun Gong practitioners to arrest them all, and because their backgrounds are too ordinary, the authorities cannot even trouble themselves to mount formal prosecutions in most cases, but instead resort to brutality (as with June 4th) in the hope that physical oppression will lead to elimination of Falun Gong.

As to the likelihood of success for the authorities' brutal methods, many observers believe the Falun Gong will outlast the CCP. As Gandhi once said, "Martyrdom is not the end of the matter, but only the beginning." A religion only really begins its existence when its followers have experienced martyrdom. Given that many traditional religions underwent suppression to the point of virtual extinction, only to revive and flourish decades later, how long will the CCP be able to maintain its suppression of the Falun Gong? Falun Gong originally had at least 10 million followers, and was already deeply entrenched among the people. Now it has spread to other parts of the world, and has its own martyrs who have left behind their own witnesses and stories. The viability and future prospects of Falun Gong cannot be underestimated.

THE FOURTH GENERATION AND FALUN GONG

After the Fourth Generation leadership took over the reins of power, it failed to correct Jiang Zemin's foolish policy, and has continued to suppress Falun Gong. From a rational point of view, it would not have been difficult for the Fourth Generation to reassess Falun Gong, because in terms of protecting the CCP's rule, it is clear that suppression of Falun Gong was a mistake. Reassessing Falun Gong would not necessarily pose a challenge to CCP rule. The current antipathy between the communist government and Falun Gong originated with Jiang Zemin; he made Falun Gong the government's enemy by declaring it so, and conversely if it is no longer considered the enemy, it will no longer be so. This is not without historical precedent; examples include the Christian church's relationship with Rome, and Buddhism's relationship with various ancient Chinese dynasties.

Having said that, it would not be easy for the Fourth Generation to declare that Jiang Zemin was in error. Given the preposterousness, the level of violence, and the depravity of the suppression of Falun Gong up to now, if the error were admitted, would the CCP be able to preserve its power base? Small errors are easier to correct, but the larger the error, the harder to correct because of fears over the ramifications. At the Luoshan conference in 1959, wasn't it obvious to everyone present that Peng Dehuai's statement was correct and that Mao Zedong's policies were a disaster? Nonetheless, all those at the meeting stood behind Mao and violently attacked Peng. In the end even Peng himself signed his own condemnation and admitted that he had committed the error of opposing the Party. This is what is called "acting in the interests of the group," and "defending the integrity of the Party and the leadership."

Yet, by failing to correct the error of suppressing Falun Gong, the Fourth Generation has effectively committed itself to continuing down Jiang's dead-end road of wickedness rather than taking the high road of benevolence.

In fact, the CCP doesn't believe it can actually eliminate Falun Gong; rather, suppression of Falun Gong is a symptom of the Party's loss of confidence in its own future. The Falun Gong issue, like June 4th, tells the outside world yet again that an authoritarian government must by its very nature extend and abuse its power and must depend on the suppression of the people to protect its existence. It also tells the outside world that the victimization of some is the victimization of all, and that when we protect the human rights of others we also protect our own human rights. I have emphasized many times that indifference is not a crime, but is the necessary condition of crime; the existence of authoritarian power lowers our moral standards. We must brace ourselves against it, for the sake of others, and for ourselves.

Translated by Stacy Mosher

This translation is an edited and updated version of six articles originally published in *Beijing Spring*.

Notes

1. In his 1984 essay "Politics and Conscience," Havel gives an example of "antipolitical politics": "I think that is an experience of an essential and universal importance—that a single, seemingly powerless person who dares to cry out the word of truth and to stand behind it with all his person and all his life, ready to pay a high price, has, surprisingly, greater power, though formally disfranchised, than do thousands of anonymous voters." See *Living in Truth,* Faber & Faber, 1987.

2. See an interview of Dai Qing and Chen Guide published in *Beijing Spring:* http://bjzc.org/bjs/bc/73/39.

3. More recently there have been many cases of self-immolation by people subjected to forced relocation in urban redevelopment schemes.

4. See Caylan Ford and Jason Loftus, "Fifth Anniversary of a Deadly Hoax in China," *The Epoch Times,* January 23, 2006, http://www.theepochtimes.com/news/6-1-23/37268.html.

5. Chen Duxiu, Qu Qiubai, Wang Ming, and Hua Guofeng were all Chinese Communist Party leaders who were eventually purged from power—Chen and Qu in the pre-PRC era, Wang in the early 1940s, and Hua following the death of Mao Zedong.

CULTURAL CHRISTIANS AND CHRISTIANITY IN CHINA

Ka Lun Leung

While the authorities continue to arrest and imprison priests and evangelists involved in China's unsanctioned churches, intellectuals intrigued by Christianity find themselves walking a fine line between faith and professional survival.

In the mid-1990s, a debate arose in Hong Kong's religious circles over "Cultural Christians." The debate focused on whether or not this mainland group of so-called or self-proclaimed "Cultural Christians" were authentic Christians, and over the difference between the Christianity they expounded and the Christianity handed down through history.

What are "Cultural Christians"? What kind of social phenomenon does their existence reflect, and what does it indicate about Christianity's future development in China? Before drawing any conclusions about "Cultural Christians," we need to examine the origins and development of the phenomenon.

The Development of Christianity

"Cultural Christians" as a social phenomenon first appeared during the 1980s, a golden age of growth for Christianity in China during which the number of followers exploded to more than 10 million within a decade. The impetus was the end of the Cultural Revolution, when the Chinese communist government implemented its Open Door policy, allowing Christians and three other religions to once again spread their teachings to a limited extent, and allowing the reopening of churches that had been closed for more than ten years. Many people disappointed with social conditions turned to religious faith, and many young people were drawn to churches out of curiosity and worship of the West. Urban churches were unable to accommodate the masses of worshippers.

As for rural areas, the development of Christianity was even more astonishing. One of the reasons was that traditional Chinese religions were still banned under the government's policy of "overthrowing feudal superstition," but peasants had strong religious needs, and Christianity was one of the options legally available to them. Throughout the 1980s and up to the mid-1990s, Christianity took over the role of folk religion in the rural areas, which means that it also developed in a way similar to folk religion. Christianity's spread in rural areas exceeded that in urban areas, with rural Christians constituting up to 80 percent of the total Christian population in China.

Interest in Christian Culture

During this same period some intellectuals also became interested in Christianity. They were people who cared about social and cultural development, and hoped through a comparison of Chinese and Western culture to determine the reasons for China's backward development and explore possible directions for the future. The questions they raised included: why did the feudal period last so long in China? Why did cruel and anti-intellectual movements such as the Cultural Revolution occur in China? This concern for global cultural trends and comparisons between East and West became common in intellectual circles, to the point of developing into a new intellectual movement referred to as "cultural fever."

Because these intellectuals possessed only a basic understanding of Western culture, they reductively referred to Chinese culture as Confucian culture, and to Western culture as Christian culture. They saw China's feudal backwardness originating in Confucianism, and the West's openness and affluence as attributable to Christianity. In their view, Christianity was the spiritual pillar of Western civilization and the progenitor of the democracy, science, human rights, and rule of law so coveted by Chinese people. One intellectual, Liu Xiaobo, believed that Chinese people's lack of a transcendent God made them unable to prevent someone setting himself up as a god.

The interest these intellectuals developed toward Christianity stemmed from their concerns about China's cultural development. For that reason, they based their understanding on Christianity as the root of Western culture, and were less interested in the religious aspects.

They were pragmatists who asked the question, "Can Christianity be of any use to China?" Eventually discussion of Christianity became a new intellectual cultural trend referred to as "Christian fever."

Scholarly Research on Christianity

At the end of the 1980s, the scholarly community's interest in Christianity began to increase markedly, and a growing number of scholars joined in on the discourse over Christianity. But their main concern was not on the cultural side (the future direction of Chinese culture), but rather arose from scholarly needs and interest. During this period the traditional topics covered in university philosophy and history departments, such as Marxist research, had lost much of their market value. On the other hand, religion, having long been banned, was a vast, uncharted territory, and research on Christianity had particular market value.

Because Christians in the West (including Taiwan and Hong Kong) exhibited tremendous interest in the revival of Christian studies in China, they were willing to provide enormous financial aid; universities and theological seminaries in Europe and North America offered free resources and research subsidies, took the initiative to cooperate with mainland research centers in developing research plans, and gave Chinese researchers opportunities to travel overseas, among other advantages. In the 1990s the number of universities and research organizations opening religious-studies courses and religious-research centers, and even stand-alone Christian research centers, multiplied to more than thirty.

These academic religious researchers were clearly different from the intellectuals who embraced Christianity in the 1980s out of a concern for the future of Chinese culture. They might still have a significant degree of concern for culture, and hope through their research to help establish Chinese society's spiritual civilization, but it was quite clear that this concern was not the primary goal of their research into Christianity. In fact, they tended to carry out fragmentary rather than comprehensive research on Christianity and routinely neglected its historical and practical aspects, focusing instead on its philosophical and theological aspects. In addition, the content of their discussions was for the most part bound by Western theological thought, with little study of local conditions and even less grasp of local topics. They claimed no aspiration for proposing comprehensive answers for Chinese society and culture.

Because of these differences, most of these academic researchers regarded Christian studies as a profession and a job. In their work at universities or research institutes, purely conceptual research was safer than on-the-ground research; and research of the West was safer than research of local conditions, with less risk of blundering into a political no-man's-land.

Here we have examined two kinds of people: the first is the intellectual who studies Christianity out of a concern for Chinese society and culture, and the second is the scholar who carries out pure research of Western religion as a profession. There was considerable overlap between these two kinds of people in the early stages, but they became more clearly differentiated over time, and at present there are many more people of the second type than of the first type.

The turning of academics toward religious studies did not escape political pressure at the beginning; but due to the major drive toward opening and reform, from the 1990s academics were given increasingly greater room for movement, whether in terms of exchanges with overseas academics, or in writing and publication within China. During this period bookstores carried more and more books relating to religion, both philosophical and for general readers, and most were the products of academics engaged in religious studies.

Since the government's controls of religious believers remained relatively strict, books published by Christian organizations could not be bought in ordinary bookstores, and religious believers were not allowed to introduce their beliefs in public places (whether in public forums or in newspapers or the broadcast media), but academics faced no such bans and controls; for that reason academics increasingly assumed the public role of religious spokespersons. In other words, apart from going to church, the public's knowledge of Christianity could only be obtained through the words and pens of these scholars.

Underground Christian Converts

We cannot neglect mentioning a third kind of person: people who through their contact and study of Christian teachings have gradually developed an interest in Christianity and have even converted to the faith. Whether we talk about intellectuals concerned about culture or academics engaged in pure research, both kinds include people who have become genuine Christians. In some cases faith came about as a result of personal feelings and convictions, and in other cases it was influenced by contact with overseas Christians, especially among scholars on overseas study or exchange programs who had an opportunity to take part in church activities.

Under China's current political circumstances, these scholars cannot easily openly identify themselves as believers. First of all, if many were good students in their youth, they might have been accepted as members of the Communist Party, and Party members are not allowed to have religious beliefs. Secondly, as believers it would be difficult for them to continue their research and study of Christianity at the university or research institute, because in the view of the government only atheists can teach religion without bias; as a person with religious faith would automatically be regarded as biased, he would probably lose his position. Thirdly, the mass of China's Christians still come from the grassroots levels, and include disproportionate numbers of women, elderly, and illiterates, and doctrinal standards in churches are generally poor; many intellectuals maintain their distance out of embarrassment at being associated with such people.

A minority of intellectual Christians conduct their own small fellowship and study groups, but the majority simply cultivate their faith privately, avoid participating in any church-related social organizations, and are not willing to lose their social position for the sake of their beliefs.

What Is a "Cultural Christian"?

With the above historical background, it is easier to determine what a "Cultural Christian" actually is.

First of all, a Cultural Christian mainly refers to someone who has accepted Christian beliefs, but who for a number of practical reasons is unwilling to join a church, and who feels uncomfortable among self-organized Christian groups. In order to rationalize their religious choice, and in order to maintain distance from ordinary Christians, such people refer to themselves as "Cultural Christians," as opposed to "Church Christians."

These Cultural Christians take their genuine religious faith and make it entirely a matter of personal conscience, with no relationship to their public life and activities. The main purpose of the faith is to acquire an ontological identity, at most to improve one's character, and has no relation to one's cultural or social role or work. This relegation of religious faith to the purely private sphere is in fact a throwback to the attitude of traditional Chinese scholars toward religion—those who alternated between Confucianism and Daoism, performing their Confucian role in the public sphere, while practicing Daoism only in their private life.

The interesting thing is that in spite of the title of "Cultural Christian," these believers actually, in a sense, go against both culture and society; that is to say, they reduce their religious beliefs to a purely personal and internal concern, with no relation to their public life. Religious faith becomes nothing more than a set of life views and values, and creates no conflict with mainstream political ideology. This writer knows quite a few of these Christians; they are not willing to openly admit their beliefs to others, nor do they withdraw from the Party. They continue to maintain their positions and every kind of political advantage, and they say, "After I retire I'll start going to church."

Secondly, there are some scholars who, focusing on Christianity as a research topic, refer to themselves as "Cultural Christians." They do not have a concealed Christian faith, but they consider themselves "associates" of Christianity because of their interest in the philosophy and theology of Christianity, and acceptance of a certain amount of Christian thought, such as the worldview and teachings of Jesus. Why do they consider themselves "associates"? What benefit do they derive from it? The main reason is that they can present themselves publicly as spokespersons for Christianity.

As noted before, because of political prejudice and the relatively low intellectual standards of the average Christian pastor and believer, in public life church members have few avenues of expression, and as a result the views of society at large regarding Christianity are formed by these scholars. It is quite a rare phenomenon for a person who is not a church member or believer to become a spokesperson for Christianity. Quite a few overseas Christians have expressed puzzlement over why such people have become representatives of Christianity, and the reply they receive is that these also are "Christians," but "Christians from the educated class" as opposed to traditional "Church Christians." These scholars see the difference between the two in that the former do not have to accept the historical Christianity expounded by the West, and can accept the portions of Christian philosophy that are appropriate. They proclaim nationalism and stress that Chinese have the right to define Christianity for themselves without referring to what has come down through Western history. These "Christians" for the most part reject Christianity's supernatural content and see Christianity as only a social phenomenon. Their designation of themselves as "Cultural Christians" arises from their equating Christianity with Christian culture.

In summation, the first and second types of "Cultural Christian" are differentiated from each other in that the first assiduously privatizes his faith and removes religion's cultural and social relevance, while the second shrinks religion into nothing more than a social or cultural phenomenon and rejects its supernatural aspects.

As a traditional Christian believer, this writer finds it hard to accept researchers of Christianity who are not believers as representatives of Christianity.

"Cultural Christians" and the Future of Christianity in China

The appearance of "Cultural Christians," in the form of either the first or the second type, reflects the circumstance of Christianity in modern China. The first type of Cultural Christian is composed of people who do not dare to openly proclaim their religious faith. They take Christianity's original character as a positive religion and shrink it into a mystical religion in order to prevent their faith from coming into direct conflict with their public life and affecting their work or their political privileges.

From this we can see that Christianity is still subject to considerable discrimination in China, and that what Christians face today is not so much direct persecution but rather open and subtle prejudice in many forms. Although China's constitution guarantees the political and social rights of religious believers, because China is ruled by a single party, and Christians are not allowed to join that party, they are bound to face discrimination in various spheres (including academia), for example hitting a glass ceiling in promotions. A person who openly proclaims his faith will pay social costs in many respects.

China's constitution prohibits the involvement of religion in politics and education, and in practical terms religion has been eradicated from all spheres of public life, not just politics and education. Religious believers can express their support for government policies, but cannot use religious criteria to criticize them. For example, Christians cannot voice opposition to the official one-child policy or the practice of forced abortion. China's Christians have no voice in social ethics.

The second type of Cultural Christian does not belong to a church but acts as a spokesperson for the church. In China it is overwhelmingly the case that Christians are not allowed to speak or act for themselves. In fact, the government appoints non-Christians to every level of the hierarchy of the official Three Self Patriotic Movement.[1] Likewise it is widely known that deputy provosts of theological seminaries are non-Christians. Under these circumstances, in which Christians are not allowed to express their views in public life, it is not surprising that academics who study Christianity take up the role of spokespersons.

In a country with atheism as one of its founding principles, religion will be marginalized as a matter of course. Consequently, religion for the most part is only able to attract people who are already marginalized, such as peasants. Since believers are unable to participate significantly in society, it is difficult for them to develop any influence in culture and society.

For a very long time nationalism has served as a source of spiritual strength to Chinese in opposing Western imperialism and colonialism. But today nationalism has become the main force within China for fighting off outside interference in the government's continued unreasonable suppression of marginalized groups. Nationalism is no longer a tool for staving off foreign hegemony, but for rationalizing internal hegemony. We can see today that the official Three Self Church uses nationalism to prevent foreign intervention in its persecution of dissident voices. Likewise, scholars use nationalism as a reason to ignore the existence of tens of millions of Chinese Christians and claim the right to declare a Chinese version of Christianity. In this way nationalism has become a tool of suppression for the powerful against the powerless.

Translated by Stacy Mosher

Notes

1. The beliefs of individual leaders of China's officially sanctioned churches (both Protestant and Catholic) remains a topic of contention. For official biographies of the current leadership of the National Christian Three-Self Patriotic Movement of the Protestant Churches in China, see http://www.chineseprotestantchurch.org.cn/1.asp. For reports of government control of authorized religions in China, see European Country of Origin Information Network, http://www.ecoi.net/detail.php?id=8587&linkid=11935&cache=1&iflang=en&country=all, and also David Aikman, *Jesus in Beijing,* Regnery Publishing, 2003.

ART FROM THE LATRINES OF THE GREAT NORTHERN WILDERNESS

Wang Ai

An artist resorts to unconventional means to preserve his artistic integrity and his art.

On October 24, 2003, the Amerasia Bank of Flushing, New York, presented an exhibition of more than fifty unusual paintings. These huge works in Chinese ink depicted repeated images of black barred windows, crystalline tears, blood dripping down the face of the canvas, twisted, dismembered corpses framed in black, and clusters of teeth and claws—ferocious images that assaulted the eye. The exhibition shocked all who went to see it.

The artist, Yan Zhengxue, was born in 1944 in Zhejiang Province. He was accepted at the Zhejiang Fine Arts Academy in 1962, and in 1990 was appointed head of the Yuan Ming Yuan Artists Colony, referred to at the time as the Soho of China. In 1993 he was elected a deputy of the People's Congress of Jiao City, Zhejiang Province. In 1994 Yan was arrested on trumped-up charges after leading opposition to the government's dismantling of the Yuan Ming Yuan Artists Colony, and was sentenced to Reform Through Labor (RTL) at the Beijing Xianghe RTL camp in the Great Northern Wilderness. There he was tortured with electrical truncheons for six hours, a sensation he compares to being skinned alive. Finally, when the camp guards saw he would not submit, they began giving him ink and paper and allowed him to paint.

Yan Zhengxue used the coarse paper and brushes he was given to express the rage in his heart. Often a camp guard would enter while Yan was in the process of painting, and Yan would quickly wad the painting up and step on it and tell the guard that it was only a useless discard. After the guard left, Yan would retrieve the crumpled painting, painstakingly smooth it out and resume painting. In this way he created more than one hundred works.

After completing a painting, Yan Zhengxue would wrap it tightly in plastic, and whenever he was sent outside of the prison to work, he would conceal a painting in his clothes. While laboring he would take an opportunity to use the latrine, and while the camp guard waited for him outside, hid the wrapped painting in the latrine. Because of the cold weather in the Great Northern Wilderness, the contents of the latrines were often frozen, and by covering his painting with debris, Yan could ensure that the camp guards would not find it. During his three years in the RTL camp, Yan Zhengxue concealed his works in several different latrines. When one of his fellow prisoners was about to be released, or when he was expecting a visit from a family member, Yan would ask them to recover paintings from the latrines and take them away. Yan knew that what he was doing was very dangerous and that if discovered he would be severely punished. But his artistic instincts told him that he must express his true feelings about life in prison to the outside world.

On April 3, 1996, three days after Yan Zhengxue was released from RTL and allowed to return to his home in Beijing, he held an exhibition of his works entitled, "Yan Zhengxue's Prison Exhibition." The exhibition alarmed the police, who closed it down that same afternoon. Prior to his recent exhibition in New York, Yan Zhengxue tried several times to bring his paintings out of China, but did not succeed. Finally, through special connections he was able to smuggle them into the United States concealed in shipments of other goods.

Traditional Chinese ink paintings are characterized by their glorification of tranquility, gracefulness, deep meaning, and reticence. Cultured people throughout Chinese history strove to suffuse their works with a lofty and otherworldly atmosphere. Even in the more realistic paintings of the Ming artist Chu Ta (1626–1705), strong feelings of pain for his country's losses were subtly expressed through images of damaged lily pads and wilted flowers or solitary, sightless birds. Chinese artists chose bamboo, orchids, plum blossoms, and chrysanthemums to express their dissent, and their sense of beauty eventually became a kind of aesthetic tradition in which viewers are pulled into superficially playful works that are actually a uniquely restrained response to suppression.

Yan Zhengxue is probably the first artist in the Chinese ink medium to use coarse black frames, tears, blood, dismembered corpses, and other such fierce images as a direct and naked expression of pain and a howl of protest from the oppressed soul. Yan Zhengxue's works replicate the characteristic spirit but not the form of traditional Chinese ink paintings: although he uses the flowing beauty of the ink to express his feelings, he chooses a monumental square format more characteristic of Western paintings and the immediacy of realistic images to give a new face to traditional ink paintings. It is through the works created by Yan Zhengxue in prison that we can see how an ink painting can be full of sound and emotion and power.

Yan Zhengxue said to a reporter at the exhibition, "I am a painter, I cannot express myself through language but only through painting. To let others see through my paintings how an artist in China is oppressed, to awaken others to the suffering I endured, that is my greatest hope." The hope of a true artist.

Postscript: Yan Zhengxue eventually returned to China, and in January 2007 was facing charges of subversion.

Translated by Stacy Mosher

AN OPEN LETTER TO MY
POLICE READERS

Yu Jie

Experiencing for the first time the naked force of dictatorship, a young writer carries away the lesson of forgiveness, not vengeance.

Gentlemen of the police, on the eve of the Hong Kong publication of my book *A Son of Tiananmen*,[1] I address this open letter to you, my loyal readers. When you interrogated me on December 13, 2004, you forced me to "voluntarily" allow you to copy essays and other materials from my laptop computer, including the manuscript for this book of essays. You have thus had the pleasure of being the first to read this book.

I appreciate how keen you are to read my manuscript. As soon as I stepped off the plane from a trip to the United States in July 2004, I was followed by a group of plainclothes policemen who were talking into their walkie-talkies. Thank you for the special welcome you accorded me. As I stood in line to go through customs, the plainclothesmen went into the customs office. A few minutes later, a group of uniformed customs officers blocked my path and told me that they had to inspect my baggage. They then proceeded to overturn the contents of my suitcase and search it for more than an hour.

When a customs officer found some books about Christianity, he acted as if he'd stumbled on a rare treasure. He asked me, "Are these Falun Gong propaganda materials?" I didn't know whether to laugh or cry over his professional standards.

Eventually, the officer noticed my notebook computer and camera. He asked, "Have you just bought this notebook computer?" I answered, "I've been using this computer for more than a year. Look at the wear and tear on it."

The officer said, "You must show us the receipt. If you can't produce a receipt, we'll just have to keep it here until you bring the receipt tomorrow. If you don't show us a receipt, we will just have to assume it's new and you'll have to pay customs duty on it."

While all this was happening, several flights landed and hundreds of travelers walked past us carrying laptop computer cases, but the customs officers ignored all of them. I knew that you wanted to keep my computer and steal the files and essays it contained, so I told you, "In that case, I'll pay the customs duty." I would rather pay some 3,000 yuan in customs duty than allow you to minutely scrutinize every word I had written to discover "treasonous" and "reactionary" essays that could be used as evidence in a future trial against me. And so on that day your ploy was unsuccessful.

On December 13, 2004, at 6 P.M., five uniformed police officers knocked on my front door. One of them handed me an interrogation warrant. As I was about to step back into my apartment to read it more carefully, one of the officers grabbed the warrant and took several steps back, evidently afraid that I was going to tear it up. All I had had the time to see was the charge, "suspected of endangering national security," and the header, "Beijing City Public Security Bureau State Security Guards Regiment."

Two big policemen grabbed me by the arms, took me downstairs, and forced me into the back of a police car, squeezed between two other officers. We were escorted by several police cars ahead and behind. I couldn't understand why such a big contingent had been dispatched to arrest me. After all, I wasn't James Bond, just an unarmed intellectual.

When we arrived at the local police station, an interrogation session began that would go on for fourteen hours. I was not subjected to physical violence. My interrogators even treated me to a McDonald's hamburger. Throughout the night, a series of policemen took turns asking me question after question. Oddly enough, policemen kept coming into the room with pieces of paper, which they would place on the desk of the head interrogator, as if there had been a big break in the case. This was clearly a form of psychological warfare.

A middle-aged policeman was given the role of Good Cop. He said he had worked in a college, and in fact did look rather professorial. Speaking with an air of gravity and earnestness, he told me, "You have a promising future. Don't continue any further on the wrong path. Your trouble is that you've fallen in with the wrong crowd and have been associating with the scum of society, people like Liu Xiaobo.[2] You've already reached the brink, and you had better step back before it's too late."

Next, Mr. Good Cop outlined a series of splendid life paths for me: "You could become an academic. Getting a job at a university is not that difficult, and someone as intelligent as you should have no trouble obtaining a professorship pretty quickly. Or else you could write novels or scripts for movies and television and become rich and famous. We would not interfere with your creative freedom. Everyone is trying to make money these days. You should also think about yourself." If this kind mentor had taken off his police uniform he could have passed for a Party youth counselor.

Mr. Good Cop admonished me, "I know you may end up turning me into a character in one of your essays. But no matter what you think of me, I'm telling you this for your own good. Even if you can't accept what I'm saying right now, once you've had time to calm down and think about it you will realize that I meant well." He said this with an air of sincerity and concern.

Having failed to persuade me, Mr. Good Cop was replaced by Mr. Bad Cop. As this young plainclothesman sized me up on entering the room, it was immediately clear that he meant business. He looked at me closely, stuck his finger in front of my face, and started berating me: "If you don't cooperate with me, I won't make it easy on you! You're a cultural hooligan. We're political hooligans. Why would we be scared of you?" He clearly wanted me to grasp that now that he was in charge, there would be no more Mr. Nice Guy.

Mr. Bad Cop cut to the chase: "Don't you start quoting the law to us. We in the Communist Party have never abided by the law. To be frank with you, we communists were hooligans from the outset. The blood of innumerable people was shed to establish our regime. Why would we hand it on a silver platter to people like you? We've never been afraid of the grumblings of intellectuals. As Chairman Mao once said, 'Let millions upon millions of intellectuals fall to the ground!' "

Mr. Bad Cop may not have had a lot of schooling, but what he said about the history of the Communist Party was more accurate than what experts in Party history tend to write. With a glint in his eyes, he added, "What's our job as policemen? Defending the state power of the Communist Party! We still have a lot of methods up our sleeves to deal with

people like you. Believe it or not, I could send you into criminal detention right now and have inmates beat the living daylights out of you. We
could make you disappear and say that you died in a car accident. We're
more ruthless than the KGB and have unlimited resources to deal with
the likes of you. And if that doesn't scare you, remember that you have a
family and close relatives. We can also destroy your family!" When he
finished talking, Mr. Bad Cop gnashed his teeth like a wolf.

My "police readers" had downloaded and printed dozens of articles
of mine from foreign Web sites. They had me put my signature and fin-
gerprints on page after page. In my opinion, you needn't have gone to
all that trouble. I published all of my essays under my own name, and
took responsibility for every word I wrote; how could I possibly deny
that I was the author of those articles?

Mr. Good Cop said, "Whenever one of your essays directly mentions
Hu Jintao or Wen Jiabao by name, it insults the top leadership, which already constitutes a threat to state security."

I couldn't help but feel how ludicrous this was. "Do you mean to say
that a dictatorship with millions of soldiers and police officers is so fragile that it's threatened by a few articles written by an intellectual? You
people don't seem to have much self-confidence."

Mr. Good Cop replied, "Your articles are full of hatred for the Party,
and your actions wouldn't be accepted even in Western countries. Even
the democratic America you so admire wouldn't tolerate your insulting
the government this way; Bush Jr. would have sicced the FBI on you
long ago." In effect, according to Mr. Good Cop, our Party had shown
real benevolence toward me.

Mr. Bad Cop, on the other hand, threatened me: "The contents of
your computer are a time bomb. If you're not careful, they could explode in your face and destroy you. The safest thing for you to do is to
let us deal with them."

When the police computer specialists finished copying all the data on
my computer, Mr. Bad Cop became very amiable. The transformation
was as remarkable as that of Hyde to Jekyll. Speaking as if we were
bosom pals, he told me, "From now on we're buddies. If you run into
any problems and come to me for help, you can be sure I'll be able to
sort it out."

My Wife's Interrogation

My interrogation was a travesty of the law. I was denied the right to legal counsel and the right to remain silent. My arrest was illegal from start to finish. Neither uniformed nor plainclothes policeman showed me any form of identification. When they finally released me, they did not give me a copy of my interrogation warrant.

Although they had no search warrant, the police forced me to sign a document stating that I had voluntarily surrendered my computer and the files it contained. They also kept me in custody for fourteen hours, although the law stipulates that twelve hours is the maximum.

When I arrived home at 8 A.M. the following day, I found out that the police had interrogated my wife for more than an hour for no other reason than that she had telephoned a few friends to tell them that I had been arrested. Banging her fist on a table, a ferocious policewoman told my wife, "Kicking up such a fuss will seriously damage your husband's case!"

As my wife recounted her treatment by the police, I recalled an interview with Danuta Walesa, the wife of dissident Polish unionist Lech Walesa. In October 1982, when Poland was still a dictatorship under General Jaruzelski, Danuta was ill-treated by the secret police while attempting with their two daughters to visit her husband, who had been taken into custody. A policewoman shoved her into a room and knocked down one of her daughters.

Danuta wrote, "The captain looked like a wild animal. I realized that he could beat me up. He had previously lost his temper and jumped up and down as if demented. The captain said that he had to write a formal report that would state how I had insulted him. I replied that I would lodge a formal complaint about the savage conduct of the police. As I was leaving I told him that despite his imposing uniform, he was nothing but a dirty pig."

Gentlemen of the police, what Danuta said is also what my wife wanted to tell you. To be sure, we wouldn't call you pigs. As Christians, we don't hate you. When you interrogated me, I prayed silently to God to give me wisdom and courage, and to forgive you for your crimes, as you didn't know what you were doing.

A plainclothes policeman who spoke Mandarin with a Cantonese accent told me in an apparent appeal to logic, "Since you've written a book entitled *Rejecting Lies* [Jujue Huangyan], and pride yourself on being someone who speaks the truth, you really must tell us the truth." A guardian of the empire of lies admonishing an ordinary citizen to tell the truth! It was a scenario more preposterous than Kafka's *Metamorphosis* or Beckett's *Waiting for Godot*.

The plainclothes policeman also asked me about my relationship with Professor Ding Zilin.[3] I asked him, "Do China's constitution and other laws forbid me from associating with Professor Ding Zilin? You murder a young man and don't let his parents mourn him. You also have children and parents. What would you do if your child had been murdered?"

The man did not dare give me a straight answer. He just mumbled, "It's not the same."

Gentlemen of the police, I believe that the dictatorship is doomed to failure. Although you still have the power to manufacture lies, there is no one left who believes your empty promises. You are currently promoting a propaganda movement under the slogan of "Maintaining the Advanced Nature of Communist Party Members." But everyone knows that once the apple is rotten to the core, there is no way to keep it fresh. Violence is the only means you have left to legitimize your rule, and sooner or later violence inevitably ceases to be effective.

Pity Instead of Hatred

Gentlemen of the police, you have tried to scare me into submission, but I can't help feeling that you are the ones who are truly afraid. I look upon you with pity, not hatred. The Polish dissident and unionist Adam Michnik put it well: "You don't regard policemen with hostility. You only feel pity for them. You know that a great many of them suffer from psychological disorders. Every one of them is ashamed to face his children."

Yes, gentlemen of the police, I look on you as readers, not enemies. As I write, my goal is not to oppose anything, or to make enemies or foment hate. It is to protect the freedom and dignity of myself and my compatriots. Naturally, this includes the freedom and dignity of police officers. As Michnik said, "Start by becoming the person you want to see in the ideal society. You believe in freedom of speech? Then work to establish it. You believe in a society rich in dignity and humanity? Then work to build it. In your struggle for truth lead a life of dignity." You can imprison my body but you cannot imprison my soul. You can impugn my character, but you cannot take away my dignity.

Gentlemen of the police, although you are my "first readers," my writings have had no effect whatsoever on you; they are like warm tears falling on a cold stone. This demonstrates the limits of written language, and my own limits as well. There is no magical "Open Sesame!" formula to further the cause of enlightenment. Your indifference makes me realize the wide chasm that separates one human soul from another. I aim to bridge that chasm. I will not treat you as you have treated me, however much I may be tempted to do so. I know that if we oppose the Community Party with the methods of the Communist Party, this world of ours will become a pigsty whose stench reaches to high heaven.

Adam Michnik offered this advice: "I don't want communists to be able to say, 'There is no difference between Michnik and us. When we were in power, we trampled them underfoot, and now Michnik's friends are trampling us underfoot.' You're a pig, I'm a pig, he's a pig, and in the views of some, the whole world is a pigsty; I can't see any point to this, and I don't believe it's true. To exist we must uphold certain principles regardless of the circumstances."

We have to begin changing this situation of living in a pigsty, and that means not treating yourself like a pig and not treating others like pigs. I believe that the day will come in China when you will be held legally accountable for everything you have done. But I will have long forgiven you, even if you refuse to repent, because doing so fulfills a personal spiritual need that has nothing to do with you.

I write this open letter to you, my police readers, not to denounce you but to call on you to listen to your conscience and recover your spirit before it is too late. I have written this open letter as a means of replacing the anger and hatred in my soul with love and forgiveness. Archbishop Desmond Tutu of South Africa says that without forgiveness there is no future, and that forgiveness brings happiness. Adam Michnik, jailed five times and severely beaten twice by the police, once wrote, "I hope that my close friends, particularly those who have been arrested and are still engaged in struggle, will be granted the strength to traverse that dark and windswept stretch between despair and hope. I hope they will be granted the patience to learn that most profound of all arts: forgiveness."

Only God can give us the strength and patience to forgive and to love those who are not lovable (and that includes you, my police readers). I yearn for a thankful heart that will make me appreciate all that I have experienced, all that I am currently experiencing, and all that I will experience in the future.

Translated by Paul Frank

Notes

1. Yu Jie, *A Son of Tiananmen (Tiananmen zi zhi),* Hong Kong: Open Magazine Publishing, 2005. Yu Jie wrote this essay as the preface to his book.
2. Liu Xiaobo is a leading Chinese dissident.
3. Ding Zilin, a retired professor at Chinese People's University, lost a son at Tiananmen Square on June 3, 1989, and has campaigned for an official accounting of the violent official crackdown.

Resource List

Human Rights

AMNESTY INTERNATIONAL (AI)
http://www.amnesty.org/
AI is a worldwide network promoting internationally recognized human rights. AI focuses on preventing and ending the most serious abuses of the rights to physical and mental integrity, freedom of conscience and expression, and freedom from discrimination. AI's China office is especially outspoken about the release of political prisoners and freedom of expression.

ASIAN HUMAN RIGHTS COMMISSION (AHRC)
http://www.ahrchk.net/index.php
The AHRC was established in 1986 by jurists and human rights activists to raise human rights awareness in Asian countries. AHRC mobilizes public opinion to put pressure on governments to end violations of internationally recognized human rights. The AHRC sponsored the Asian Human Rights Charter, a declaration of rights for people in Asian countries, and has focused attention on recent Hong Kong issues.

CHINA DEVELOPMENT BRIEF (CDB)
http://www.chinadevelopmentbrief.com/
Widely considered the most authoritative Web site devoted to NGOs in China, CDB is produced by a small nonprofit organization in Beijing. A quarterly journal is available by subscription, and articles from past issues can be read free of charge on the Web site. The CDB also provides English translations of Chinese laws relevant to NGOs and a database of international NGOs operating in China.

CONGRESSIONAL-EXECUTIVE COMMISSION ON CHINA (CECC)

http://www.cecc.gov/

The CECC monitors human rights and rule of law in China for Congress and the U.S. president. Its Web site provides extensive materials on legal reform in the PRC, posting English translations of key Chinese laws and regulations, as well as papers and transcripts from the commission's regular roundtable discussions.

HUMAN RIGHTS IN CHINA (HRIC)

http://www.hrichina.org/

Human Rights in China is a Chinese international nongovernmental organization that works to promote universally recognized human rights and advance the institutional protection of those rights in China. HRIC implements programs to generate institutional and systematic change while engaging in critical-advocacy strategies on behalf of individuals in China, with the overarching goal of increasing independent civil space within China. HRIC works with international and domestic Chinese activists to develop multilateral, bilateral, and domestic human rights strategies, while engaging multiple international actors.

HUMAN RIGHTS WATCH (HRW)

http://www.hrw.org/

Human Rights Watch is an independent nongovernmental organization that monitors and exposes human rights violations around the world. HRW calls for holding abusers accountable, as well as challenging governments and those who hold power to end abusive practices and respect international human rights law. It enlists the public and the international community to support human rights worldwide.

INTERNATIONAL CENTER FOR HUMAN RIGHTS AND DEMOCRATIC DEVELOPMENT (ICHRDD)

http://www.ichrdd.ca/

Also known as Rights and Democracy, ICHRDD is an independent Canadian organization that promotes, advocates, and defends human rights and democracy around the world. Programs focus on reinforcing laws and democratic institutions mainly in developing countries.

INTERNATIONAL FEDERATION OF HUMAN RIGHTS (FIDH)

http://www.fidh.org/

Founded in 1922, FIDH is a federation of NGOs from all over the world created to protect human rights as proclaimed in the Universal Declaration of Human Rights. It is a nonpartisan group promoting human rights education, protecting victims of human rights abuses, and preventing the violation of fundamental liberties.

INTERNATIONAL SERVICE FOR HUMAN RIGHTS (ISHR)

http://www.ishr.ch/

The ISHR provides services for human rights defenders and NGOs through reports, training, strategic advice, informational and logistical support, and protection. One of its areas of expertise is informing NGOs about United Nations proceedings and procedures, United Nations Covenants, and individual country ratifications.

HUMAN RIGHTS FIRST (HRF)

http://www.humanrightsfirst.org/

HRF works internationally to defend cases of human rights violations, advocate respect for the rule of law, and build a strong international system of justice and accountability. Examples of the group's work include representing human rights activists who fight for basic freedoms and peaceful change at the local level, protecting refugees in flight from persecution and repression, and creating safeguards for workers' rights.

MINNESOTA ADVOCATES FOR HUMAN RIGHTS

http://www.mnadvocates.org/

Minnesota Advocates has received international recognition for a broad range of innovative programs to promote human rights and prevent the violation of those rights. Minnesota Advocates provides investigative fact-finding, direct legal representation, collaboration for education and training, and a broad distribution of publications.

TRANSPARENCY INTERNATIONAL (TI)

http://www.transparency.org/

TI works on both national and international levels to prevent corruption and reform the systems that create and foster corruption. IT advocates for policy reform and multilateral conventions as well as monitoring compliance by governments and corporations.

UNITED NATIONS OFFICE OF THE HIGH COMMISSIONER OF HUMAN RIGHTS (OHCHR)

http://www.unhchr.ch/

The Office of the High Commissioner of Human Rights is the department of the United Nations Secretariat devoted to the promotion and protection of human rights established within the Charter of the UN and other international treaties. Through its publications and reports, the Office of the High Commissioner of Human Rights aims to raise awareness of human rights on the international level.

Detention/Labor Camps

CHINA MONITOR

http://www.chinamonitor.org/

Operated by a Chinese student living in the United States, this Chinese-language Web site posts news, interviews, and essays on executions and death sentences in China. China Monitor also examines attitudes toward the death penalty elsewhere in the world.

THE LAOGAI RESEARCH FOUNDATION

http://www.laogai.org/

Established in 1992, the Laogai Research Foundation gathers information and spreads public awareness on the Chinese *laogai,* or prison labor camps. The foundation publishes the annual *Laogai Handbook* and other reports, and its books can be accessed in full on its Web site. The organization has more recently expanded its focus to document and report on other systemic human rights violations in China.

Corporate Social Accountability/Trade

ASSOCIATION FOR SUSTAINABLE AND RESPONSIBLE INVESTMENT IN ASIA (ASRIA)

http://www.asria.org/

ASRIA promotes socially and environmentally responsible investing in the Asia Pacific region through portfolio screening, shareholder engagement, and community investing. A primarily Web-based resource, it publishes country reports and holds workshops in Asian countries.

BUSINESS AND HUMAN RIGHTS RESOURCE CENTRE (BHRRC)
http://www.business-humanrights.org/
The Business and Human Rights Resource Centre is an information clearinghouse for resources on issues relating to business and human rights. Its section on investment, trade, and globalization links business and human rights concerns with trade and investment themes. Numerous China-related resources are available, many of which focus on labor rights and foreign business practices.

BUSINESS FOR SOCIAL RESPONSIBILITY (BSR)
http://www.bsr.org/
BSR is a global nonprofit organization that works with individual companies and multiple industries to develop models for commercial success in line with ethical values and the protection of communities and the environment. In March 2002, BSR held workshops on labor practices and standards and corporate social-responsibility issues for suppliers in Shanghai.

CENTER FOR REFLECTION, EDUCATION, AND ACTION, INC. (CREA)
http://www.crea-inc.org/
CREA is a faith-based, social-and-economic research, education, and action organization that uses the Purchasing Power Index (PPI), a multicultural means of measuring the purchasing power of wages, to determine sustainable living wages in any country. It provides CREA Focus, a service assisting investors and investment managers in carrying out socially responsible investing.

THE CONFERENCE BOARD
http://www.conference-board.org/
The Conference Board, headquartered in New York and Brussels and with branch offices worldwide, is a global, independent membership organization that creates and disseminates knowledge about manage-

ment and the marketplace to help businesses strengthen their performance and better serve society.

CORPORATE RESPONSIBILITY AS YOU SOW
http://www.asyousow.org/
As You Sow is a nonprofit organization dedicated to promoting progressive social and environmental policies through dialogue between socially concerned investors and U.S. corporations. The organization has focused on McDonald's and the Gap, two companies currently manufacturing in China.

CSRWIRE
http://www.csrwire.com/
The U.S.–based Corporate Social Responsibility Newswire Service highlights positive corporate initiatives through press release distribution, e-mail alerts, corporate reports, and event promotion to a targeted audience of socially conscious investors, financial professionals, consumers, and employees.

FOUNDATION PARTNERSHIP ON CORPORATE RESPONSIBILITY (FCPR)
http://www.foundationpartnership.org/
FCPR is an association that facilitates and provides technical assistance to foundations that want to be more active in social and environmental issues.

GLOBAL ETHICS MONITOR (AFX-GEM)
http://www.globalethicsmonitor.com/
A service of Agence France-Presse, Global Ethics Monitor provides information on corporate responsibility and governance within financial markets, companies, and global economies.

HONG KONG PEOPLE'S ALLIANCE ON WTO (HKPAOWTO)
http://www.hkpaowto.org.hk/wordpress/
The HKPA is a network of grassroot organizations including trade unions, community labor groups, and organizations representing workers, students, women, and religious groups based in Hong Kong. The

Alliance Web site hosts a compilation of documents and news analyses relating to the WTO.

INTERFAITH CENTER ON CORPORATE RESPONSIBILITY (ICCR)

http://www.iccr.org/

ICCR presses companies to be socially and environmentally responsible through the financial influence of 275 faith-based institutional investors, including national denominations, religious communities, pension funds, endowments, hospital corporations, economic development funds, and publishing companies. The ICCR Web site provides statistical and monitoring reports on companies investing in China.

THE INTERNATIONAL BUSINESS LEADERS FORUM (IBLF)

http://www.iblf.org/

The International Business Leaders Forum is an international educational charity set up by the Prince of Wales in 1990 to promote responsible business practices, particularly in new and emerging market economies. The forum's sixty-five-member multinationals represent a broad range of business sectors and world regions, all having strong interests in developing or transition economies. The forum has published a number of management primers and source books.

INTERNATIONAL CHAMBERS OF COMMERCE WORLD CHAMBERS FEDERATION (WCF)

http://www.iccwbo.org/

WCF works closely with multilateral aid organizations such as the World Bank Group and the United Nations Development Programme (UNDP) to develop sustainable capacity-building projects in developing countries. It also provides services such as the International Court on Arbitration.

INTERNATIONAL FEDERATION OF CONSULTING ENGINEERS (FIDIC)

http://www.fidic.org/

FIDIC represents the international business interests of suppliers of engineering and technology-based consulting services and promotes compliance with a Code of Ethics that calls for impartial advice, competence, and fair competition. The association's values are in line with the Global Compact, which enables the business community "to accept and uphold our responsibilities to society."

INVESTOR RESPONSIBILITY RESEARCH CENTER (IRRC)
http://www.irrc.org/
Founded in 1972, IRRC provides research on corporate-governance, proxy-voting, and corporate-responsibility issues to more than 500 subscribers and clients representing institutional investors, corporations, law firms, and other organizations, with the goal of enabling clients to make informed decisions that reflect their investment philosophies.

SOCIALLY RESPONSIBLE INVESTING (SRI)
http://www.socialinvest.org/
SRI is a personal finance site that encourages investment in companies that are environmentally and socially responsible, and aims to influence the policies of irresponsible companies through the withholding of investment. This Web site also provides links to socially responsible investing institutions.

THIRD WORLD NETWORK (TWN)
http://www.twnside.org.sg/
TWN is an international network of organizations and individuals involved in issues relating to development and North-South issues. It conducts research on economic, social, and environmental issues pertaining to development, and provides a representative platform position. The Web site posts its books, articles, and position papers, as well as background information on related issues.

3D TRADE—HUMAN RIGHTS—EQUITABLE ECONOMY
http://www.3dthree.org/
3D aims to promote an equitable economy by strengthening the connection between human rights advocates and policymakers in trade. The Web site provides information on issues linking trade and human rights, and posts position papers, presentations, and articles on relevant topics.

TRANSNATIONALE.ORG

http://www.transnationale.org/

This Web site of the Transnational Corporations Observatory, a French NGO, provides comprehensive information on 9,500 companies around the world, including their social and environmental behavior (such as violations of ILO conventions), financial data, membership in influential lobbies, management information, and plant locations.

UNITED NATIONS DEVELOPMENT PROGRAM: CHINA (UNDP)

http://www.undp.org.cn/

The UNDP is a UN agency that seeks to ensure the most effective use of UN and international aid resources in working with 166 countries on their own solutions to global and national development challenges. The mission of the UNDP China office is to reduce poverty in China by supporting initiatives to achieve growth with equity, gender equality, and environmental sustainability. The Web site includes online editions of the agency's reports on development in China.

UNITED NATIONS GLOBAL COMPACT

http://www.unglobalcompact.org/

Launched on July 26, 2000, the Global Compact is an initiative bringing together companies, UN agencies, labor groups and civil society. The initiative includes a set of ten voluntary principles relating to human rights, labor standards, the environment, and anti-corruption, which companies agree to promote and abide by in their business activities. The Global Compact aims to use dialogue as a means to catalyze action in support of UN goals and mainstream the ten principles.

VERITÉ

http://www.verite.org/

Verité is a U.S.–based independent, nonprofit, social-auditing-and-research organization aiming to ensure that people worldwide work under safe, fair, and legal working conditions. It develops concrete steps to correct safety violations and exploitation of workers through a combination of training for management and workers, education programs, and remediation programs. Its research products include labor-law digests, country labor assessments and in-depth issue reports, all of which have been produced for China.

WORLD ECONOMIC FORUM (WEF)
http://www.weforum.org/
The WEF, funded by the membership fees of 1,000 multinational companies, works in partnership with academia, government representatives, international organizations, labor leaders, media, NGOs, and religious leaders to identify strategic issues and provide a platform for decision makers to effect constructive change. The WEF's flagship is its annual meeting in Davos, Switzerland, which focuses on crucial global, regional, and industry issues.

WORLD MONITORS INC. (WMI)
http://www.worldmonitors.com/
WMI is a consulting group based in New York City that provides expertise to multinational companies, nongovernmental and multilateral organizations seeking to align their business practices with human rights standards around the world. It seeks resolution of the conflicting needs of business enterprises and their stakeholders with human rights concerns.

Labor Issues

ALL-CHINA FEDERATION OF TRADE UNIONS (ACFTU)
http://www.acftu.org.cn/
The ACFTU is the only officially recognized labor union in China, representing 135 million workers in 31 regions and 10 national industries. Any unions established must be registered under it. As a mass organization of the Chinese Communist Party, its role is to facilitate and support the implementation of government policies.

ASIAN MONITOR RESOURCE CENTRE (AMRC)
http://www.amrc.org.hk/
Focusing on Asian labor concerns, AMRC researches, documents, and publishes reports on gender equality, transparency, labor solidarity, and education.

BEHINDTHELABEL.ORG

http://www.behindthelabel.org/

Sponsored by an alliance of clothing workers, religious leaders, and students, BehindTheLabel.org is a multimedia newsmagazine and online community that focuses attention on the deplorable conditions of workers in the clothing industry.

BUREAU VERITAS QUALITY INTERNATIONAL (BVQI)

http://www.bvqi.com/

BVQI is a third-party management-accreditation firm working to give credible certificates to international companies in the labor industries. Accredited by thirty accreditation bodies, including Social Accountability International and the Fair Labor Association, BVQI operates from offices in Beijing, Guangzhou, Hong Kong, Shanghai, Taipei, and Qingdao.

CHILD WORKERS IN ASIA (CWA)

http://www.cwa.tnet.co.th/

This Thailand-based NGO aims to raise awareness of child labor in Asia, and includes children in its advocacy campaigns. The Web site includes online editions of the organization's quarterly newsletters, annual reports, and published books.

CHINA LABOR WATCH (CLW)

http://www.chinalaborwatch.org/

CLW is a New York–based NGO that seeks to empower Chinese factory workers and promote a general awareness of the current labor conditions in China. CLW advocates the enforcement of PRC domestic labor laws as well as international standards. CLW's Web site provides information on the status of workers' rights in Chinese factories and on foreign companies operating factories within China.

CHINA LABOUR BULLETIN (CLB)

http://www.clb.org.hk/

Hong Kong–based China Labour Bulletin provides news and information on labor issues and relevant laws in China, as well as bulletins regarding labor abuses and the arrest and imprisonment of labor activists.

It also provides an archive of radio interviews carried out by labor activist Han Dongfang with workers and others regarding workplace accidents, conflicts with management, and labor demonstrations.

CLEAN CLOTHES CAMPAIGN (CCC)

http://www.cleanclothes.org/

The Clean Clothes Campaign is an international coalition of autonomous consumer organizations, trade unions, human rights and women's rights organizations, researchers, solidarity groups, and activists that coordinates campaigns and other activities aimed at improving conditions for garment workers, home workers, and migrant workers.

CSR ASIA

http://www.csr-asia.com/

Established in 2004, CSR Asia is a Hong Kong–based organization that provides information concerning corporate social responsibility within the Asia Pacific Region. The Web site includes the organization's reports on responsible investing in China, and offers research services and training for individual companies.

ETHICAL TRADING INITIATIVE (ETI)

http://www.ethicaltrade.org

http://www.eti.org.uk

The ETI is a U.K.–based alliance of multinational corporations, NGOs, and trade unions promoting implementation of a code of conduct for good labor as a standard for ethical sourcing. ETI focuses on the ending of child labor, forced labor and sweatshops, and examining worker health and safety, labor conditions, and labor rights.

THE FAIR LABOR ASSOCIATION (FLA)

http://www.fairlabor.org/

FLA is a nonprofit organization established to protect the rights of workers in the United States and around the world. The FLA Charter Agreement is an industry-wide code of conduct and monitoring system that holds companies publicly accountable for their labor practices. The FLA accredits independent monitors, certifies that companies are in compliance with the Code of Conduct, and serves as a source of information for the public.

HONG KONG CHRISTIAN INDUSTRIAL COMMITTEE (CIC)

http://www.cic.org.hk/

The CIC is a faith-based organization working for labor rights of industrial workers. CIC services include advocacy, direct service, empowering workers, promoting independent trade unions and policy change, and monitoring conditions of workers in Hong Kong and mainland China.

INTERNATIONAL CONFEDERATION OF FREE TRADE UNIONS (ICFTU)

http://www.icftu.org/

Founded in 1949, the ICFTU is an association of organizations striving to create independent labor unions throughout the world. It also campaigns against child labor, pushes for trade and labor standards, and monitors the effects of globalization. The ICFTU publishes several reports a year, including its annual Survey of Trade Union Rights.

THE INTERNATIONAL FEDERATION OF CHEMICAL, ENERGY, MINE, AND GENERAL WORKERS UNIONS (ICEM)

http://www.icem.org/

The main function of the ICEM is to negotiate on a global scale with multinational companies and sectors to ensure international standards on trade union rights, health, safety and environment, and equality at work. ICEM's Asia division has a working relationship with China's official All-China Federation of Trade Unions.

INTERNATIONAL LABOR ORGANIZATION (ILO)

http://www.ilo.org/

A United Nations specialized agency, the International Labor Organization (ILO) aims to promote social justice and internationally recognized labor rights. ILO programs include the occupational safety and health-hazard alert system and the labor standards and human rights programs. The Web site offers information on country-specific labor standards and trade union activities as well as resources on linkages with trade issues.

ILO DECLARATION OF FUNDAMENTAL PRINCIPLES AND RIGHTS AT WORK (1998)

http://www.ilo.org/public/english/standards/index.htm

The conventions outlined in this document concern international labor standards as well as the rights of workers. The topics covered include forced labor, freedom of association and protection of the right to organize, the right to organize and collectively bargain, equal remuneration, abolition of forced labor, and minimum age of workers.

INTERNATIONAL ORGANIZATION OF EMPLOYERS (IOE)

http://www.ioe-emp.org/

The IOE represents the interests of business in the labor and social-policy fields, including United Nations agencies and other international organizations. It ensures that international labor and social policy is feasible for employers in the developing and transitional countries. The IOE organization in China is the Chinese Enterprise Confederation.

THE NATIONAL LABOR COMMITTEE (NLC)

http://www.nlcnet.org/

With headquarters in New York and offices in Central America and Bangladesh, the NLC addresses the economic issues that are shaping conditions for democracy and social justice worldwide. It carries out public education, research, and social activism in support of worker movements in Asia, Africa, and the Americas.

PLAY FAIR AT THE OLYMPICS

http://www.fairolympics.org/

Play Fair is an organization that works with other international organizations such as Oxfam, Clean Clothes Campaign, and Make Trade Fair to campaign actively against the abuse of workers' rights in the sportswear industry.

SOCIAL ACCOUNTABILITY INTERNATIONAL (SAI)

http://www.cepaa.org/

SAI creates and implements independent workplace quality standards for companies in the labor industries. Besides the creation of the SA8000 performance standard, SAI also runs conferences, trains and certifies accreditation organizations, and presents awards for compliance.

SOLIDARITY CENTER

http://www.solidaritycenter.org/

This Web site of the AFL-CIO's American Center for International Labor Solidarity has a special section on China and a list of Chinese labor activists in prison. The organization promotes democracy, freedom, and respect for workers, and it publishes research and reports, including one focusing on labor rights in China.

SWEATSHOP WATCH

http://www.sweatshopwatch.org/

Sweatshop Watch is a coalition of various interest groups fighting for the elimination of sweatshop conditions in the global garment industry. Its Web site provides information on campaigns and reports focusing on companies using sweatshops in China.

ZHOULITAI.COM

http://www.zhoulitai.com/

Chonqing-based lawyer Zhou Litai offers legal assistance to workers, and provides news and information on labor issues on the Chinese-language Web site.

June Fourth

64MEMO VIRTUAL ARCHIVE

http://64memo.org/

A project of Human Rights in China (HRIC), 64Memo is the most comprehensive Chinese-language archive documenting the history of the 1989 Tiananmen democracy movement. The archive provides extensive research information, audiovisual reports, photographs, and firsthand accounts of the June 4th crackdown.

AIDS/Health

BEIJING AIZHIXING INSTITUTE

http://www.aizhi.org/

The Web site of China's most prominent AIDS NGO includes multiple resources on HIV/AIDS. Part of the organization's mission is to provide assistance to children affected by the disease.

THE CHINA AIDS ORPHANS FUND (CAOF)

http://www.chinaaidsorphanfund.org/

A Minneapolis-based organization provides humanitarian relief to children and orphans in Henan Province whose families have been affected by AIDS. The organization's relief initiatives include educational funds for orphans, medical care and training, and foster care and orphanage programs.

CHINA AIDS SURVEY

http://www.casy.org/

This California-based Web site provides information on policies, attitudes, and medical advances relating to AIDS in China, noting that nearly 10 percent of China's HIV victims are under 19 years old. The site's database contains summaries of Western and Chinese news articles, AIDS-related glossaries, and backgrounder briefs concerning the issues of AIDS in China.

CHINA HIV/AIDS INFORMATION NETWORK (CHAIN)

http://www.homeaids.org/

An NGO established by the Salvation Army and Yunnan Red Cross Society, CHAIN works with government departments, NGOs, medical professionals, and other relevant bodies to provide current news about HIV/AIDS prevention and awareness.

UNITED NATIONS POPULATION FUND (UNFPA)

http://www.unfpa.org/

The United Nations Population Fund is the world's largest international sponsor of population and reproductive-health programs. The UNFPA's 2002 country program for China can be accessed at the following link: http://www.unfpa.org/asiapacific/china/5chi0305.pdf.

Censorship/Media

CHINA INTERNET NETWORK INFORMATION CENTER (CNNIC)
Information Center
http://www.cnnic.net.cn/
CNNIC, the state network information center of China, provides officially sanctioned information on China's Internet use, including surveys, and also registers domain names in China.

CITIZEN LAB
http://www.citizenlab.org/
Citizen Lab is an interdisciplinary laboratory, based at the Munk Centre for International Studies at the University of Toronto, focusing on the intersection of digital media and world civic politics. In addition to exploring the relationship between media and state control, Citizen Lab also summarizes news concerning the latest developments within the field.

COMMITTEE TO PROTECT JOURNALISTS (CPJ)
http://www.cpj.org/
The New York–based Committee to Protect Journalists gathers information on censored journalists through independent research, fact-finding missions, and reports from individual journalists. The site contains databases of journalists who have disappeared, or who have been executed or imprisoned.

DYNAMIC INTERNET TECHNOLOGY, INC. (DIT)
http://www.dit-inc.us/
This Web site provides the DynaWeb application that allows China-based Internet users to gain access to forbidden Web sites.

ELECTRONIC FRONTIER FOUNDATION (EFF)
http://www.eff.org/
Founded in 1990, EFF is a group of lawyers, technologists, and volunteers that challenges legislation that threatens to impose pricing or official controls on Internet access. The organization's site summarizes relevant news and highlights current legal cases dealing with electronic censorship.

FREENET

http://www.freenet-china.org/

U.S.–based Freenet provides free software to help Chinese Web users access the Internet without fear of censorship. The Web site also provides uncensored news articles and links to overseas media.

GLOBAL VOICES ONLINE

http://www.globalvoicesonline.org/

Global Voices is a non-profit global citizens' media project, sponsored by and launched from the Berkman Center for Internet and Society at the Harvard Law School. It is a forum for interesting conversations, information, and ideas appearing around the world on various forms of participatory media such as blogs, podcasts, photo sharing sites, and videoblogs.

HACKTIVISMO

http://www.hacktivismo.com/

Hacktivismo attempts to circumvent government-sponsored censorship with software released under the HESSLA license, which forbids use for any purpose that does not respect human rights. The Web site also provides current news on cases of human rights defenders.

PRIVATERRA

http://www.privaterra.org/

Privaterra, supported by Computer Professionals for Social Responsibility, provides Internet technological support in data privacy and protection for civil society organizations and human rights NGOs. Its Web site provides relevant news, links, and other resources.

REPORTERS WITHOUT BORDERS (RSF)

(Reporters sans Frontieres)

http://www.rsf.org/

Reporters Without Borders is an international organization working to document and condemn attacks on press freedom. In addition to its annual report, the organization also produces publications and databases detailing imprisoned journalists.

Poverty/Rural

ACTIONAID CHINA

http://www.actionaid.org/china

Founded in 2001, ActionAid International is an international develop-ment agency aimed at fighting poverty, injustice, and inequality world-wide in partnership with local groups. With staff in Hebei, Guizhou, and Beijing, the group has launched initiatives in rural areas to en-hance farmers' capacities for facing the challenges of China's rapid inte-gration in the global economy, notably the impact of China's WTO membership.

THE ASIA MIGRANT CENTRE (AMC)

http://www.asian-migrants.org/

The Asian Migrant Centre is a Hong Kong–based NGO that operates as a monitoring, research, training, and support center dedicated to the promotion of the human rights and empowerment of Asian mi-grant workers and their families. AMC has recently increased advocacy efforts related to trade and its impact on migrant workers, including the sponsorship of a regional conference on the WTO, Development, and Migration.

CHINARURAL.ORG

http://www.chinarural.org/

Sponsored by the Carter Center, this Chinese-language Web site pro-vides information on village governance, relevant laws and policies, and news and resources relating to rural life.

Religious Repression

CARDINAL KUNG FOUNDATION

http://www.cardinalkungfoundation.org/

The Cardinal Kung Foundation aims to bring awareness of the under ground Catholic church in China and to end the religious persecution. The organization's work includes the education of seminarians, creation of underground orphanages, and public education. The Web site con-tains a brief history of the underground church and a list of imprisoned Catholics.

CHINA AID ASSOCIATION (CAA)
http://www.chinaaid.org/
Established in 2002, China Aid Association focuses on the fate of China's underground Christian church, and promotes religious freedom in China through field investigation, public advocacy, and academic research.

COMMITTEE FOR INVESTIGATION ON PERSECUTION OF RELIGION IN CHINA (CIPRC)
http://china21.org/
The Committee for Investigation on Persecution of Religion in China is a New York–based organization that documents the persecution of Christians in China.

MING HUI NET
http://www.minghui.org/
http://www.clearwisdom.net/
The main Web site of the Falun Gong spiritual movement, Ming Hui Net details the tenets and activities of Falun Gong, and provides information on individuals who have been detained, imprisoned, or executed by the Chinese government.

VOICE OF THE MARTYRS (VOM)
http://www.persecution.com/
Based in the United States and with over thirty affiliated international offices, Voice of the Martyrs is an interdenominational organization striving to aid Christians who are being persecuted for their religious beliefs worldwide.

Uyghur Issues

EAST TURKESTAN INFORMATION CENTER (ETIC)
http://www.uygur.org/
Based in Nurnberg, Germany, the ETIC Web site provides information on the culture and human rights situation in Xinjiang. The Web site includes testimonies of abuse and links to relevant reports by NGOs and the U.S. government.

THE GOVERNMENT OF XINJIANG UYGHUR AUTONOMOUS REGION (XUAR)

http://www.xj.gov.cn/

The official Web site of the Xinjiang Uyghur Autonomous Region provides information on government structure, official policies and announcements, development plans, and related organizations.

INTERNATIONAL UYGHUR HUMAN RIGHTS AND DEMOCRACY FOUNDATION (IUHRDF)

http://www.iuhrdf.org/

The IUHRDF was established in 2005 by former political prisoner Rebiya Kadeer and Uyghur intellectuals in the United States. The main purpose of IUHRDF is to promote human rights, religious freedom, and democracy for the Uyghur people, with a particular emphasis on Uyghur women and children.

UYGHUR AMERICAN ASSOCIATION (UAA)

http://www.uyghuramerican.org/

Based in McLean, Virginia, the UAA works to promote human rights and self-determination for Uyghurs and to protect their culture and environment. The Web site provides NGO, government, and press reports on human rights in Xinjiang, as well as the latest news on persecution of the Uyghur population.

UYGHUR HUMAN RIGHTS PROJECT (UHRP)

http://www.uhrp.org/

A research, reporting, and advocacy organization, the UHRP was founded by the Uyghur American Association (UAA) in 2004. UHRP's mission is to promote human rights and democracy for the Uyghur people, and to raise awareness of human rights abuses that occur in the Xinjiang Uyghur Autonomous Region (XUAR).

Tibetan Issues

FREE TIBET CAMPAIGN

http://www.freetibet.org/

Founded in 1988, London-based FTC provides information on international campaigns and exhibitions relating to human rights in Tibet as well as updates on imprisoned Tibetans, and encourages individual involvement in campaigns.

MONGOL-AMERICAN CULTURAL ASSOCIATION (MACA)
http://www.maca-usa.org/
Founded in 1988, MACA provides charitable and humanitarian support and promotes Mongol culture in the United States. It operates the Mongolian Children's Aid and Development Fund (MCADF), which supports children's institutions, orphans and other groups through various public cultural programs and the publication of a newsletter that carries articles related to current events and Mongol culture.

SOUTHERN MONGOLIAN HUMAN RIGHTS INFORMATION CENTER (SMHRIC)
http://www.smhric.org/
SMHRIC gathers and distributes information concerning the human rights situation in the Inner Mongolia Autonomous Region. It also works to promote and protect human rights and democracy in Inner Mongolia, and to improve the international community's understanding of the situation.

FRIENDS OF TIBET
http://www.friendsoftibet.org/
Friends of Tibet is a global movement using direct action in support of Tibetan independence. Its Web site provides information on current campaigns and activities.

GU-CHU-SUM
http://www.guchusum.org/
The Gu-Chu-Sum movement is dedicated to assisting former Tibetan political prisoners in exile. The Web site provides profiles of existing political prisoners, prisoners who died as a result of official persecution, and information on the main detention centers.

INTERNATIONAL CAMPAIGN FOR TIBET (ICT)

http://www.savetibet.org/

Based in Washington, D.C., the ICT works to promote human rights and self-determination for Tibetans and to protect their culture and environment. The Web site provides news, position papers, and multimedia resources.

STUDENTS FOR A FREE TIBET (SFT)

http://www.studentsforafreetibet.org/

SFT is a chapter-based network of young people and activists around the world. Through education, grassroots organizing, and non-violent direct action, it campaigns for Tibetans' fundamental right to political freedom. SFT's goal is to empower and train youth as leaders in the worldwide movement for social justice.

TIBETAN CENTRE FOR HUMAN RIGHTS AND DEMOCRACY (TCHRD)

http://www.tchrd.org/

Based in Dharamsala, India, the TCHRD provides information on political prisoners and other human rights issues in Tibet.

TIBETAN WOMEN'S ASSOCIATION (TWA)

http://www.tibetanwomen.org/

The Tibetan Women's Association (TWA) was originally founded on March 12, 1959, in Tibet. TWA's main objective is to raise public awareness of the abuses faced by Tibetan women in Tibet. Through publicity and involvement in national and international affairs, TWA alerts communities to the gender-specific human rights abuses committed against Tibetan women.

TIBETAN YOUTH CONGRESS (TYC)

http://www.tibetanyouthcongress.org/

The largest and most active nongovernmental organization of Tibetans in exile, the Tibetan Youth Congress promotes reform and change to enhance the development of democracy in the Tibetan community.

Hong Kong

CIVIC EXCHANGE
http://www.civic-exchange.org/
Civic Exchange is a Hong Kong–based public-policy think tank established in October 2000, to promote civic education, conduct research, and contribute to public debate on economic, social, and environmental issues. Civic Exchange issues regular bulletins on current developments in Hong Kong, and provides links to Web sites of other major civil society and pro-democracy groups in Hong Kong.

HONG KONG HUMAN RIGHTS MONITOR (HKHRM)
http://www.hkhrm.org.hk/
HKHRM is a local monitoring organization that aims to promote better human rights protection in Hong Kong. It provides tools and resources, and updated news information on its website regarding current human rights issues.

Environment

THE ALLIANCE FOR ENVIRONMENTAL INNOVATION
http://www.environmentaldefense.org/
The Alliance for Environmental Innovation works with companies to improve environmental performance while yielding substantial business benefits. Such partnerships include United States Parcel Service, Starbucks Coffee Company, and SC Johnson Wax.

CENTER FOR ENVIRONMENTALLY RESPONSIBLE ECONOMICS (CERES)
http://www.ceres.org/
The CERES Coalition is a U.S.–based network of more than eighty organizations, including environmental groups, investors, advisors and analysts, and public interest and community groups working together for a sustainable future. CERES's Web site contains copies of its publications concerning the interaction of environment and corporate responsibility.

GREENPEACE INTERNATIONAL

http://www.greenpeace.org/

Founded in 1971, Greenpeace International is an environmental watch-dog organization campaigning against environmental degradation and pressuring governments and corporations to improve their environmental policies. In China, Greenpeace has focused on the Three Gorges Dam project and nuclear testing.

INTERNATIONAL COUNCIL ON MINING AND METALS (ICMM)

http://www.icmm.com/

CMM works with the world's mining and metal industries to articulate, develop, and promote sustainable development in line with economic, social, and environmental goals.

INTERNATIONAL INSTITUTE FOR ENVIRONMENT AND DEVELOPMENT (IIED)

http://www.iied.org/

The IIED uses research, policy studies, networking, education, and advocacy to affect change on all policy levels, with particular focus on mining, the paper industry, and food systems. The IIED's Web site includes reports on projects on China concerning the plastics industry and deforestation.

INTERNATIONAL INSTITUTE FOR SUSTAINABLE DEVELOPMENT (IISD)

http://www.iisd.org/

The IISD presents policy recommendations on international trade and investment, economic policy, climate change, measurements and indicators, and natural resource management. Many of its programs center on research and capacity-building in developing countries.

INTERNATIONAL PETROLEUM INDUSTRY ENVIRONMENTAL CONSERVATION ASSOCIATION (IPIECA)

http://www.ipieca.org/

IPIECA is a voluntary nonprofit organization comprised of petroleum companies and associations at the national, regional, or international levels. IPIECA's mission is to develop and promote scientifically sound, cost-effective, practical, socially and economically acceptable solutions to global environmental issues pertaining to the petroleum industry.

INTERNATIONAL RIVERS NETWORK (IRN)
http://www.irn.org/

IRN was established in 1985 as a nonprofit all-volunteer organization of activists experienced in fighting economically, environmentally, and socially unsound river intervention projects. It has focused on China's Three Gorges Dam project, and has encouraged international investors and institutions to consider the harmful environmental and social impacts of the project.

PROBE INTERNATIONAL
http://www.probeinternational.org/

This Canadian NGO exposes the environmental, social, and economic effects of Canada's aid and trade abroad. Its Three Gorges Probe Web site focuses particularly on environmental and human rights issues connected with China's Three Gorges Dam project.

RAINFOREST ACTION NETWORK (RAN)
http://www.ran.org/

The Rainforest Action Network strives to protect the world's rainforests and the people living in and around them through education, local organizing, and peaceful direct action. One of its largest campaigns targeted Citigroup for its funding of the Three Gorges Dam project.

RESOURCE RENEWAL INSTITUTE (RRI)
http://www.rri.org/

The Resource Renewal Institute is a collaboration between NGOs and local and national governments dedicated to solving environmental and social problems through a systemic, multisector management process.

UNITED STATES AGENCY FOR INTERNATIONAL DEVELOPMENT, US–ASIA ENVIRONMENTAL PARTNERSHIP (USAEP)
http://www.usaep.org/

The USAEP is a public-private initiative tasked under the auspices of USAID to bring environmental sustainability to Asian countries through resource-efficient projects and pollution reduction. The USAEP is involved with government and industry in both Hong Kong and Taiwan in projects such as waste management and infrastructure.

WORLD BUSINESS COUNCIL FOR SUSTAINABLE DEVELOPMENT (WBCSD)
http://www.wbcsd.ch/

WBCSD is a coalition of 160 international companies from more than thirty countries and twenty major industrial sectors that holds annual meetings where business leaders can analyze, debate, and exchange experiences on all aspects of sustainable development.

WORLD CONSERVATION UNION (IUCN)
http://www.iucn.org/

The World Conservation Union partners with government agencies, NGOs, scientists, and experts from 181 countries to influence, encourage, and assist societies throughout the world to engage in equitable and sustainable utilization of ecosystems. It has worked in China to create a regional action plan for administering protected areas, with a focus on tropical and subtropical forests.

WORLD RESOURCES INSTITUTE (WRI)
http://www.wri.org/

WRI is an environmental think tank that uses scientific research, economic analysis, and real-life experience to find practical ways to protect the earth and improve people's lives. WRI projects include developing a sustainable transportation strategy in Dalian, and reports on China's health and environment.

WORLD WILDLIFE FUND (WWF)
http://www.worldwildlife.org/

The WWF focuses on protecting and saving endangered species, as well as determining global threats. The WWF works closely with China's parks department to establish and maintain protected areas. WWF's China reports focus on topics such as southern subtropical evergreen forests, northern plain deciduous forests, studies on the South China Sea, and endangered species.

Chinese Articles: Web Site Sources

Following are some prominent overseas Chinese-language Web sites that publish articles by some of China's leading dissident thinkers and commentators. They are the sources of many articles translated for *China Rights Forum*.

BEIJING SPRING
http://www.bjzc.org/

CHINAEWEEKLY
http://www.chinaeweekly.com/

CHINA INFORMATION CENTER
http://www.observechina.net/info/index.asp

CHINA MONTHLY
http://minzhuzhongguo.org/

DEMOCRACY NET
http://www.asiademo.org/

THE EPOCH TIMES
http://www.dajiyuan.com/

NEW CENTURY NET
http://www.ncn.org/asp/zwginfo/index.asp

OPEN MAGAZINE
http://www.open.com.hk/

PEACEHALL
http://www.peacehall.com/

REN YU RENQUAN
http://www.renyurenquan.org/

About the Contributors

Chen Guidi and **Wu Chuntao** *(Rule by Terror)* are a husband and wife who work for the Hefei Literature Association. They spent three years and most of their savings researching and writing their banned best-seller, *Chinese Peasantry: A Survey,* which was published in English in 2006 as *Will the Boat Sink the Water?: The Life of China's Peasants* (Public Affairs).

Gao Ertai *(Address Unknown)* is a dissident artist and writer. He is currently a visiting scholar at the University of Nevada, Las Vegas.

He Qinglian *(Media Control in China; Draining the Pond to Catch the Fish),* an economist, is also the author of *China's Pitfall.* She is a senior researcher in residence with HRIC.

Hu Jia *(A Tale of Two Crises: SARS vs. AIDS)* is director of the Beijing Aizhixing Institute, a nongovernmental organization devoted to protecting the rights of people affected by HIV/AIDS.

Hu Ping *(The Falun Gong Phenomenon)* is a New York–based political commentator and chief editor of the Chinese-language monthly, *Beijing Spring.*

Huang Xiang *(The Power of a Red Rose)* is a respected poet whose works are now banned in China. After suffering persecution in China, Huang and his wife obtained political asylum in the United States. They now live in Pennsylvania.

Jin Yanming *(A Mother's Story)* is the wife of dissident Liu Jingsheng, who was sentenced to fifteen years in prison for his involvement with the China Freedom and Democracy Party.

Ka Lun Leung *(Cultural Christians and Contemporary Christianity in China)* is president of the Alliance Bible Seminary of Hong Kong and specialist on the Christian church in China.

Leng Wanbao *("Resurrection" Exposes Confession under Torture)* was imprisoned for five years for his participation in the 1989 Democracy Movement. Based in Jilin, he has published numerous articles on human rights issues.

Liu Xiaobo *(The Rise of Civil Society in China; China's Robber Barons)* is a leading dissident intellectual based in Beijing.

Qiu Yueshou *(Mineshaft: Our Black Home)* was a lecturer in Chinese at Shantou University, and is a Ph.D. candidate in international relations at the University of Technology, Sydney.

Ren Bumei *(A Migration of Souls)*, formerly operator of the *Bumei Zhiye* Web site in Beijing, emigrated to Canada in late 2004. He now works for overseas Chinese Web sites.

Wang Ai *(Art from the Latrines of the Great Northern Wilderness)* graduated from Beijing Normal University with a degree in Chinese language and literature. She is now a writer and translator based in New York.

Wang Juntao *(June 4th and Human Rights in China)* was imprisoned as a "black hand" behind the 1989 Democracy Movement. Released on medical parole in 1995, Wang recently earned a doctorate in political science at Columbia University.

Wang Yu *(Someone Outside the Door; To the Students at Tiananmen)* is a poet who lives in New York.

Yan Li *(Rotten Rope; Give It Back to Me)*, a poet, novelist, and painter, was a founding member of the avant-garde Stars art group during the 1970s. He now lives in New York.

Yang Chungguang *(The Age of Mammoths)*, one of China's most important underground poets, was imprisoned for eighteen months for his participation in the 1989 Democracy Movement. Subsequently operating a literary Web site, Yang was subjected to official harassment until he died in September 2005 following a stroke.

Yang Hongfeng (*A Tiananmen Mother Vows to Fight On*) is a reporter for *The Epoch Times.*

Yang Yinbo (*A Migrant Family's Accounts*) is a young Internet essayist based in Guangzhou. His parents are migrant workers.

Yi Ban (*The View Beneath the Bridge*) is the pen name of a writer based in Beijing.

Yu Jie (*An Open Letter to My Police Readers*), based in Beijing, gained great popularity in China as a young firebrand because of his political essays. He is now banned from publication in China.

Zeng Linlin (*Death Row Study Session*) is the daughter of Zhang Zhixing, a cadre who was executed for her political beliefs during the Cultural Revolution.

Zeng Renquan (*Broken Flowers*) is the pen name of a freelance journalist based in China.

Zhang Lin (*The End of the Rope*) is a political dissident and prolific Internet essayist based in Bengbu, Anhui Province. In June 2005 he was sentenced to five years in prison on charges of endangering state security.

Zhang Youjie (*An Inside View*) is a Beijing-based sociologist who has written a number of reports on human rights issues.

Index